The Price of Fear

The Film Career of Vincent Price

In his own words

†

Joel Eisner

BLACK BED SHEET

The Price of Fear:
The Film Career of Vincent Price in His Own Words
A Black Bed Sheet/Diverse Media Book
April 2013

Library of Congress Control Number: 2013935605

ISBN-10: 0-9886590-2-6
ISBN-13: 978-0-9886590-2-5

The Price of Fear

THE FILM CAREER OF

VINCENT PRICE

In his own words

†

Joel Eisner

A Black Bed Sheet/Diverse Media Book
Antelope, CA

Acknowledgements

I would like to thank the following people for their assistance and help with this book: Michael Lederman, Zachary Zito, Ken Landgraf, John Donaldson, Robert Byron, Fangoria's Tony Timpone and Starlog's Dave McDonnell.

My gratitude and thanks to Tom Weaver and the late Steve Swires for allowing me access to many of their interviews (including never before published material) they have done over the years.

All photographs used in this book are from the personal collection of the author.

The following magazines, newspapers and books proved to be invaluable research materials used in the writing of this book and are listed here with the thanks of the author to all of those writers, editors and publishers involved in their creation.

MAGAZINES

Cinefantastique, Fangoria, Monsterland, Films and Filming, Video Watchdog, Life Magazine, American Cinematographer. Scarlet Street, The Dark Side, Famous Monsters of Filmland, Filmfax, Screenland, Photoplay, Photoplay Film Monthly, Movieland, Midnight, Hollywood, Cinemagic, True Story, ABC Film Review, Illustrated London News, Shriek!, Hello!

NEWSPAPERS

Citizen News, Toronto Star, The N.Y. Times, Baltimore Evening Sun, N.Y. Herald-Tribune, N.Y. Newsday, L.A. Daily News, Screen International, N.Y. Post, L.A. Times, N.Y. World-Telegram, Variety, Virginia News Leader, Philadelphia Inquirer.

BOOKS

I'd *Love to Kiss You...Conversations with Bette Davis* by Whitney Stine, *Vincent Price: Actor And Art Collector* by Riverside Museum Press, *Horror People* by John Brosnan, *Box Office Champs* by Eddie Dorman King, *The Films of Roger Corman* by Ed Naha, *Fast & Furious: The Story of A.I.P.* by Mark Thomas McGee, *The Movie World of Roger Corman* by J. Philip de Franco, *The Films of Christopher Lee* by Robert Pohle, Jr. & Douglas C. Hart, *James Whale* by James Curtis.

Horror Film Stars by Michael R. Pittsm *Vincent Price* by Vincent Price, *Roger Corman: How I made a 100 movies in Hollywood and Never Lost a Dime* by

Roger Corman & Jim Jerome, *The Motion Picture Guide* by Jay Robert Nash & Stanley Ralph Ross, *The Films of Peter Lorre* by Stephen Young, James Bigwood & Raymond Cobana, *Quinlan's Film Stars* by David Quinlan, *Universal Pictures* by Michael J. Fitzgerald, *The R.K.O. Story* by Richard B. Jewell & Vernon Harbin, *The Universal Story* by Clive Hirschhorn, *Basil Rathbone: His life and His Films* by Michael B. Druxman, *Heroes of the Horrors* by Calvin Thomas Beck, *Boris Karloff & His Films* by Paul M. Jenson, *Step Right Up! I'm Gonna Scare the Pants off America* by William Castle, *Boris Karloff: A Critical Account of his Screen, Stage, Radio, Television & Recording Work* by Scott Allen Nollen, *Universal Horrors: The Studio's Classic Films 1931-1946* by Michael Brunas, John Brunas & Tom Weaver, Ronald Colman, *Gentleman of the Cinema* by R. Dixon Smith , *Interviews with B Science Fiction & Horror Movie Makers* by Tom Weaver, *Science Fiction Stars & Horror Heroes* by Tom Weaver, *Vincent Price Unmasked* by James Robert Parrish & Steven Whitney, *The Films of Reginald LeBorg* by Wheeler Winston Dixon *Dark Visions* by Stanley Wiater, *Christopher Lee and Peter Cushing and Horror Cinema* by Mark A. Miller, *Peter Cushing: The Gentleman of Horror and His 91 Films* by Deborah Del Vecchio and Tom Johnson.

The following materials from Vincent Price's private collection were invaluable in the creation of this book:

The Villains Still Pursue Me by Vincent Price: transcript of lecture given at De Anza College, Northern California, circa 1979.

The Villains Still Pursue Me by Vincent Price: handwritten early draft of lecture circa 1969.

Autobiography of a Villain by Vincent Price: early draft of lecture cira 1958.

I would like to thank the following people (both living and dead, or possibly undead) whose memories of Vincent are included in this book: Peter Cushing, John Carradine, Christopher Lee, Ian Ogilvy, Fiona Lewis, Caroline Munro, Roy Ward Baker, Louis M. Heyward, Robb White, Reginald LeBorg, Rose Hobart, Charles Bennett, Samuel Z. Arkoff, Roger Corman, Charles B. Griffith, Boris Karloff, Bette Davis, Jack Nicholson, Michael Pate, Robert Hutton, Linda Hayden, Robert Quarry, Christopher Wicking, Valli Kemp, Gordon Hessler, Barbara Steele, Hazel Court, Nancy Kovack, Milton Subotsky, Richard Matheson, Andre de Toth, David Hedison, Edward Bernds. Lindsay Anderson, Michael Armstrong, Brenda Vaccaro, Jeff Burr, Yvonne Craig, Art Linkletter, Charlton Heston, Jane Russell, Red Buttons, Douglas Fairbanks, Jr., Anne Baxter.

Special thanks to Victoria Price for her approval and support in this tribute to her father.

And of course my heartfelt thanks goes to the Merchant of Menace himself: VINCENT PRICE, whose help, encouragement, and support of this project kept it alive long after his untimely departure.

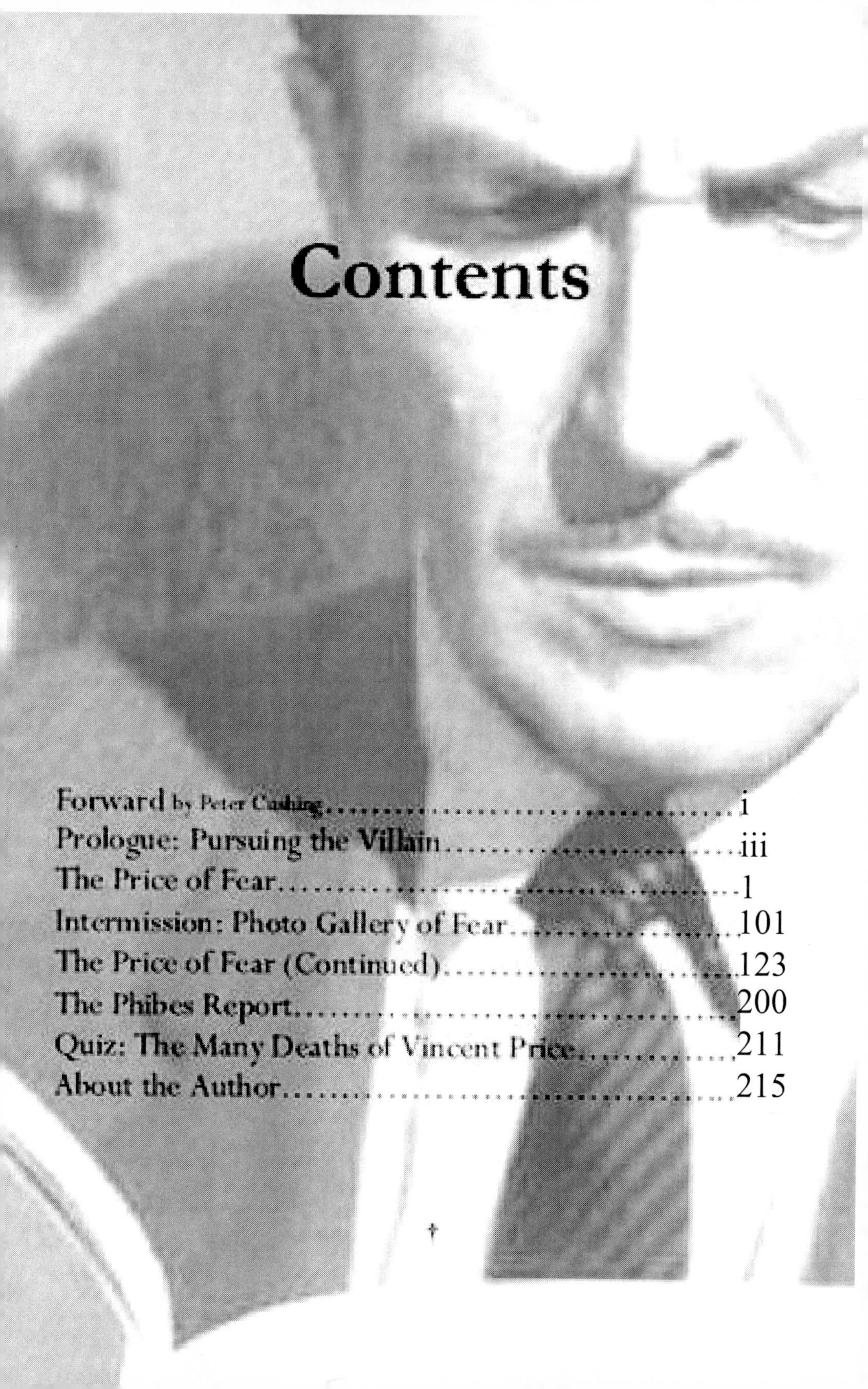

Contents

The Price of Fear:

The Film Career of Vincent Price

In his own words

†

Joel Eisner

FORWARD

Vincent, dear old son,

Mr. Joel Eisner asked me to write a forward for his homage to you and your work, but that seemed to me far too formal and impersonal when speaking about such a dear old friend and colleague, so I hope he will use this 'open' letter instead.

"The Price of Fear," eh! Usually, actors fear the price won't be good enough, but in your case, it is -- invariably. You give and have given your best, often making silk purses out of sow's ears, and your efforts have given enormous pleasure to audiences all over the world, be it on the wireless (radio is too modern a term for the likes 'o me!), the stage, television and film; and -- bully for videos -- they will go on doing so for ever and ever amen.

It's one of my lasting regrets that we didn't work together more often, but it is with great joy that I recall those rare occasions when we did. A very special one is our last movie, "House of the Long Shadows," when, in company with dear old Christopher Lee and the late lamented John Carradine, we faced the rigors of an English summer down in deepest Hampshire. (Very damp, Hampshire). Your kindness and thought for others were an example to us all.

I don't think I've ever told you this. Just before the outbreak of the Second World War, I came over to the States in search of fame and fortune, like a fool stepping in where angels fear to tread. (No one knew me except my parents.) Being skint, I presented my Equity Card at the box-office, and was given a freebie seat in the theatre on Broadway, where you were starring in Patrick Hamilton's play "Gaslight." Your performance impressed me tremendously, and, years later, when I appeared on B.B.C. television as the same character, I used bits of your 'business' which had remained in my memory all that time! (Motto: If you're going to pinch, pinch only the best!)

Well, old Darling, it gives me a warm and cozy feeling to know that we're all destined to meet again some sunny day. (Destination unknown, but what a cast!)

Recently, Mr. Mark Miller, a fellow countryman of yours, brought to my notice the following lovely excerpt from Tennyson's 'Ulysses' and I can think of nothing more apt with which to bring this tribute to a close.

'...Tho' much is taken, much abides; and tho'
We are not now that strength which in old days
Moved earth and heaven; that which we are, we are;
One equal temper of heroic hearts,
Made each weak by time and fate, but strong in will
To strive, to seek, to find, and not to yield....'

With my love, dear Vincent, and may God's blessing be with you always.

As ever,
Peter Cushing, O.B.E.
Whitstable,
Kent, 1992

Peter Cushing passed away on August 11, 1994, at the age of 82 after a long battle with cancer. Although Vincent never saw this completed book, I did send him a copy of this letter, it was so moving I thought it would cheer Vincent up and I am sure it did.

†

PROLOGUE

"PURSUING THE VILLAIN"*

When I was about five years old, I had the chance to see *House on Haunted Hill* broadcast on television. To this day, I have fond memories of being scared by this film (especially the scene with the blind woman scaring Carolyn Craig in the cellar) but it also was my first Vincent Price film. Over the years I have had a chance to see almost all of his films and in writing this book I have had the opportunity to see at least two dozen, which for one reason or another I had never seen (thank goodness for video and cable television). It was like finding buried treasure. Many of these films I regret not having seen before, and of course there are a few that should have remained buried. Regardless of how good or bad a film might be, I have never been disappointed by Vincent's performance.

I don't know exactly why I became fascinated by Vincent Price; it might have something to do with his acting style, the way he never quite took himself too seriously even in the most horrifying moments (as you will learn, he really thought of himself as a comic, and in particular a slapstick comic). The characters he portrayed always had a moment of self-satisfaction in whatever they do, and in these moments (usually accompanied by a sinister smile and/or a light chuckle), Vincent seemed to be enjoying himself the most and I have always been able to identify with that. He had always been able to invest in the characters he portrayed a sense of humanity, so that unlike many of the more recent slasher/gore films, Vincent's pictures do not overpower you with special effects but instead they slowly draw you into the story, so that long after it is over, you still manage to bring a part of it away with you; whereas current films all begin to seem alike after awhile. This is the reason why the old Universal horror films and many of Vincent's films of the 1950's and 1960's hold up so well...they left something to the imagination. After all, you go see a film to be entertained and not to be grossed out by blood and guts (or do you?).

To the general public at large, Vincent Price was an actor who spent most of his career playing villains in an assortment of horror films and television shows. To some he will be remembered for his expertise in cooking, and his knowledge of art. But to the current generation he is only known as the voice on Michael Jackson's *Thriller*, Edward Scissorhands' creator and as a character seen in a series of parodies on the Saturday Night Live television series.

But Vincent was much more than his films and television shows (which, sadly, is really the only surviving proof of his acting career). I first came to know in 1985 when he granted me an interview for the *Official Batman Batbook*, which I was working on at the time. As he played Egghead in the 1966 television series, it gave me the opportunity I needed to speak with him, as I not only wanted him for the Batman book but I wanted to work with him on a book about his own film career. I was very fortunate to have him agreeable to both projects. Vincent adored the Batbook, in fact he called it "EGG-cellent!" I won't go into the long process it has taken to get this book to print, the research, the rewrites, the interviews, and of course Vincent's own death. However, in doing this book, I came to understand the man who called himself Vincent Price.

While he came from, in his own words, "a well-to-do" upper middle class family, he was the most down-to-earth person I have ever encountered. There was not one person who didn't love Vincent (at least I couldn't find any.) He portrayed some of the most evil and terrifying villains ever created, and yet in real life he was anything but the villain.

Like Boris Karloff before him, Vincent was a gentleman who could get along with anyone from any background and any walk of life. And like Boris, embraced the "boogeyman" persona with a sense of humor and did everything he could to, in his own words, "send himself up."

When Vincent began his acting career, he spent most of his early stage and screen appearances as the good guy, the aristocrat or the cultured gentleman. It wasn't until he accepted the role of the villain, Mr. Manningham in the play Angel Street did his career began to take a villainous turn.

At the same time, that Vincent was finding success as a villain on Broadway, Boris was mere blocks away, playing up his own monster image as the villainous Jonathan Brewster in the stage comedy, Arsenic and Old Lace. Both men would spend the next few years balancing their villainous images by appearing in comedic roles. Karloff, in feature films with Danny Kaye, Lucille Ball and Abbott & Costello and Vincent on radio with Jack Benny and Red Skelton.

Several more years of costumed characters (of the good guy, bad guy and royalty types) followed but it wasn't until Vincent starred as the burned mad sculptor in the *House of Wax* did his career take a horrific turn. Turning down a low-paying role on Broadway in lieu of the well paying big studio 3-

D epic, Vincent unknowingly set himself on a path that would change his life forever.

House of Wax, was nothing new, it was a remake of the 1933 film *Mystery of the Wax Museum* starring Lionel Atwill (who, like Vincent, was a popular stage actor who later found a niche as a horror movie villain). The only real difference was that it was going to be made in the new process of 3-D. Like the first version, the cast was primarily made up of B-level movie actors, no major stars (although Charles Bronson, then known by his real name of Charles Buchinsky, still many years away from his own stardom, appeared as Vincent's mute/brute assistant Igor).

Why Vincent was cast in *House of Wax* is something of a mystery based on his track record in films. He was not a scene-stealing villain, at least not at this point in career, he had little experience in horror films and he wasn't a major drawing star, as he had only been playing leads in small or low budget features. Yet, he was able to instill in the character of Henry Jarrod a sense of humanity and culture that many other actors would not have been able to pull off. Vincent's interest in art and his warm personality played well in the first half of the film and proved a nice balance in the second half when he had to portray burned madman with twisted sensibilities. *House of Wax* was one of the top grossing films of 1953, and would have made Vincent a star. He received numerous offers to appear in horror films but he turned them down. He returned to the theater and to mainstream films and with the exception of the *Mad Magician* did not venture in the genre for several years.

Vincent spent the rest of the 1950's appearing on TV quiz shows, comedy variety programs with Jack Benny and Red Skelton and the occasional drama. It wasn't until the end of the decade that he found himself forever cast as a horror actor. *The Fly*, *The Return of the Fly*, *House on Haunted Hill* and *The Tingler* established Vincent as the successor to Boris Karloff, as the reigning king of horror.

While the above-mentioned films were all B-Features, and Vincent wasn't the villain in any of them (he was the Fly's brother in the first film and the uncle to the son of the Fly in the second. He was a millionaire trying to stop his cheating wife and her lover's plan to use the setting of the *House on Haunted Hill to* kill him, and he was a doctor who discovered the title creature in the *Tingler*), his association with these films established his image with the general public and sealed his fate forever.

Beginning with the *Fall of the House of Usher* and continuing for over the next two decades, Vincent (much to his chagrin) became America's favorite boogeyman. Realizing there was money in horror films, Vincent signed a long term deal with American International Pictures to appear in numerous horror films based on the work of Edgar Allan Poe. Together with some of the greats of the horror film genre, Basil Rathbone, Lon Chaney, Jr. Peter Lorre and Boris Karloff, Vincent would create some of the most memorable films in the history of horror films. And yet, he would have been happier making comedies (he did get a chance with the two Dr. Goldfoot films but they were not very successful).

With each and every villain he portrayed, Vincent began to lose his identity. He became famous as a fiendish villain but in real life he was anything but a fiend. He balanced his professional career by becoming the art buyer for the Sears Department stores. He spent years scouring the world's famous art galleries to fill the needs of Sears' customers. Vincent threw himself into his vocation by trying to bring affordable artwork to the American consumer (and by using the large salaries from his Poe films to further his own art collection as well. Although according to Vincent, "I really never made that much money, because I would do things for very little money if they were a challenge and exciting, and fun to do.")

"I think a lot of people thought my career, being as varied as it was, to be a little suspect," reflected Vincent. "Why didn't he concentrate on this or that, or the other thing? I was an art historian before I was an actor, and I couldn't give that up for anything in the world because the history of art is the history of man!"

"I was never a super star," Vincent admitted. "If I had been the kind of fellow that said I would only do things that were as good as the part of Prince Albert in *Victor Regina*, I might still be sitting there waiting for that part to come along." Vincent instead had a wide and varied career in all areas and all mediums (stage, radio, television, film, books, cooking, and art). He was more than a movie villain, he was a gracious and talented performer who brought happiness to millions of people the world over. And in conclusion, I will leave you with a quote from the late John Carradine, who, every time he found a Vincent Price film running on television, would exclaim, *"The Price is Right* is on!"

*Author's Note: "Pursuing the Villain" is a reference to the title of Vincent Price's most popular lecture topic "The Villain Still Pursues Me!" in which he discussed his work in the world of horror films and yet led a very quiet and cultured life, a topic which pursued him until the end of his life.

Chapter One

The Candy Kid Meets the Golem
or
How to Become an Actor without Really Trying

He is known to the world as the Master of Movie Menace, the King of the Shockers, and the Crown Prince of Horror. He is thought by many to be the rightful heir to the throne of Horror King, Boris Karloff. He was born Vincent Leonard Price, Jr. on May 27, 1911, in St. Louis, Missouri, the fourth child of Vincent Leonard Price and Margaret Cobb Wilcox Price.

Unlike many actors in Hollywood, Vincent came from a very stable and loving home. Both his parents, and the other Price children, Harriet (age 17), Mortimer (age 14) and Laura-Louise (age 10), were always looking out for the baby of the family.

From the day he was born, everyone knew the boy was special, especially Vincent's father who was the President of the National Candy Company, a firm that specialized in jawbreakers and jellybeans. On the day of young Vincent's birth, the office workers presented the elder Price with a plaque proclaiming the boy to be "The Candy Kid," a title which in later years Vincent found quite handy. Vincent fondly recalled, "When my father was elected President of the National Confectioners' Association of America, candy manufacturers all across the country would send us samples, which made me very popular with the girls at Christmas Time."

It is not surprising that Vincent grew up to be a 'King' as he sprouted from a very old and distinguished family tree. "My first ancestor in this country was a fellow named Peregrine White. (My grandmother's maiden name was White). He was born on the Mayflower the day it landed at Plymouth Rock (if they had known about me, they might have thrown him overboard!) and, as the first child in the Massachusetts colony he received a grant of land which today is one of the farms which supplies the Howard Johnson's restaurant chain.

"My grandfather invented baking powder and went on to found the Chicago based Price Baking Soda Company. He later sold it for a handsome profit to the Royal Gelatin Company in 1890, which unfortunately, he later lost in the crash of 1892."

As a result, Price's father was taken out of Yale to run the family candy company. "My father made it successful," Vincent remembered, "but by then he had children, and he felt he had to stay in the business. So he never did what he really wanted to do, which was to become a lawyer and to write poetry."

Towards the end of his life Vincent admitted it was very risky to make acting his career and art his hobby. "But I was always a risk-taker," he said. "I suppose because I sensed my father's disappointment in his own life. That's why I vowed never to feel trapped by my life."

Vincent often claimed that his mother was a descendant of the Frenchmen who traveled with Pere Marquette, the priest who discovered the Mississippi River before finally settling down in the French colony in what is now Detroit, Michigan. "She wasn't," Vincent admitted. "I've been known to stretch the truth and it almost had me end up wearing feathers. Much as I would like to have Indian blood in my veins, I can't really claim it. The Frenchmen who founded my mother's family either brought their French wives with them or waited until some arrived on the next boat.

"In telling myself a tale about mother's ancestors coming over with Pere Marquette, which they didn't, I did happen on an early member who was an artist craftsman and one of the early silversmiths in this country. His name was Pierre Desnoyers, and he settled in Detroit, Michigan. One interesting fact I came across is that Pierre Desnoyers did a thriving business in silver headbands complete with single silver feather - made for the Indians."

With his Broadway debut still decades away, Vincent, (aided by his Aunt Minnie), found himself starring in a local Kindergarten production of *The Angel of the Annunciation*. This quickly won him a nice long 'rave' column in the local paper.

After listening to his aunt read his good review (he was still too young to read it himself), Vincent declared, "I'm going to be an actor!"

His parents (who were far more open-minded than most parents of that time period) replied, "Go ahead, we want you to be anything you have the nerve and courage to become."

Many years later when Vincent once again brought up his dream to become an actor, his parents were not as enthusiastic as they were before. "When you are brought up in the Middle West as I was," Vincent pointed out, "and you wanted to be an actor, you had to harbor it, because it was something that just was not done. I told my mother and father, who were good Episcopalian business people that I wanted to be an actor and my mother said 'But you can't dance!' I think ever after I opened in Victoria Regina on Broadway, that she really was disappointed that I didn't do a song and dance number in it."

While Vincent was raised in a devoutly religious atmosphere, his life was not devoid of the supernatural elements which would foreshadow his future career in horror film business. Vincent believed "there are mental powers men have scarcely tapped and little understand." He was certain "there are spiritual powers that come to warn us, to humble us, perhaps, when we become arrogant and are carried away with our own importance. Individuals, as we are aware, are as variable as the weather. They seldom enter or leave our lives in precise fashion. In certain unique cases, a presence may seem to appear to us after death. This "spirit" or "unbidden guest" -call it what you will—seems reluctant to relinquish his hold on life."

Vincent recalled two unusual incidents that occurred in his early life. The first happened (as he learned later), when he was a baby, "I slept in a room by myself in a crib. Over it was hung a heavy brass lighting fixture. One evening, well after midnight, my mother woke up and made an unprecedented trip to my room. Apparently I was a child who never woke up at night. But this night she came to my room, reached above my crib to turn on the light, and the whole fixture dropped into her hands. She put the heavy object carefully by my crib and went back to her room and to bed. The next morning she asked my father to test that fixture, saying she had dreamt that it was loose. Upon discovering the fixture safely on the floor, my father recalled Mother's nocturnal visit to my room and reminded her of it. When the implication of this near-accident reached her consciousness, she fell into a dead faint and never could be induced to mention that incident again."

The second incident had a more ghostly tone to it as Vincent recalled, "*As* a child, I never tired of hearing and rehearing the tale of my young uncle, and how his uneasy spirit was comforted. This story was first told to me when I was just past my tenth year, and I accepted it wholeheartedly with a child's faith. Nothing has happened in the intervening decades to make me discount what I at first accepted so readily.

"My father's brother was accidentally killed on a hunting trip and the news of his death greatly affected his mother, my grandmother. She took to her room and did not emerge for months. Then suddenly, one evening, she appeared for dinner and joined the family, apparently recovered from her grief. That night, in the drawing room, she quietly rose from her chair and, as if acknowledging an unseen request, went to the piano, sat down and played a piece no one had ever heard before. When she had finished, she smiled and conversationally thanked her dead son for requesting that piece. Needless to say, the others were stunned, mainly because they knew she could not play a single note of music, and never *had!*

'She repeated the same performance every night for a week, playing the piano beautifully, always a different tune. Then on the last night, she spoke once more to her dead boy, thanked him again, and this time said: 'Good night. and rest, my dear one, I shan't play for you again.'

"This story was told to me as gospel. Those who witnessed the event, while amazed, nevertheless accepted it as a blessing, because it brought the poor lady solace. It cured her grief and, they felt, comforted the young man's spirit and put him to rest.

"My reaction to the tale was one of pride to know my family, while worldly in all the best ways, had enough spiritual imagination to be grateful for this miracle, and accept it without question. Possibly the only Doubting Thomas in the group was my father, who racked his brain time after time for a possible explanation, but could find none.

"I grew up hearing many stories of this kind concerning the fate of certain members of the family. Later, when I was well advanced in my career, I found myself cast in various film roles that caused me to ponder the inexplicable, and yet I prefer to believe in my philosophy of life because, frankly, it makes the world a far more varied and exciting place."

By the time he was school age, Vincent's mother, dissatisfied with the St. Louis public school system, created (along with other concerned parents) the St. Louis Community School; a progressive institution which encouraged its students to read anything they wished and pursue any subject matter that peaked their curiosity. And as part of the school's unique curriculum, Marguerite Price would lead the students on frequent trips to the St. Louis City Art Museum. It was here that Vincent received his initial exposure to what would become his first love: ART!

"I didn't want to be swallowed up by my older sisters' and brother's interests," Vincent remarked. "Everyone but me was musical, so my interest in art gave me an identity, and set me apart from the others."

When he was not attending school, Vincent loved to go to the movies. Of course, he always managed to get his mother or one of his sisters to take him whenever he wanted. (After all, he was royalty, even if they didn't know it yet). Ironically, the first film Vincent recalls seeing was *Der Golem* the 1920 German Horror film starring Paul Wegener as a stone statue that came to life. Although he loved every minute of it, Vincent admitted he was so terrified, "I wet my pants." Which ironically is something his own films later caused future moviegoers to do, although I am sure there are very few who would admit it as freely as Vincent did.

After graduating from the Community School, Vincent's father decided the now-twelve-year-old Vincent should attend the St. Louis Country Day School, an advanced boy's prep school, in the belief that it would properly prepare Vincent should he wish to follow in the family tradition and attend Yale University like his grandfather, himself and Vincent's brother Mortimer. But school was the farthest from Vincent's mind. He had recently become fascinated by American Indian art and wanted his parents to take him on a vacation trip to the Old West. His parents opted instead to send him to a dude ranch in Southern Colorado for the summer.

Despite the numerous activities, Vincent found time to go exploring in the nearby hills; and it was during one of these frequent treks that Vincent uncovered some ancient Indian artifacts. Believing he had found something important, he reported his discovery to the authorities. After closer examination, they found that Vincent had discovered an ancient Mesa Indian burial ground and before he knew it, Vincent was holding his first press conference (a sign of things to come). The significance of his find was so great it reached even the newspapers in St. Louis.

At the end of the summer, Vincent entered the prep school, where he quickly won the leading role of Sir Galahad in the school play. But even with a starring part, he wasn't comfortable in the role of the hero, as "I spent most of the rehearsal time backstage shooting craps," recalled Vincent.

Believing a trip to Europe would broaden his son's education, the elder Price sold his vacation home in Canada and used part of the money (the rest went to the other children) to send seventeen-year-old Vincent on a summer tour of Europe, where he spent the next several weeks exploring museums and cuisine of seven world capitals. While the tour was quite hectic, he did find enough time for a romance with in his words, "an extremely interesting young blonde girl."

Returning home he soon found himself "consumed with the idea of being an artist." And he did in fact find work as an artist on the school yearbook. But it wasn't until after he painted a portrait of his mother that he realized he didn't have any artistic talent. His mother, however, thought differently and had the painting framed and then hung on the parlor wall for all to see. For years it was a constant and painful reminder to Vincent of his lack of artistic talent, so when his mother died years later, he had the painting taken down and burned.

In the fall of 1929, Vincent entered Yale University as an art history major but later turned his attention to the study of English, when he decided to become an actor. Having had no formal training as an actor, he considered joining the Yale Drama School but he changed his mind when he found the group to be too "precious."

While at Yale, Vincent had his first adult encounter with the supernatural which set the path for the future king of horror films. "It was at a very formative period in my life," Vincent recalled. "I was faced with the choice of going out into an academic life or a creative artistic life; I just didn't know what decision to make.

"One night I was pondering over the matter and I asked my room mate, a very square, staid sort of fellow, for advice. *He* started to advise me against choosing an artistic career when suddenly he turned into an absolute flaming bush. No, I'm not kidding. To me he seemed to be on fire to the point where I had to back out of the room."

"Now, naturally, my room mate thought I was absolutely out of my square head, but I went out and walked for about an hour, preceded by this sort of flame."

"It was an extraordinary and wonderful experience, and afterwards I knew just what direction I had to take. Like most manifestations it was symbolic. I knew that if I did what this fellow suggested, it would burn me up as he had seemed to me to be burned. After that I knew I had to go into something which would give me an artistic outlet."

It was Vincent's contention that the only way to learn how to become an actor was to learn from the professionals. So, when he wasn't pursuing his studies he spent his time going to the theater.

"I think I saw every movie, good and bad, that played in New Haven, Connecticut, between the years 1930 and 1933. And I didn't miss many concerts, plays or revues, either. At the time, many, of the plays previewed, in New Haven."

While he gave up the idea of being an artist, he never gave up buying art, something he had been doing since he was twelve years old. As a young boy, Vincent used to *haunt* the shop of a particular art dealer, where he would spend hours studying and admiring the work of many famous artists, until one day he decided he would save up enough money to buy himself a piece of art.

Prices for artwork during the early part of the 20th Century were far more affordable than they are today, but even then Vincent had to scrimp and save to raise the down payment for an original Rembrandt etching, entitled "Two Academical Nudes, One Standing."

Using the installment method (something he would later promote during his tenure as the art buyer for the Sears Department stores), he put five dollars down and arranged with the art dealer to pay off the balance of $32.50 over a period of six months. ($37.50 was still quite a bargain for an original Rembrandt etching). Vincent did everything he could to pay off the dealer, including selling newspapers and magazines and even old junk, but by the end of six months the etching was paid off and Vincent was now the only twelve year old boy in St. Louis (if not the entire country) with an original Rembrandt, a piece he owned until his death seventy years later.

Through his contacts at the university, Vincent met and befriended the famous writer and cartoonist James Thurber (the creator of Walter Mitty), who introduced him to many of the art galleries and dealers found in New York City. But after seeing what treasures were available to him, Vincent decided, "I would only buy what I liked. I didn't want, and couldn't afford, to buy famous works or things that would certainly become more valuable as time went by. Some of them did, but they were things that I admired because I admired them, not because I wanted to make a buck."

In 1933, he graduated from Yale and moved to New York in the hopes of making it as an actor. But without formal training he was unable to find an acting job, so to make ends meet "I drove a bus for the students at Riverdale Country Day School (in Yonkers)," Vincent recounted. "After that I was an assistant teacher of English, German, dramatics and art. I had to eat. I could have written home for funds, but somehow that wasn't playing the game." He also helped out by coaching the students in school plays.

When the school year ended, Vincent decided to pursue his master's degree in art history. Using the money he earned as a teacher (and the eleven hundred dollars his father gave him as a graduation gift), he traveled to England (traveling third class. "The best way to travel," Vincent pointed out. "You have much more fun that way than when you go first class.") to attend the University of London's Division of Fine Arts located in the Courtauld Institute. It was here that his life changed forever. Until this point in time, he could have had just about anything he wanted. He came from a loving and supportive (not to mention well-to-do) upper middle class family, he had traveled throughout Europe, he attended an Ivy League university and was now in London pursuing his master's degree. He could have easily returned home to become anything he wanted, even a businessman like his father, but instead something happened to alter his life forever. He was bitten by the deadly sting of the acting bug!

"I don't think I would have been so determined to make something of myself if it hadn't been for the Depression. When my brother, Mortimer, graduated from Yale 14 years before, the world was his oyster. He was an enchanting man, but he never took advantage of all his opportunities."

Years later when Vincent was cast as the aging Russian aristocrat in the film *The Whales of August*, he used his late brother as the basis for the character. "I used my memories of him to show a man who is very charming but in no way working toward anything.

"When I graduated, there were no jobs," he said sadly. "The world was not my oyster but a very small pebble you had to push around with your nose. So I realized you have to seize every opportunity that comes your way.

"I was down, all right," Vincent admitted, "but not out and it occurred to me that maybe if I went to London and saw the stage producers there I'd be able to wrangle some sort of an acting job. I knew London like a book, knew just where to go and whom to see so it wasn't like going into a strange land. I'd spent several summers abroad during my college vacations. I had been a research student in the universities of Nuremberg, Vienna, Frankfort, and London. In 1932, during one of these vacation periods I had spent my days piloting tourists through museums and art galleries, tutoring in history and English while at night I had sung in a Vienna night club. I knew my way around—but that's about all. But my knowledge and acquaintance of Europe never fazed the London producers at all! They said, even more politely than the American producers: 'You can't get a professional stage job without professional experience and you can't get professional experience anywhere outside of a professional theatre,' all of which not only left me more than slightly bewildered but completely determined to find an acting job. Then about a week later, I lied my head off to English producer Norman Marshall and with such good effect that in no time at all I was given a part in the London production of Chicago produced by John Gielgud. That was in 1935 and I made my professional bow at the Gate theatre (in a non speaking role) as a Squeaky-shoed cop, doubling as the judge in the last act! Now, I slapped myself on the back, I was actually getting somewhere in this acting business!"

Years later, Vincent recalled his early career, and he came to the conclusion that he did not get the part because of his acting ability. But instead "the real reason I was hired was that I was an American and I could assist the director in a way. There were all these English girls playing American chorus girls and they didn't know how to chew gum. They would swallow it all the time. I not only taught them how to chew gum, but also how to talk with gum in their mouths!"

Despite having no lines, he did manage to attract attention. "Each time I crossed the stage, I would get a laugh from the audience." However, it wasn't his acting ability at work here but a pair of very squeaky shoes. This went on for several performances, until the rest of the cast decided they had had enough of it. So, when he arrived for the next performance, "I found my pair of shoes boiling in oil. After that, they never squeaked again!"

Two months later, Vincent returned to the Gate Theater in "a highly ambitious production of Laurence Housman's lovely little series of one-act plays based on the life of Queen Victoria, entitled *Victoria Regina,"* but this time it was not a walk-on part. The now twenty-three year old Price, who had no formal acting training, auditioned and won the lead role of Prince Albert, the German nobleman who married Queen Victoria. Of course, it may have been that he looked a lot like Prince Albert and that he spoke fluent German, which won him the part. After all, this was not a large scale production as the Gate Theater was "a small, private theater club (the whole theater including the backstage area wasn't much bigger than a large living room). It had to be a club because you couldn't portray royalty in the theater until they'd been dead for three generations and George V was still alive!" Vincent pointed out.

"The Gate Theater was located right across the bridge under Charing Cross Station. The theater was bombed during the war and has never been rebuilt."

While he got the part with no problem, he soon found that playing Prince Albert was in Vincent's own words "A wonderful part, wonderful character, but the problem for the actor really was, while challenging, not very exciting. My main problem with playing a character like Prince Albert was that Prince Albert was so good! In fact, he was called Albert the Good!

"So, I set out to find some kind of humanity about Prince Albert. I read everything about him, and you know he was an ideal kind of human being. I finally did find out that there were certain elements of humanity in him, after all, he and Victoria had nine children, so there had to be a certain amount of humanity required there! And he was not above having a good temper, and he was a man who was not too kind to his son, Edward VII. He had frailties, and on those, you could hang a character, a cloak of acting.

"But one of the things of playing a historical character is to try and look like him. But Prince Albert was somebody who really fooled me. Every time you see a picture of him or a statue of him or even a tobacco can, there he is! And he's absolutely unbending and inflexible. And the director in the play in London kept saying, 'Mr. Price! Vincent, you know you really do have the German accent. You look like Prince Albert, but you're a slob.' I couldn't stand up straight that long. I really couldn't! And the girl who was playing with me was four feet eleven inches and I'd start the scene standing straight and I'd end up bending over.

"So I went over to the Victoria and Albert Museum to do some research, and I went up to the curator of the costumes there. And I said, 'I'm an American slob--actor! And I'm playing Prince Albert. Help me! How did he look like that?

"So he said, 'Well, it's perfectly easy, Mr. Price.' He said, 'I think I can help you. We have many of Albert's uniforms from the time that he was here in England, right from when he first came and married Victoria. And if you'd like to see them, I'd like to show them to you.'

"And I said, 'That's Fine.'

"He said, 'We also have some of Queen Victoria's.'

"And I said, 'No, Albert's will do for now.'

"I went over, and he opened a big closet, and he pulled them out. And here were all Albert's uniforms. It looked like he was still in them.

"I said, 'Can I touch one?' I then knew why Albert was so unbending. There was a steel rod right from under his armpits to his hips. Well, if he'd bend over, he'd have sprung right back into place! That's what held him up. And I thought, well if that's the way Albert did it, then, I can do it.

"So on my way down to rehearsal that day. I went in an athletic store, a place where they sell things to athletes. And I bought one of those little sort of half corsets that middle-aged men wear when they play golf to keep everything from falling out. And I went to the men's room, and I put on this little corset, and I laced it up. And there I was...Prince Albert!

"So I went down to the theater, and I started to rehearse the scene. And the director said, 'Ah now, Vincent, now, you have it. Now, you really look like Albert. You sound like Albert. You are Albert.'

"And I said, 'Yes, thank you very much' and passed out cold.

"Well, about a half hour later, when somebody had enough sense to unbutton something other than my shirt, they found me in the Iron Maiden of Nuremberg and released me.

"But you know, I found an extraordinary truth about it from that corset. Yes, I did get some stays put into my clothes because they reminded me to stand up straight. Albert really wore those corsets. Now also, he had great military training. He was German. You know, his presence was that. But he needed it. I needed it!"

Chapter Two

Broadway, Here I Come
or
Helen Hayes, Furniture Mover

Once he had solved his posture problem, Vincent was then thrilled to be in his first real professional play and in the lead role, at that, but the fates had something more in store for him. Gilbert Miller, the Broadway producer/director was in London looking for a new project for his then current star Helen Hayes and as fortune would have it, attended a performance of the play and fell in love with it. He immediately bought the American rights to the play, and cast Miss Hayes in the title role (originated by British actress Pamela Stanley). Impressed by Price's performance, Miller brought Miss Hayes over to England to check out the leading man. And it was on Hayes' insistence that he hired Vincent to recreate his role on Broadway. But at first Miller was reluctant to hire Price because he was under the misconception that he was British ("I was an English discovery, I was discovered in England, but I was an Englishman from St Louis. St. Louis is a curious town being at the confluence of these two great rivers and being neither Southern nor Middle Western. Our speech pattern is quite unique, strangely enough, and they use records of mine to teach English in foreign colleges because I don't have an accent. I have a couple of veneers of an English accent which come from playing English parts.") But after reading in the London Times about Vincent's altercation with the British actor's union, that Miller realized his mistake and quickly offered Vincent the part.

Prior to Miller's offer, Vincent had been offered the parts of Orsino in *Twelfth Night* and of Orlando in *As You Like It*. The plays were to be produced by Sydney Carroll and given during the summertime at the Open-Air Theater in Regent Park. Thinking it would help his career to appear in the classics, Vincent accepted. Unfortunately, British Actor's Equity, upset that an American was given the parts over many qualified and unemployed British actors, complained to the Ministry of Labor, who was responsible for giving Vincent his work permit.

Summoned before the minister, producer Sydney Carroll quickly explained that Vincent was appearing in the productions for no money, believing the experience was his only needed compensation. Carroll also agreed to donate the salary he had proposed to pay Vincent to the Actor's Benevolent Fund. At first the minister was going to allow Vincent to have his permit, but the Union refused to let the matter rest and in the end the Ministry refused to give Vincent the necessary permit.

Vincent however did not need a permit to appear at the Gate Theater as it was a private theater club, supported by subscription and not with government and/or public money. So, instead of playing in *Twelfth Night*, Vincent took the small roll of Max in Schnitzler's *The Affair of Anatole*, before moving to New York and Broadway.

With a signed contract offering him two hundred and fifty dollars a week in his pocket, Vincent wired Miller to send him the cost of his passage home. Miller, however, believing Vincent was well off, ignored his request. Unbeknownst to Miller, players in all Gate Theater productions were working for prestige, since all of them got the same magnificent salary (even the stars) of $15 a week. So Vincent, though he was being hailed as a great star in England, could barely get up the price of passage to New York.

When Miller sent him a wire reprimanding him for stalling, he picked up his one suitcase and black cat Albert and arranged to travel to New York by steerage. He then informed Miller that he was coming in on the steamship *Aquitania.* Miller told the *New* York press about the great star he had signed up, and advised them to be at the gangplank and get the story of a lifetime.

So, when Vincent walked through steerage carrying his extra coats on one arm, and his suitcase and extra pair of shoes in the other, not a reporter saw him. *It* never occurred to Vincent that reporters were waiting. So, the next day, when he arrived at the theater, an upset Miller laced into him with "Who the devil do you think you are, refusing to speak to the press?"

"Refusing to speak to the press?" a surprised Vincent replied. "You mean reporters were waiting for me?"

It turned out that the reporters were waiting where the first class passengers docked. It hadn't occurred to them that "the story of a lifetime, one of the biggest stars in England," would arrive by steerage.

Vincent opened in the play on the day after Christmas 1935, to rave reviews. Also in the cast were actors George Macready, who years later would share his love of art (and other things) with Vincent by opening one of the first major art galleries in Beverly Hills, and George Zucco, who years later would become a horror star in his own right, although not on Vincent's level.

This was a dream come true for Vincent (or any young actor). He was twenty-four years old, and starring on Broadway in what was essentially his first acting role, opposite the great star Helen Hayes without any training and receiving great reviews. But he was soon to learn a lesson about what it takes to be a Broadway actor.

"I was young, inexperienced, and Helen was wonderful to me. Helen was about thirty-five years old and had been in show business since she was five. By the time she was seven she was already a star. She gave me what I might call my first real acting lessons. She was also the first one to teach me what 'upstaging' means.

"In one of my scenes with Miss Hayes, we were supposed to start, sitting in chairs on the stage, talking to each other. She was slightly upstage, but she kept moving farther and farther upstage until the end of the scene she was at the back wall and I had my back to the audience. Helen Hayes was a tiny woman, but she could move furniture marvelously!"

Intimidated by his costar, Vincent conceded that he once took acting lessons. Like many of his contemporaries, he was intrigued by the Stanislavsky method. "But I didn't tell Helen I was taking classes, Vincent recalled. "I'd been portraying Prince Albert as a rather simple, straightforward fellow. Then, as my teacher suggested, one night I played him in a more emotional way. After the first act, Helen stopped me backstage. 'What's come over you?' she asked. 'Whom do you think you're playing, the Russian Czar?'" That put an end to my acting classes, and I went back learning from the best in the business, Helen Hayes."

When the play closed for the summer of 1935 (most theaters back then did not have air-conditioning so they shut down for the summer months), Vincent was rushed off to Hollywood to make a screen test, which quickly brought him several film offers, but he wisely turned them all down to remain on Broadway, believing he was still too inexperienced to act in films. Vincent spent the summer of 1936 appearing with summer stock companies all over New York state as well as Westport, Connecticut and Showhegan Maine) in such plays as *Elizabeth the Queen* as Lord Essex with Mildred Natwick as Elizabeth, *What Every Woman Knows*, *The Passing of the Third Floor Back* and *The Firebrand.*

While in Skowhegan, Maine, he was offered the title role in a production of *Parnell.* Playing opposite him in the role of Katie O'Shea was an Irish brunette with very dark hair and dark brown eyes, named

Edith Barrett. During the course of the play, Vincent and Edith fell in love with each other. But as the summer season ended and the play closed, Vincent had to return to New York to continue in his role of Prince Albert.

When the play closed for the summer of 1937, in order to prepare for the national tour, Helen Hayes advised Vincent against his touring the country in the part. "I want very much to have you come with us," she said when the play was ready to go on tour, "but if you did that, personally, you will be very sorry. You will be typed forever after in Prince Albert parts. My advice to you is to stay here in the East and play summer stock for all you are worth. All sorts of parts and every part you can get. Vary them much as possible. It will be the greatest experience for you."

Vincent wisely decided to bow out. After 517 performances, he had had enough, but rather than return to summer stock he chose to try his hand at movie making. He returned to Hollywood where he was offered a long term contract by MGM, an offer he chose to reject in favor of a lesser paying seven year contract with Universal, as it allowed him six months off each year to return to Broadway.

A little-known fact about Vincent was that he was almost cast as Ashley Wilkes in the classic film *Gone with the Wind*. As Vincent recalled, "I was doing *Victoria Regina* on Broadway and they thought I'd be right for Ashley Wilkes. I was playing a German in the play, with an accent, and George Cukor (who was the first director of *Gone with the Wind*) had just seen the play and came backstage to see me. I said to him, (using a southern accent), 'Hello Mr. Cukor, how are you?' Now I'm from Missouri, and I naively have not a southern accent but an accent of that area, but he thought I was putting him on!, I didn't get the part, of course, I wish I had. I think I would have been better than Leslie Howard, because I never thought he was anything but English. He just was wrong. Everyone else was perfect. It would have been fun." (Several years ago, Vincent's screen test for Ashley Wilkes finally resurfaced in the MGM archives).

With Vincent now under contract, Universal soon found itself hard pressed to find a suitable project for him to make his screen debut. He was first scheduled to appear in a film called *Road Movie* opposite actress Wendy Barrie. The film which was later renamed *Prescription for Murder* was recast with Kent Taylor when the studio executives decided to give Vincent a better starring vehicle. He was then considered as a co-star for Universal's teen star Deanna Durbin's latest film, *That Certain Age* which was being produced and directed by Joe Pasternak. However, Vincent was deemed too young for the part of the older man, so Melvyn Douglas was given the part instead. Lastly, Universal offered him a role in a remake of *The Storm* opposite Nan Grey, Barton MacLane and Charles Bickford, but once again he lost out to contract player, Preston Foster.

Unable to find him a suitable part, Universal let Vincent's return to Broadway in a play entitled *The Lady Has a Heart*. The play was a flop and closed after about ten weeks and 91 performances. "It almost broke my heart," Vincent remembered. "When you are a big success in the beginning of your career, it's difficult to swallow adverse criticism. All actors are criticized from time to time, of course. But we still resent it, and we are hurt by it." Three months later, in January 1938, Vincent was recruited by Orson Welles to join his troupe of Mercury players in a production of *The Shoemaker's Holiday* playing opposite Joseph Cotton. The play ran for 69 successful performances which prompted Welles to offer Vincent a role in his next production, George Bernard Shaw's *Heartbreak House* opposite Geraldine Fitzgerald and Welles himself.

"I thought Orson Welles could have been the greatest director the theater ever had," Vincent declared. "He was 21 years old at the time, and to work with him was so exciting! He was fresh and full of wonderful ideas. He played Shodover in *Heartbreak House*, but he was not very good in it, because he never rehearsed with us. The company was marvelous, but Orson was completely undisciplined. I had a contract to do five plays with him, and went to rehearsal for the second play, after *Shoemaker's Holiday* had opened and Orson never showed up!"

It was during the production of Shoemaker's Holiday that Vincent rekindled his romance with actress Edith Barrett, whom he had met the previous summer during a stock company performance of *Parnell*. While they appeared in the cast together, they weren't lovers as they were in *Parnell*. But it didn't matter because every time they looked at each other, they knew that there was something between them which they wanted to pursue.

Orson Welles worked all his players fantastically hard. They had barely time enough to do anything but act. Still, during the lunch hour, Vincent and Edith went to *Longchamps* restaurant, ate and looked at each other. They discovered that they liked doing both.

They were delighted when they got a day off during rehearsals. It was spring; love was in bloom, and so was the countryside in and near New York. They got into a car, and Vincent drove into Connecticut. On the way home, he told Edith how he felt about her. She felt the same way about him.

Vincent and Edith were later married on April 22, 1938 at the St. Thomas Episcopal Church on New York's 5th Avenue. He was 26 and she was 31. In attendance were many of the Mercury players including Orson Welles, who arranged for the Wedding party to be held at the Mercury Theater after the regular Friday evening performance. "The wedding reception," laughed Vincent, "was so full of actors it looked like a revival of '*Trelawney of the Wells*.' I didn't know so many actors, since I had been acting only a few years, but Edith's grandfather, Lawrence Barrett, had been a famous actor in his day and Edith's family knew all the famous actors of two or three generations. And they all came."

The bride and groom enjoyed only a weekend honeymoon. The following Monday, Vincent and Edith were back hard at work.

Chapter Three

Hollywood, at Last
or
They Serve Coca-Cola at the Tower of London

In June of 1938, Vincent was recalled to Los Angeles by Universal to finally make his debut, in the screwball comedy *Service Deluxe.* "It was my first picture," recalled Vincent. "But I didn't know anything about *movie acting* so I went to Laura Elliot to study the technique. It involved learning how to control your face, so that you didn't mug or exaggerate your expressions, for the camera. Actors from the theater tend to mug a bit. Everybody from the theater who came to Hollywood studied with Laura."

Helen Murphy (played by Constance Bennett) runs the Madison Service Bureau, which provides a variety of services for its rich clients. When old man Wade (Lionel Belmore) hears his country bumpkin nephew Robert Wade (Vincent Price) is coming for a visit, he orders Helen to prevent his arrival. Robert who has invented a new type of tractor is traveling to New York in order to find a financial backer for the invention. While on board a ferry headed for New York City, Helen, finding who she thinks is the nephew, convinces a hapless yokel to return home and avoid New York. Confident she had done her job, she unknowingly befriends a handsome stranger, Robert Wade.

Robert, who has been raised in an all-female family, refuses to allow women to run his life, so unaware that Helen runs a service bureau, immediately falls for her. Once back in New York, Helen learns of his identity, but as she has fallen for him, she refuses to let him know the truth about her.

Robert learns that Helen's bureau has been hired to look after him. His uncle refuses to see him, immediately turns them down and goes off on his own, spending most of his free time with Helen (unaware that she is also Dorothy Madison of the Madison Service Bureau). But after weeks of disappointments, Robert, unable to sell his tractor, decides to return home. Upset over the possibility of losing Robert, Helen calls upon client Scott Robinson (Charlie Ruggles), a rich industrialist-turned-amateur-chef to look at Robert's invention.

After meeting Robinson's man-hungry daughter, Audrey (Joy Hodges) and his eccentric Russian cooking instructor, Bibenko (Mischa Auer), Robert makes a deal with Robinson. Needing a working model to show his board of directors, Robinson gives Robert the unlimited use of his basement machine shop to construct one. He also arranges for Helen's bureau to set Robert up with an apartment nearby.

Later, Audrey traps Robert into marrying her; Robinson, thrilled with the idea of having him as a son-in-law, quickly contacts Helen and orders her to make the arrangements for the wedding.

Upset over losing Robert, Helen confronts him and tells him her true identity. Furious over Helen's interference in his life, Robert throws her out after telling her that he is going to marry Audrey.

The next day, Robinson calls Helen to make the arrangement for a party at which he plans to unveil Robert's invention as well as announce his engagement to his daughter. In return for her fine service, Robinson also invites Helen to the party.

Robert, who resents the constant attention Audrey is giving him, begins to regret his decision to marry her. Learning that Bibenko is in reality an exiled Russian Prince, Robert arranges for him to attend the party in his full regalia.

Audrey falls for the Prince and when the day of the wedding arrives, she runs off with Bibenko to get married. Robert left at the altar proposes to Helen and together they agree to let him run the service bureau thereafter.

On the first day of shooting, director Rowland V. Lee planned to do a love scene between Vincent and star Constance Bennett. "I was scared out of my wits," Vincent recalled. When it came time for Vincent to perform, his overstated stage technique proved too much for Miss Bennett's custom-made dress. Vincent's rough handling of the dress nearly shredded the fragile material. So, while a prop man went off to find Vincent a pair of gloves to wear, the director enlightened Vincent to the proper way in performing a love scene for the camera. He then rearranged the cameras so he could shoot the scene from a different angle thus preventing Vincent's gloves from being seen in the film.

The picture suffered at the hands of the critics and died at the box office. But Vincent remembered, "It was wonderful experience for me but it was dreadful picture. It did however nearly ruin me; they made me buy a thousand dollars worth of clothes, so that I would look very elegant, but it took me the rest of the year to pay for them but not before they immediately went out of style."

While on the film he did get a chance to work with the King of Horror Makeup, Jack Pierce, who created the Frankenstein monster makeup. "Jack Pierce could make just about anyone look like a monster, Vincent remarked. "He shaved my eyebrows and I asked him 'Why!' He said, 'Actors don't have eyebrows like yours.' He shaved my mustache. Then I made him stop, right there, because it looked to me like I was just going to be shaved. It was terrible I looked like an Airedale."

Howard Barnes of the New York Herald Tribune called *Service Deluxe* "a floundering farce" although he thought "Vincent Price was moderately good at the romance," but "quite baffled by the extraneous antics."

While Bosley Crowther of the New York Times believed "Vincent Price seemed a likely screen hero" he did think Vincent was a too tall to "get into the camera field vertically."

"The executives at Universal had an idea," Vincent said. "Because I was tall, I could be turned into a second Gary Cooper. I told them, 'The only person who can be a second Gary Cooper is Gary Cooper,' but they didn't listen to me."

While the film did little to help his career, it did give the audience a glimpse of his wonderful singing abilities, something he honed at home years earlier while performing with his musically inclined siblings. In fact, he would continue to use this talent over the next five decades to the surprise and delight of his audience.

"I don't know what Universal thought of my performance, but for some reason they let Warner Brothers borrow me for my next film, *The Private Lives of Elizabeth and Essex*. The film dealt with the love-hate relationship between Queen Elizabeth I (Bette Davis) and Robert Devereaux, the Earl of Essex (Errol Flynn). Elizabeth who was torn between her love for the younger Essex, a flamboyant adventurer, (who plans to woe the queen and take control over her throne) and her inherited duties to the throne of England. Vincent was given the small but colorful role of Sir Walter Raleigh, who was jealous of both Essex's relationship with Elizabeth and his position over him in the royal court.

"It was a terrifying experience," remembered Vincent. "It was almost my first picture and I was playing Sir Walter Raleigh. I had played Essex with Mildred Natwick about three weeks before in summer stock. I thought I was pretty good as Essex, but I got the part of Raleigh because Errol Flynn was playing Essex. Every time, when Errol wouldn't learn his lines, the director, Michael Curtiz, would say (imitating Curtiz's heavy Hungarian accent) 'Errol, you better be careful, Vincent just played it three weeks ago, and so I can replace you.' Now you can imagine how it makes an actor feel. Errol loathed me. He finally got even with my by signing me up to do a picture in the south of France, which was an experience (*The Adventures of Captain Fabian*).

"Michael Curtiz *was* a caricature of a director." Vincent acknowledged. "He was a very good director, but he was a caricature and all those marvelous things you might have heard about him were all true. It was during Warner Brothers' heyday. Here I was doing a film with Bette Davis and Errol Flynn. How much bigger can you get? You can't. On the set were little page boys, all dressed up who could get you anything, girls, Cokes, anything, they had plenty of them too. Hot girls and cold Cokes! This one time Mike Curtiz said to one of the page boys, 'I want a Coca-cola!' The boy left, and we all heard him order this because it was during a big crowd scene and the boy never came back with the Coke. Finally, Mike got furious, which was part of his stock and trade, and he screamed at the top of his lungs. 'Next time I send some son of a bitch to get a Coca-cola, I go myself!'"

One of the most unusual events occurred off camera when the cast members held a contest to see who had the shapeliest calves. And as Vincent recalled, "Everyone was surprised when Donald Crisp won over Errol Flynn."

Vincent returned to Universal for his next film to co-star with Boris Karloff and Basil Rathbone, in the costume shocker, *The Tower of London*. He was offered the part of Edward IV, (which was later given to actor Ian Hunter) but instead opted for the smaller yet colorful part of the Duke of Clarence, a role which almost cost Vincent his life.

The film depicted the story of Richard, Duke of Glouster, a humpbacked tyrant who became King of England, by doing away with the members of his family who stood between him and the throne. Along the way to the top, Richard (played by Basil Rathbone) challenges his brother Clarence (Vincent Price) to a duel of drink. Going into the wine cellars, the brothers try to drink each other under the table, with the winner gaining Clarence's valuable land holdings.

While viewing the completed film, you get the impression that both men were having the time of their lives but as Vincent recalled, things were not always as they appeared. "Basil and I had to rehearse that drinking scene over and over again. I nearly threw up after drinking goblet after goblet of fake wine, which was in reality diluted Coca-Cola."

At first it appears that Clarence is the winner of the duel, but Richard manages to recover and together with his henchman, Mord the bald-headed club-footed executioner (Boris Karloff), they drown Clarence in a vat of wine. Well, things didn't quite go the way it was planned and it was Vincent who almost drowned. "There was a scene in the film where Basil and Boris drown me in a vat of wine and being young and foolish, I insisted on going into the vat myself. The stunt coordinator instructed me to grab onto a bar at the bottom of the vat, count ten, and then come up for air. The ten count would allow Basil to finish the take and, also give the crew enough time to reopen the lid of the vat. The liquid in the wine vat was actually water, but Basil and Boris had used the barrel to deposit cigarette butts and old Coca Cola bottles in. Anyway, while I was down at the bottom of that tank...holding onto the bar and counting....I heard the crew breaking into the vat with axes. It seems that my friends, Boris and Basil, had sat on top of the lid and the thing was stuck. Luckily for me, they got it open before I was in any serious danger.

"After they yanked me out of the vat by the heels, I got a round of applause from the crew, but I was disappointed to find my two co-stars, who had been very nice to me, so far, not on the set. I thought the least they could have done was to lead the applause. But they appeared a few moments later with a beautifully wrapped gift---a carton of Coca-Cola!"

One of the positive aspects of the film for Vincent, however, was that it enabled him to develop longstanding friendships with Karloff and Rathbone, which would continue until their deaths in the 1960's. Despite the numerous monsters and villains he portrayed, Karloff was in reality a kind and gentle man, a fact which reminded Vincent about the first time he met Boris Karloff. "He was in full makeup. He had one shoe that was built up into a clubfoot which caused him to wobble when he walked. He also had a shaved head and a hump on his back. He came up to me with his little daughter seated on his shoulder and said,' I just want you to know that I'm not as mean as I appear'."

Now Basil Rathbone was more the practical joker type: "he would do wonderful things to keep everyone's spirits up. The crew on that picture loved Basil and in particular there was one Grip, who always made good-natured insults about England. So, Basil would feign anger and chase the man up into the catwalks of the soundstage.

"One day Basil gathered the entire cast together and said, 'Let's make an agreement amongst ourselves, that we never tell a dirty joke that we didn't hear after we were fourteen.' So, we all went home that night and thought about all the jokes we heard before we were fourteen. They were not particularly dirty, but they were very funny. So, we came on to the set the next day and told each other these stories. He was a sweet man, but a great prankster and joker and a wonderful actor."

Except for Vincent, the majority of the male cast members were all English and as actress Rose Hobart (who portrayed Anne Neville) recalled, "All those English actors were terrible womanizers who were always telling stories about their conquests. Well, we always stopped for afternoon tea and I was the only one of the women invited to join the four guys (Rathbone, Karloff, Price and Hunter). And their conversation was getting dirtier every day. It was really getting obscene! One day, when they had just finished one really bad one and they were laughing and having a ball, I asked, "What are the three most insulting words that a woman could say to a man?" And the answer was, "Is it in?" The reaction was fantastic, because I knew exactly who had been asked this question and who had not. And they were so shocked that all conversation ceased on the subject for the rest of the time I was invited back. They were trying to outdo each other, of course. The boys were showing off and were lying through their teeth!"

Also in the cast was Basil Rathbone's son John Rodion (Rathbone) as Lord Devere and Donnie Dunagan portrayed Basil Rathbone's son in the film *The Son of Frankenstein*.

The reviewer for the Brooklyn Daily Eagle thought "Vincent Price turned in an encouraging portrait of the Earl of Clarence, the bon-vivant of the family, who meets his fate in a tank of Malmsey wine."

But Variety, the show business newspaper went further with their praise by proclaiming "Vincent Price is excellent as the weakly Duke of Clarence."

After completing the film, he returned in December 1938 to New York to appear in the Broadway revival of *Outward Bound*. Vincent called it, "A strange and very dated play about people who are dead and get on this ship and pass over into the next world. It had been a big success the year before with Leslie Howard. It was being revived as a comeback vehicle for an actress named Laurette Taylor who, as Vincent recalled, "was the most talented actress I ever worked with. She had retired from the theater, but made a comeback in *Outward Bound*. It was directed by Otto Preminger. Laurette hadn't been in the theater for a number of years. Her husband had died about 20 years before, and she'd been drunk ever since. It was the longest wake in history!

"Otto was able to give her a sense of security, which she was lacking. On opening night, when she made her entrance, the audience gave her a standing ovation for a good ten or fifteen minutes. It was one of those extraordinary moments. To have brought this incredible star back into existence was really a great triumph for Otto.

"While I was appearing in *Outward* Bound at the National Theatre in Washington, we gave the very first benefit performance on behalf of the

March of Dimes. This was a favorite charity of President Roosevelt, who invited the entire company to come and take supper at the White House with him and his First Lady.

"We were shown throughout the various rooms by Mrs. Eleanor Roosevelt herself. When we reached the Lincoln bedroom, one of the ladies in our troupe shivered, and murmured she felt the place was 'haunted.' Mrs. Roosevelt admitted that she felt that way, too, and told of an incident that had occurred just a few days before.

"'I was sitting in my study downstairs when one of the maids burst in on me in a state of great excitement," Mrs. Roosevelt recalled. "I looked up from my work and asked her what was the trouble.

"'He's up there—sitting on the edge of the bed, taking off his shoes!' she exclaimed.

"'Who's up where, taking off his shoes?' I asked.

"'Mister Lincoln!' the maid replied.

"Shortly afterwards, Mrs. Roosevelt elaborated on the Lincoln legend in her own newspaper column, '*My Day*.' Her theory was that anyplace where someone had lived *hard* would quite likely be haunted by their personality.

"I consider this quite a plausible theory. Nor does a person have to have lived an unhappy existence to make his presence felt."

The play (which also featured actress Helen Chandler, who was the female lead in 1931 film version of Dracula opposite Bela Lugosi) ran for 255 performances before Vincent had to return to Universal in the summer of 1939. While appearing in the play he supplemented his income by joining the cast of the then popular radio serial, *Valiant Lady* as Paul Morrison, the resident villain. The cast also included Joan Blair, Judith Lowry and fellow Mercury theater player Everett Sloane. It was also during this time period that he began lecturing on art to local schools and colleges, something he would do throughout the rest of his life.

Chapter Four

The Invisible Actor
or
I Should Look So Good in a Coma

Once back in Hollywood, Vincent did a one day test for a part in an Irene Dunne film, but when the film was postponed, he was put into *The Invisible Man Returns* which marked his first appearance in a science fiction/horror film.

When Geoffrey Radcliffe (Vincent Price) is falsely accused of murdering his brother and is sentenced to death. Dr. Frank Griffin (John Sutton), the brother of Jack Griffin, (the original invisible man played by Claude Rains in the 1933 film), turns him invisible, which allows him to escape prison and find the real killer, before the invisibility drug drives him mad. (Years later, Vincent and Claude Rains would work together for the first and only time on the *Suspense* radio series in the episode *The Hands of Mr. Ottermole.*)

Learning that Willie Spears (Alan Napier, making his American film debut and later known for his portrayal of Alfred the Butler on the *Batman* television series) has recently been promoted from night watchman to a management position, he begins to suspect his cousin, Richard Cobb (Sir Cedric Hardwicke) is behind it. Tricking the superstitious and drunken Spears that he is a ghost come back to haunt him, he gets him to admit that he saw Cobb murder his brother and agreed to keep silent in return for a better job.

Radcliffe confronts his cousin, who flees for his life, but not before killing Spears. Despite interference from the police, Radcliffe finds Cobb and chases him back to the family mining company, where he traps him atop a coal elevator. Radcliffe is shot by the police, while Cobb falls to his death but not before admitting his guilt and his cousin's innocence.

Having escaped the same fate as Cobb, Radcliffe manages to find his way back to Dr. Griffin, despite having lost a lot of blood. Unable to find a suitable antidote to the invisibility drug, Griffin gives Radcliffe a transfusion, which restores him to visibility, thus allowing him to receive a lifesaving operation.

At first Vincent was excited to be playing the title role until he learned that the film was going to be directed by German immigrant Joe May who as Vincent recalled was "difficult to understand, as he spoke very little English. I spoke German, which gave me something of a rapport with him. At least we were able to curse at each other. He was a great director in his day in Germany, but he really did have a bad time here because he didn't speak very much English at all." Joe May was one of founders of the German cinema and is credited for giving director Fritz Lang his start in films.

There have been great improvements in special effects over the many years since the invisible man returned, and no one was more grateful for this than Vincent, especially after recalling what it took to make him invisible. "There was a scene in the film where I had to undress a scarecrow and put its clothes on myself, because I am only invisible when I'm naked and it was very cold outside. The scene took nine hours to film but it lasted less than a minute on the screen. In those days the set was filmed with the camera anchored firmly in place and then they draped the whole set in black velvet, I was then draped in black velvet and so whatever I put on myself, I draped around the black velvet. It took forever because if your hand went too far in any direction, it would become visible to the camera."

While making the film was a "laborious and boring experience" the final product was the photographic marvel of its time. But not everyone was able to appreciate the time and effort that went into the invisibility effects, as Vincent learned. "I liked to sit behind people in the theater, while they were watching the film. At the end of the film, when I become visible again, there were two fellows seated in front of me and one of them turned to the other one and said, 'That will teach him not to drink ten cent whiskey!'"

William Boernel of the New York World Telegram found the film to be a highly exciting, if preposterous, thriller which will leave you pale around the gills with its eerie shudders," with Vincent Price playing his part with "intense sincerity."

Having found someone who could understand him, director Joe May cast Vincent in his next film, an adaptation of Nathaniel Hawthorne's *House of the Seven Gables.* In which Jeffrey Pyncheon (George Sanders) returns home to discover his father, Gerald (Gilbert Emory), at brother Clifford's (Vincent Price) insistence is planning to sell their ancestral home to pay off his bad debts. Jeffrey, believing there is a valuable land grant hidden somewhere in the house, grows furious.

Clifford, who plans to marry his cousin Hepzibah (Margaret Lindsay) and move to New York, could care less and would rather be rid of the house, which is said to be cursed by the ghost of Matthew Maule, who was swindled out of his land and his life by the Pyncheons' ancestor.

However, before the house can be sold, Jeffrey convinces his father to reconsider, which in turn causes Clifford to argue with his father, who suddenly suffers an attack and collapses, hitting his head as he falls. Clifford rushes to his side, but the old man dies moments later.

Jeffrey, deciding to get the house for himself, accuses Clifford of murdering their father and manages to get him sent to prison for life. When the time comes for Jeffrey to take control of the house, he learns that his father, in order to keep his creditors from taking the house, signed the deed over to Hepzibah, who in turn banishes him from the house. She quickly closes up the house and intends to live in it like a prison, just like her fiancé Clifford.

Twenty years later, Clifford returns home after the new governor commutes his sentence and, together with Hepzbiah and Matthew Maule's descendant (Dick Foran), trick Jeffrey into clearing Clifford of his father's murder before he himself dies from the same ailment that killed the elder Pyncheon, leaving Clifford to finally marry Hepzibah.

As Vincent recalled, "It was a good film, but the two main characters were brother and sister in the novel yet they wanted to add a little sex to the film, so in the movie they were lovers." Vincent would appear years later in a more faithful (but abridged) version in the anthology film, *Twice-Told Tales*.

During the course of his long career, and due no doubt to his cultured voice, fine manners and the type of parts he played, Vincent was often mistakenly believed to have been English. Not just by the viewing public but by his peers and members of the press such as actress Rose Hobart and Elizabeth Copeland, the film reviewer for the *Richmond Virginia New Leader* who in her review of the film refers to George Sanders and Vincent Price as "two poised and personable Englishmen." Vincent, as you now know, was born in Missouri, while Sanders was in fact born in Russia.

While Vincent and Joe May got along well enough, co-star George Sanders did not. As Vincent recalled "George hated Joe May, he just couldn't stand him. I don't know why because George was such a dear and wonderful man. I knew him really intimately and was very, very fond of him. He only pretended to be a dreadful man, but he was a brilliant raconteur, spoke Russian superbly, he was a wonderful pianist and had a beautiful singing voice."

Vincent's next film *Green Hell* was directed by James Whale, the man responsible for the films *Frankenstein* and *The Old Dark House*. He was considered to be one of the best directors in Hollywood, but by the time

Vincent came to work with him, he was past his prime and this proved to be one of his last films.

Archeologists David Richardson (Vincent Price), Keith "Brandy" Brandon (Douglas Fairbanks, Jr.) Forrester (George Sanders), Dr. Emil "Nils" Loren (Alan Hale, Sr.), Graham (Gene Garrick) and Jim "Tex" Morgan (George Bancroft) head off into the South American jungles to search for a hidden Incan Temple and buried treasure. After trekking through the jungles for months, they finally locate the temple and set up camp. They soon uncover the burial tomb of the Incan chiefs and their horde of golden treasures. However, before they can return with the gold to civilization, Richardson is killed by a hostile tribe of Indians. Problems arise when their friendly Indian workers return to camp with supplies and Richardson's widow, Stephanie (Joan Bennett).

The lonely men soon begin to fight among themselves for her attentions with Forrester coming out on top. When Stephanie and Forrester prepare to return to town, Brandy makes his move on Stephanie. Suddenly, their Indian workers desert them and they soon find themselves under attack by the hostile Indians. Deciding to stand their ground, they barricade their campsite and shoot it out with the Indians. When Brandy sneaks out to retrieve the rest of their ammunition, he is struck down by poison darts. Upon seeing Brandy apparently dying, Stephanie turns her affections towards him. Forrester, having lost the girl and believing they are all doomed, shoots himself. Minutes later, the friendly Indians return with reinforcements and wipe out the hostile Indians, allowing Brandy (who survives the poison) to return with Stephanie, the treasure and the others to civilization.

"We were all interested to see what Whale would make out of it," declared Vincent. "Whale had been one of the great directors of Hollywood. All of us felt it, when we were working on the film. But even he could not disentangle himself from the bad story. The script was written by Frances Marion, who was one of the great lady scenarists of Hollywood, but it was a really ordinary story."

Despite the bad script, Vincent still had a fondness for this film because "It was one of the funniest films ever shot anywhere in the world and one of the ten worst pictures ever made. I'm rather proud of that one because it was hysterical. Joan Bennett (later the matriarch of the Collins family on the gothic television soap opera *Dark Shadows*) was lost in the jungle and she's later found made up in a beautiful hairdo and beautifully dressed. The doctor leans over her and says, 'don't worry, it's just a coma.' Just a coma! We should all look so good in a coma!"

"Then there was a scene in which I was going up the Amazon with Douglas Fairbanks, Jr., who was playing a character called Brandy. For some unknown reason, while going up the Amazon, I say, 'Brandy, do you think it is possible for a man to be in love with two women at the same time, and in his heart be faithful to each, and yet want to be free of both of them?" Well, opening night, the audience fell on the floor with laughter. It was the funniest picture in the whole world."

Vincent was fortunate to be killed off early in the film, but not so fortunate is its star Douglas Fairbanks, Jr. who remembered that "Harvard University voted *Green Hell* the worst picture of the year."

"I think it is one of the worst I ever made," recalled Fairbanks. "It was produced by a friend of mine named Harry Edington and we were all clients and friends of his so he sort of appealed to us all on a friendship basis to do it. The dialogue was so absolutely dreadful, it was funny. Nobody took the film seriously that I can remember other than James Whale himself, who thought it was pretty good. But we all felt obliged to Harry Edington. It was a bad script written by a wonderful writer, Frances Marion, who had done a lot of work with my step-mother Mary Pickford.

"However, I admired Vincent Price as an actor and I thought he was terribly good in the things I had seen him in, like the play *Victoria Regina*. I thought he was first class actor and a very genial and nice fellow to work with. But the film was so bad I think I made a deliberate effort to forget as much of it as I could."

While Universal couldn't save the film, it did manage to reuse the Mayan Temple set as it later turned up as an Egyptian Temple in the film *The Mummy's Tomb*.

Chapter Five

Vincent, the Playwright
or
Pearl Harbor Gets the Gaslight Treatment

After the completion of *Green Hell*, Universal (which was in financial trouble) terminated Vincent's contract. Vincent quickly signed with Darryl F. Zanuck's 20th Century-Fox, who offered him the same salary terms and conditions as Universal had given him. Eager to make use of their new star, Fox rushed him into two historical costumers, *Brigham Young, Frontiersman* and *Hudson's Bay* before he returned home to St. Louis to appear before sold out crowds in a production of *The American Way* at the St. Louis Municipal Opera House.

Brigham Young, Frontiersman was based on the true story of how the Mormons escaped persecution by traveling to Salt Lake City, Utah to set up their church. Joseph Smith (Vincent Price) the Church founder and prophet is found guilty of treason in Illinois and sentenced to death but is soon murdered when a mob storms the jail where he is being held. Disciple Brigham Young (Dean Jagger) takes over leadership and takes the people to Utah. Also in the cast were John Carradine, Brian Donlevy, Jane Darwell and a young Tyrone Power (whose death years later caused a very unusual if not unnerving incident in Vincent's life).

Hudson's Bay had exiled British nobleman Lord Edward Crew (John Sutton) teaming up with French Canadian trappers Pierre Radisson (Paul Muni) and Gooseberry (Laird Cregar) after escaping from jail to start a fur trading business with the Indians of Hudson's Bay. But when the government of French Canada attempts to take the profits, Lord Edward takes them back to England to ask King Charles II (Vincent Price) for help.

King Charles is at first reluctant but when he learns of the great profits he will receive, he changes his mind. Lord Edward returns to Canada with his friends to form the Hudson's Bay Company. Also along for the trip is Lord Edward's fiancée Barbara's (Gene Tierney) spoiled rich brother, Gerald (Morton Lowry), who against direct orders gives alcohol to the Indians. Alcohol causes the Indians to go crazy and fight among themselves. Without the Indians' help, Pierre will not be able to deliver the fur pelts to

King Charles, so in order to appease the Indians, he orders Gerald executed against Edward's wishes.

Once back in England, King Charles orders them thrown into jail for executing a British subject without his permission. However, once he learns that the Indians will refuse to deal with him without Pierre and Gooseberry, the greedy King Charles agrees to free them and send them back to Canada. Leo Mishkin of the New York Morning Telegraph thought "only Vincent Price, as King Charles himself, tried to set an example of what good acting should be."

While Vincent was busy setting an example of good acting, actor Laird Cregar in his film debut, was busy stealing the show. Cregar, who would later gain fame as Jack the Ripper in the classic film *The Lodger*, was a giant of a man who would die tragically at the age of 31, due to a massive heart attack brought on by years of excessive dieting.

"Laird was an extraordinary man," Vincent recalled. "He was also an enormous man. He was a giant, and his family were all giants. I happened to know his mother and his brothers. He was about six foot three and he weighed about 300 pounds, but it wasn't fat. It was muscle. He tried desperately to get thinner, but he just couldn't. He couldn't take it off without removing some bones or something!

"I read the eulogy at his funeral, strangely enough, though I didn't know him that well. His mother wanted me to do it because I'd been with him in his first picture. He was a wonderful actor and died much too young."

Despite its benign subject matter, the film did have a problem with the motion picture censors. According to Vincent, "I was playing a scene as Charles II with Nell Gwyn (Virginia Field) and we had some Charles II Spaniels on the bed and she leaned over and they cut the entire scene out, with no explanation."

Vincent later traveled to Skowhegan, Maine to oversee the production of his own play, a screwball comedy entitled, *The Poet's Corner*. "I loved it. I had a wonderful time. I was at a famous summer theater in Maine and I showed the play to the director (I'd had worked there before) and he said, 'Well, it needs some work, but I like it and I'll do it, if you'll play in it.' I said, My God, I can't play in it; I'd be so nervous and self-conscious. So, he put me in a small part.

"Well, it was a disaster, because every time somebody else would open their mouth and say one of my brilliant lines, I'd gasp with awe or if it was a funny line, I'd belly laugh and I wasn't meant to laugh! But it was fun to do, but I never tried another one."

In the spring of 1941, Vincent and Edith welcomed the birth of their son, Vincent Barrett Price. A few short weeks later he returned to Los Angeles to assume the Jose Ferrer role in the West Coast production of *Mamba's Daughter* starring Ethel Waters.

From the time he was a small boy, Vincent's greatest idol and perhaps the man who has had the strongest influence in his life was John Barrymore. When he grew older, he saw in Barrymore not only the great artist but also the most colorful and exciting personality on both the stage and screen. Vincent's greatest ambition up to this time had been to play the Barrymore role in "Topaze." "Not only because he played it, remarked Vincent, "But because it is a great role. And he showed an actor the way."

On December 5, 1941, Vincent opened in the lead role of Mr. Manningham in the New York version of the British play *Gaslight* (a role Charles Boyer would later inherit in the 1944 film version). The play, re-titled *Angel Street,* starred Judith Evelyn (who later co-starred with Vincent in *The Tingler*) as the wife and Leo G. Carroll (future star of TV's *Topper* and *The Man From U.N.C.L.E.'s* Mr. Waverly) as the detective.

"Aristotle had a theory of drama," declared Vincent. "It also became the story of my life, in which part of it was that the villain, the man who must pay for his sins at the end of the drama, should not be a drab man. He should not be a skulking man. He should not be an ugly man. He needn't be the *Hunchback of Notre Dame.* He needn't be that kind of man. Actually, according to Aristotle, the villain should be a man of great nobility, of great high birth, of wealth, of education because Aristotle felt if that man has to pay for his sins---this educated, beautiful, noble human being, if he must pay for his sins, then, you and I---the hoi polloi---know that we must pay for ours.

"Well, Prince Albert was a noble man. But the fellow in *Angel Street* was an ignoble man, and yet, there was a kind of nobility of badness about him. He was the kind of villain...an ideal villain in a way. He believed in himself, in his own charm, in the fact that he could get away with anything. And he almost did.

"The story of *Angel Street* is a fascinating story and it also changed my life. It was set in Victorian London about the year 1890. And it's set in a Victorian mansion, so when the curtain goes up, you see a Victorian living room with the fire burning and the gaslights flickering. And on the couch is a rather arrogant, handsome man very sort of sure of himself, and his fluttery wife, Bella is flying around doing all those lovely things for him that *You* liberated women no longer do for us men: bringing him his slippers and the paper. And Jack Manningham is lying there, accepting it all as though it were his due. And you get a kind of clue from the dialogue that everything is not all sweetness and light in the Manningham household, that Bella has been kind of silly and kind of irresponsible.

"And Jack said, 'But Bella, you know, my dear, you are much better. You aren't losing things quite as often. You haven't misplaced things as you usually do. And to reward you, I read in the paper here that your favorite actor is opening next week in London in the West End, and I'm going to take you to the theater.'

"Well, Bella is hysterical with joy, a little too hysterical. She said, 'Oh, Jack, if you do that, I promise I won't do all those terrible things. I promise you I'll keep my wits about me.'

"He said, 'Well, that's fine, Bella. I'm going to take you to the theater.' And he said, 'By the way, Bella, what did you do with that watch that I gave you to take to be repaired?'

"And she said, 'Oh, Jack, oh, you know, you gave me that watch, Jack. Just three days ago, Jack, you gave it to me. I took it, and when you left, I put it right in that drawer. And I've looked everywhere in the house.'

"Well, Jack gets into a fit of temper, and he says, 'Why am I taking you to the theater? You're just exactly as you were. You lose everything. You're losing your mind.' And he said, "Of course, I'm not going to take you to the theater now. I'm going out for my evening walk. And by the time I get back, you find that watch or else!'

"Well, the poor lady is hysterical with frustration and heartbreak because she really thought that she'd been forgiven, and she wanders around the room. And behind the books, she finds a picture that he's accused her of taking down and hiding. She finds the grocery bill that he accused her of losing, and she finally just falls into a collapse by the front door and is sobbing there. Jack has gone for his walk.

"And there comes a knock on the front door. She open it and a little man is standing there with a little cape, hat, and he says, "Mrs. Manningham?"

"And she said, 'Yes, yes. What is it? What is it, please?'

"He said, 'I wonder if I might speak to you for just a moment.'

"She said, 'No, please, please, not tonight. I'm not feeling well. Please, come back another time.' And she shuts the door.

"The little man says, "Just a minute, Mrs Manningham. It will only take me a minute. May I talk to you?'

"She says, 'Well, come in. Come in quickly. My husband's out for his walk. He mustn't find you here. Come in.'

"So the little fellow comes in, takes his coat and hat off, and puts them down.

"She says, 'No! No! You mustn't do that. Now, you must leave.'

"He says, 'but it's so hot in here, Mrs. Manningham.' So he puts his coat back down on the chair, and he starts to tell her a story. He is a retired sergeant from Scotland Yard, and he tells her a story that's really quite alarming, that here in this house where she, Bella and Jack Manningham live -- about five years before they moved in, a horrible murder had taken place.

"And she said, 'Why are you telling me this?'

"And he said, "Well, Mrs. Manningham, I must tell you this because I have kept up an interest in this case. You see, this old lady who lived in this house, your house, Mrs. Manningham -- was murdered right here in this very room, right where you're standing, Mrs. Manningham. Her body lay there. Her body was brutally ripped apart, and everything in the whole house was ripped apart. And the blood was all over there.'

"She said, 'Please, don't tell me this. Please!'

"He said, 'Mrs. Manningham, I must tell you because I really want to know. You all have only lived here a little while, and I've waited until you were settled in. I want to know. Have you ever seen anything suspicious? Have people come to the door and talked to you -- people you didn't know. Have you seen anyone standing across the street?'

"She said, 'No. Why?'"

"He said, 'Well, you see, Mrs. Manningham. Our theory is because the murderer was never caught, and because we discovered, through friends, that the old lady had a very famous collection of rubies, that perhaps the reason the house was ransacked was that the man was looking for the rubies.'

"And she said, "No, I've never seen anybody. Now, please go because my husband is out, and when he comes back, he must not find you here.'

"Well, he goes on telling her more of his theories, and suddenly, while he's talking, the gaslight begins to grow dim, dim, dim. He says, 'What's that?'

"She said, 'Oh, that's the gaslight. It happens every night just exactly this same time. I'm sitting here, and the gaslight begins to grow dim.'

"He said, "Every night?'

"And she said, 'Yes, every night.'

"He said, 'Every night at the same time?'

"Yes, every night at the same time, the gaslight grows dim.'

"He said, 'Well, how do you explain it?'

"She says, "Well, I've called the Gas Company. They say it's just the pressure. But don't worry about it.'

"So he says, 'Every night at the same time? How do you know?'

"And she said, 'Well, you see, my husband is a very punctual man. Every night, exactly the same minute, he goes out and has his walk. And after he's been gone for about three or four minutes, the gaslight grows dim, and it stays that way for five or six minutes. And then, it starts to go up, and in three or four minutes, he comes back.'

"He said, 'Both very peculiar.' Well, he starts to tell her more about his theory, and she becomes really fascinated by this whole story. And as they're talking, suddenly, the gaslight goes up.

"She says, 'There. You see? He'll be coming back now in a minute. Now, you must go. Please, take your coat and hat. Go out the front door. Go to the right because he comes from the left, and hurry.'

"Well, the old fellow won't go. And he starts talking to her, and finally, you hear a key in the front door. And the husband is coming back.

"She says, 'Now, he's here. Now, please! Take your coat and hat. Go hide in that closet in there. He never goes in there at night. After he's gone up to bed, I'll come and let you out.'

"So the old fellow takes his coat and goes and hides in the closet.

"Well, if you have ever been to a New York opening night, then you know it's a disaster. The audience is dead. You have a feeling they don't know what they're doing. They're there for all the wrong reasons, but not this opening night!

"That opening night, the audience had become so involved in this murder, in this extraordinary relationship between the husband, the wife and the detective, that when the old fellow took his coat and went and hid in the closet, the whole audience yelled, 'You forgot your hat!'

"Well, I'm standing in the wings with the key in the door ready to come in. I turned to the Stage Manager. I said, 'My God, they're alive!'

"You forgot your hat!"

"So the old fellow comes out and gets his hat and goes back into the closet.

"Anyway, it gives you an idea of the involvement that the audience had; well, anyway, to make the whole story short, I come back, and I accuse her of more things. And obviously, I'm the villain. Every night, I go out for my walk. I go around the block. I go up into the attic. I turn on the gaslight. The gaslight goes down. Then, I turn it off, and it comes back up. And I come back and in. And finally, the detective catches me, and they find the rubies, and they put me in prison. That's the end of it. Well, anyway, that's the plot.

"The extraordinary thing was that opening night in New York; not only was the audience at the edge of their seats throughout the entire play. It probably was the greatest success of a play of its kind ever in the history of the American theater. And the audience --- when Judith Evelyn, who played the wife brilliantly, came out, they screamed and yelled ---- Leo G. Carroll, who played the detective, came out, and the audience yelled 'Bravo!', but when I came out, the whole audience stood up and hissed! Oh, it was marvelous. It really was.

"After that, I thought now, maybe if I go to Hollywood and can find a good villain maybe that will put me across as an actor, and give me the identity that I want.

"I like any kind of role in which I can lose myself, and that can happen just as easily in a role as a murderer or criminal as in a romantic part. I should hate to be limited to just playing myself. That, I think, would be very dull, since most of the fun in acting is getting out of yourself."

The play ran for over three years and 1292 performances, which surprised the Shuberts who produced the play (and owned the theater) as Vincent fondly recalled. "The Shuberts hated the play so much when they came to see a run-through that they refused to print tickets for the Monday performance. The play opened Friday, and Saturday the reviews were raves, one hundred percent. I'd never read reviews like that in my life --- 'the best melodrama of all time' ---- and so forth. And there were no tickets. There was a line outside the box office so the girls in the office had to write the seat numbers down on slips of paper!

"Finally Sunday came around. My wife was out on the West Coast and I called her from New York and I said: 'Isn't it wonderful?' There was a dead silence and then she said, 'what do you mean wonderful? It's the greatest tragedy of all time.' I said, 'The play is a hit! It is the biggest hit in town! What's this tragedy bit?' She said, *'PEARL HARBOR!'* I had read the papers, but I'd only read my own notices, I hadn't read about Pearl Harbor. Isn't that a terrible story? Almost every show in New York closed sooner or later right after that, except *Angel Street* which ran for years."

When MGM approached Shepherd Trow, who owned the rights to the play (as well as being one of its producers) in the hopes of transferring the play to the motion picture screen complete with the entire Broadway cast. Trow agreed to sell them the rights on the condition that he be allowed to direct the film. Trow was relatively unknown in Hollywood, and had had no experience as a film director. Therefore MGM was forced to turn the project down, which disappointed everyone in the cast, which as Vincent recalled "was very sad. Strangely enough, when Ingrid Bergman and Charles Boyer finally did *Gaslight*, we all got very good notices for it, because the film was not nearly as good as the play. The minute you open it up and take it out of that room, it loses its claustrophobia."

During the run of the play, Vincent made several ventures into radio including a recurring role on the serial *Helpmate* which also featured his *Angel Street* co-star Judith Evelyn as well as actress Arlene Francis (of TV's *What's My Line?* fame) and actor Myron McCormick (later to co-star in the Andy Griffith film *No Time For Sergeants*).

"Radio was such a great medium," remarked Vincent. "because you have to imagine everything." "One time during the war," Vincent recalled, "Lynn Fontaine, Helen Hayes and a whole bunch of us who were in the theater in New York did a broadcast that went around the world. It was absolutely amazing; it was being picked up all the way around the world and came back to us. We are the only country in the world that destroyed radio when television came along."

Vincent stayed with *Angel Street* for only one year due to his obligation to Fox. He was replaced in the role by his close friend and future *Mad Magician* co-star John Emery.

Chapter Six

Vincent, the Art Expert

or

Vincent, the Upper Class Scum

Once back at Fox, Vincent was cast in the film *The Song of Bernadette* (wife Edith also received a part in the film as well), a fact-based story of a French peasant girl Bernadette Soubirous (Jennifer Jones), who witnesses recurring visions of the Virgin Mary and through them uncovers the healing springs of Lourdes. After years of testing and disbelief, she is eventually believed by the church and admitted to a convent where she soon dies. Vincent portrayed the disbelieving town prosecutor Dutour who tried to get Bernadette confined to a sanatorium but in the end when he is dying of cancer he prays to Bernadette for help.

"Vincent Price does an impressive job as the implacable imperial prosecutor," reported Edgar Price (no relation to Vincent) in the Brooklyn Citizen. While John McManus of P.M. New York thought Vincent Price, was a "perfect symbolization of ruthless intellect as the ultra-cynical Imperial Prosecutor."

When various production problems caused the film's shooting schedule to expand to a then-unheard-of nine months, Vincent found himself with nothing to do for weeks in between shots, so together with actor George Macready he opened *The Little Gallery*, one of the first art galleries in Beverly Hills.

During the two years the gallery was open, it played host to the show biz elite as well as featuring twenty-two solo artist shows. But it also gave Vincent a new persona, that of "one of those show business freaks -- *The Art Expert!*"

After finally completing his work on *The Song of Bernadette*, Vincent ventured into new ground with one of his first real good guy roles, that of Private Francis Marion in the film adaptation of Maxwell Anderson play *The Eve of Saint Mark*. It was the story of a group of young men who train together in the army before being sent to fight the Japanese in the Philippines during World War II. The title referred to the old legend (quoted in the film by Vincent) that "On St. Mark's Eve if a maiden stands in a door of a church she will see inside the church all those who are going to die that year. In the film, a young island girl prays outside a large cave while the soldiers huddle inside waiting to die."

The film proved to be one of Vincent's all time favorites, "I loved that part. It was one of my few good guy roles. I played a Dixie-bred luxury lover who had spent most of his pampered life waiting to inherit a family fortune that must first pass to a grandfather, three aunts, two uncles and seven cousins. He was always in debt. Private Marion couldn't figure out why he was in the war. He was rather poetic and he really didn't belong. He should have never been a soldier.

"I had one line in the film which was unforgettable. I turned to my friends and said, 'How close does a man have to come to being horizontal before he earns the right to remain perpendicular?' That's a very complicated sentence. But it really means, 'How close does a man have to come to dying before he earns the right to live?' Almost every soldier that I met during World War II would quote this line to me, and they all loved it."

So did critic David Lardner who wrote in *The New Yorker*:

"Vincent Price wins an uphill fight by making an attractive character out of about the most unpromising one that Mr. Anderson has invented, the hero's poetic pal from the Deep South."

Vincent's next film saw him as President Woodrow Wilson's son-in-law William G. McAdoo, in director John M. Stahl's *Wilson*, the fact-based life story of the 28th President of the United States.

While the part was nothing memorable, Vincent did take something away from it. "Directors like John Stahl and Henry King (who directed *The Song of Bernadette*) taught me moviemaking. They knew how to fit you into the middle of something when you really should have been in at the beginning. They were so wise about moviemaking that the film was almost edited before it was developed. Nowadays, the kind of permissiveness where people shoot fifteen versions of a scene is just ridiculous. These people were on budgets and on schedules. They shot without wasting any time at all."

The biggest problem that arose during the filming happened after the dress rehearsal, when it was discovered that Vincent was wearing a brown tie with a blue suit. Since this was a color film, it wouldn't do. And as the wardrobe man was unable to find another blue tie except the one Alexander Knox (who played President Wilson) was wearing. The director decided to give Knox a black tie, and give the blue tie to Vincent.

Vincent's good reviews in *The Song of Bernadette* won him a featured role; in the future screen classic *Laura*. The film had its own share of production problems starting with its director Rouben Mamoulian, who during an early stage of the production walked off the picture.

After working on the film for six weeks, Vincent came home, "one Saturday night, (because in those days you worked six days a week), and received a call to report Monday morning to start the picture again. I mean right from the beginning, Rouben had been replaced by our producer Otto Preminger, Lucien Ballard, our cameraman was out and Joseph LaShelle was now in."

Then to make matters worse, Preminger immediately set out to rewrite the script. This in turn upset author Vera Caspary who threatened to sue the studio over the changes Preminger made. New writers were quickly brought in to create a compromised version that both Caspary and Preminger were happy with.

Vincent, however, had the time of his life on the film because of Shelby Carpenter, "the role I played in *Laura.* He was a wonderful character, a real 'upper-class scum!' but really elegant. Everything about him was charming but he was still a sleazy character. He was a terrible man and he was such fun to play because he didn't know it. (Most villains don't know they're villains at all). The great thing about the film was that everybody in it was a little sleazy. I thought that was one of the marvelous things that Preminger achieved in that film and the best film he ever made.

"What Otto added to the film and none of use could figure it out at first, was the ability to give each one of the characters an underlying sense of evil. Nobody in that picture is normal. Mamoulian hadn't done that, he was a very good director and a nice man, but he had no concept about these kinds of upper class scum people. Otto gave our characters a feeling of evil underneath this sophistication, a facade these high society people had. And it worked. When you saw the picture you realized these characters were essentially very, very evil, yet with their high society veneer, you'd never guess it.

"After the film was out and the film was a huge success. I asked Otto how you knew, these people were evil." "He said, 'You know, Rouben is a nice man.'" "I said, yes, he is a nice man." "Otto said, 'I'm not, most of my friends are these kinds of people.'

"The dialogue wasn't good and the characterizations weren't that good but he gave the film a suspense that was missing from Vera Caspary's very good story. That's what Otto gave it and it came off like gangbusters."

One of the things that Vincent particularly remembers about Otto Preminger was that "he didn't have a sense of humor when it came to actors breaking up. There was an important scene where Dana Andrews, the detective, is accusing all of us of Laura's murder. It was a serious dramatic moment. As Preminger moved along overhead on the crane, he said, 'Now Vincent, as the detective is talking I want you to put your hand down. And when the camera goes by, I want Judith (Anderson) to grab your hand.' She had to grab my hand in order to give me courage, because she thought I was the murderer. But as the camera went by, I kept forgetting to put my hand down. So Judith suddenly leaned over to me and said, 'For Crissakes, put it where I can get at it!' Well, that did it. I looked at her and it broke us up to such an extent that every time Otto did a take, we started laughing. Otto threw us off the stage, for about an hour, until we could regain our composure."

On the subject of his co-star Vincent remarked, "Gene Tierney is completely un-dated. She looks like the most modern girl of today. There was something extraordinary about this girl. I ended up doing six pictures with her and she never seemed to date. She seemed to remain constant. She was not pretty girl, her teeth sort of crossed over and Darryl Zanuck would not let her smile or frown. But she really came out as one of the great beauties of the motion picture industry"

Vincent's next three films were big hits but his roles were small by comparison although he did make the best of them. In director John M. Stahl's *The Keys of the Kingdom*, the story of an Irish boy who grows up to become a Catholic priest, who is assigned to start a mission in China. Despite a lack of faith by the locals and an ongoing civil war, Father Chisholm (Gregory Peck, in his second motion picture role) creates a growing mission with the help of Mandarin Mr. Chin (Leonard Strong) and Chinese believer Joseph (Benson Fong). Vincent portrayed Father Chisholm's boyhood friend, Angus Mealy, who grows up to become an ambitious but snobby church official. It was during this film that Vincent befriended a young sixteen-year-old Roddy McDowall, a friendship that lasted until the day Vincent died. Roddy, in fact, was in attendance at Vincent's funeral.

In *A Royal Scandal* produced by the great Ernst Lubitsch and directed by Otto Preminger, young cavalry officer Lt. Alexei Chernoff (William Eythe) arrives at St. Petersburg to warn Czarina Catherine the Great (Tallulah Bankhead) of an attempt to overthrow her régime by two army generals. Catherine soon falls for the officer and he quickly advances through the ranks of the army to become a general.

Alexei later falls for lady-in-waiting, Countess Anna Jaschikoff (Anne Baxter), but Catherine soon finds out and sends the girl away. Alexei, who is still loyal to the czarina, stays behind and helps her save her thrown from the plotting generals. Grateful, Catherine reunites Alexei and Anne, while she falls for new love, the Marquis de Fleury, the French Ambassador (Vincent Price).

"Otto wasn't originally scheduled to direct *A Royal Scandal*," recalled Vincent. "Ernst Lubitsch was supposed to direct, but he had suffered a heart attack. So Lubitsch became the producer of the film, and handed the direction over to Otto, who didn't have much of a sense of humor.

"Lubitsch was present on the soundstage during filming. It must have killed him to watch a serious Otto Preminger direct his comedy in an entirely different way than he had intended. It wasn't anyone's fault; it was just an unfortunate situation. But *A Royal Scandal* didn't turn out to be a bad picture at all."

The most interesting thing, however, about *A Royal Scandal* was that Tallulah Bankhead, Anne Baxter, Otto Preminger and Vincent all went on to portray villains on the *Batman* television series.

And in *Leave Her To Heaven* Ellen Berent (Gene Tierney) falls for and eventually marries writer Richard Harland (Cornel Wilde), but unknown to him she is extremely jealous and possessive, so when his crippled brother, Danny (Darryl Hickman), comes to stay with them, she does everything she can to send him away, but when he refuses to leave, she lets him drown while swimming.

After the death of his brother, Richard becomes cold towards Ellen, causing her to believe he is no longer in love with her and is planning to leave her for visiting adopted sister, Ruth (Jeanne Crain).

Ruth convinces Ellen that Richard misses his brother and needs someone to care for, so Ellen decides to have a baby in the hopes of regaining his attentions. But when she believes he prefers the child over her and, not wanting to share his affections with anyone, she deliberately throws herself down a flight of stairs, causing a miscarriage.

Richard becomes suspicious and confronts Ellen, who admits she killed his brother and their baby, because she didn't want to share him with anyone else. Disgusted, Richard packs his bags and plans to move out. Believing he is planning to run away with Ruth, Ellen plans to kill herself and throw the blame on to her sister.

Ruth is subsequently arrested and put on trial by Ellen's former fiancé, Russell Quinton (Vincent Price), now the district attorney, but she is found innocent when Richard tells the court of his wife's murder of his brother and son. Richard, however, is sent to jail for two years for hiding the knowledge of the murder of his brother. When he is released, he returns home to his new love, Ruth.

When the film was finally released, Vincent took his young son Barrett to a movie theater to watch his performance during the courtroom scene. He timed their entrance so that the boy would not see the rest of the picture; he didn't want him to be saddened and frightened by the sight of a young boy drowning, but he thought that Barrett might like to see him, delivering one of his typical performances. As he watched, Barrett squirmed in his seat. Vaguely he realized that his stern attorney, who was playing at the top of his pace, represented a performance on Vincent's part, but he was shocked by the fact that the role was so completely out of character.

"I frightened him, I'm afraid," Vincent confessed "He couldn't understand why I should be so stern and different. I'm usually pretty easy-going at home."

You see, at home Vincent was a mild, bland man. But as Vincent liked to point out (although he said this with a twinkle in his eyes), "Most murderers are also mild, bland men to the casual observer. One time I was preparing for a role as murderer, so I began to study the psychology of real murderers and dipped deep in Kraft Ebbing's histories of abnormal cases. To my amazement, I found that murderers rarely look the way you expect them to look. They generally look like simple, mild men. That's why they get away with murders so repeatedly. No one, looking at their guileless faces, can possibly suspect them. It is nearly always a guileless face—like mine, for instance (oh, what have I said?) which conceals a heart bent on murder."

Of course, whenever you met Vincent, the twinkle in his eyes always assured you, that the only place you had to fear him was on the stage or screen.

During the war years the Price family came face to face with a villain close to home, in fact it *was* their home. A housing shortage overtook the country and they had just received an eviction notice from their landlord. Vincent and his family decided that owning a home was the only solution, since any time you rented one, the landlord could get OPA permission to move into the place himself and move you out. But real estate prices were staggering upward and many of the homes in California were out of the Prices' reach. Vincent told the real estate agents, "I won't pay such prices. I'd rather live in a tree." For a time it looked as if the Price family might've had to do just that, until a real estate agent who was a friend of the family's said to Vincent: "I know a place that no one will consider buying, but somehow I feel you might like it."

In an event that would foreshadow many of his 'House' films to come, the day Vincent and Edith went to look at the house, it was raining. Rain poured through the open windows, which were inadequately stuffed with rags to make up for the absence of window panes. Rain poured through the leaking roof. But the tumbledown adobe house itself was entirely made of concrete. The house and the acre or so of garden landscape looked hopeless. It was a mass of weeds and poison ivy. However, the sycamore trees nearby, with a little trimming, could be made to look beautiful. The fruit trees, when cared for, would yield a delicious bounty. The dirty little pond, a hazard for Barrett, could be filled up. Believing he could restore the house to its once magnificent splendor, Vincent told the agent, "I'll take it," he said, "If the price is reasonable." Since nobody else wanted the place at any price, Vincent got his house.

He also bought a 1928 pickup truck, "It came in mighty handy for moving around cement, and the ladders and other things I bought, which can't conveniently be carried in the usual automobile. Vincent used to find himself the butt of his famous Hollywood neighbors when he would show up at some big Hollywood parties in the pickup truck. That is until some of his movie co-stars like Gene Tierney and Cornel Wilde, began asking to borrow the truck to aid with their own construction and moving projects.

In no time they fixed the leaking roof. They put ninety window panes in the previously empty windows. Then they asked for an estimate on the painting of the rooms. On learning that it would cost at least $1500 to hire a professional painter, they decided to do the job themselves. They did it, at a cost of $90.

Vincent adopted a novel color scheme for the house, instead of painting all the walls in one room the same color. They painted two of the living room walls yellow, one white and one grey. These colors gave light and warmth to the room which had once felt cold. There was a guest room that seemed almost too bright. Two walls were painted black to match the black fireplace in the room, and two walls white. They painted the beams red and then added Vincent's collection of masks in bright colors against the black walls makes for exciting contrast.

They made all the curtains for all the rooms themselves. For the living room, Mrs. Price sewed by hand striped curtains, eighteen feet long. They bought their string rugs at Sears Roebuck but couldn't buy any couches for the living room, but there was a wooden partition with two cabinets on either side. In Between these recesses they placed three old mattresses which they found in the house, and which they washed and aired thoroughly before using them. For upholstery they used some monks' cloth made from an old curtain which Vincent Price once used to partition the art gallery he ran in Beverly Hills before a tripled rent caused him to decide to give up the gallery. Bookcases were expensive, so Vincent made some himself out of the packing cases in which furniture from New York was sent. He also used the packing cases for wood with which to construct a fence.

(Sometime later Vincent did hire someone to put in some fences for him and the result was that he found himself completely lost one evening when he returned from the studio. The workmen had erected an eight-foot redwood fence across the front of the property "It looked just like Alcatraz!" he reported later, so that he drove a mile or so past the home up the canyon. He began stopping people and asking them if they could direct him to where he had imagined he lived.)

Over a period of several months, Vincent and Edith managed to turn this 'abandoned death trap' into a very colorful home worth more than four times what they paid for it. But most amazing thing about this entire project is that Vincent was color blind!

"When I got my physical examination for the Army, they told me that I was color blind," Vincent recounted. "I couldn't believe it. I asked a doctor how I could be color blind and yet be so violently sensitive to color and even shades of color. He told me, 'A great many painters are born color blind but because of an intense interest in color, they learn to know it better than those who are not color blind. That may be true of you, too.''

Chapter Seven

A Shocking Experience
or
Vincent Meets the Amazing Colossal Man

Having developed a screen image of a cad, producer Howard Koch gave Vincent his first starring part in the 1946 *B* thriller *Shock*. Awaiting the return of her husband, Lt. Paul Stewart (Frank Latimore), after being released from a Japanese prisoner of war camp, Janet Stewart (Anabel Shaw) waits for him in their hotel room. When he fails to arrive at the appointed time, she becomes upset and anxious, so when she happens to look out of the window, and spies Dr. Cross (Vincent Price) in the window opposite hers murder his wife, she goes into a state of shock.

When Paul finally arrives and finds his wife in shock, he calls the hotel manager, who in turn calls the house psychiatrist (he has an office in the hotel) Dr. Cross. Anabel relates what she has seen but is unable to identify Cross. Believing her impaired memory will soon return, the doctor convinces Paul to allow him to take her to his private sanatorium for treatment.

When district attorney O'Neill (Reed Hadley) begins to suspect Cross of murdering his wife, the doctor's nurse and mistress Elaine Jordan (Lynn Bari) convinces Cross to do away with Anabel, before she can regain her memory. However, when Cross suffers a guilty conscience, Elaine decides to complete the treatment herself. Paul comes to the rescue and stops the treatment.

"One of the things that got me stuck in that picture was that I was able to learn my lines. Howard Koch came to Lynn Bari and myself and said, 'These pictures are taking too long to make and we're going to have to cut down.' That was when we did *Shock*. He said, 'you are the only two people I know in the whole studio who will take the trouble to learn their lines.' We shot it in eighteen days."

"A funny thing about that film, it was a sort of science fiction story which came true. An exact replica of the murder and following circumstances happened in San Francisco just two weeks after we completed the film. It was a famous case and didn't hurt the box office at all I might add."

Vincent got mixed reviews but it won him the male lead in the now classic film *Dragonwyck* opposite his frequent co-star Gene Tierney, who played a naive farm girl Miranda Wells, who goes to live with her mother's distant cousin Nicholas Van Ryn (Vincent Price) in his mansion, Dragonwyck, on New York's Hudson River in the Spring of 1844.

Nicholas is a patroon, who rents his lands to farmers in return for a share of their profits. He lives in the huge mansion with his overweight wife Johanna (Vivienne Osborne) and young daughter Katrina (Connie Marshall). Miranda becomes Katrina's companion and when Johanna dies she eventually marries Nicholas.

Miranda quickly becomes pregnant, but the child dies soon after birth, driving Nicholas over the edge. Town doctor Jeff Turner (Glenn Langan, who years later would star in the title role of the cult classic, *The Amazing Colossal Man*) becomes suspicious when Miranda, like Nicholas' first wife, begins to suffer from the same ailment and begins to believe that she is being poisoned by Nicholas.

Meanwhile, Miranda discovers her husband is a drug addict, and has been driven over the edge by the death of his son and the loss of his lands to the tenant farmers by a new law passed in New York. Confronted by Miranda, Nicholas tries to strangle her, but is rescued in the nick of time by Dr. Turner. Now completely unhinged Nicholas confronts the farmers and attempts to shoot them, but is killed instead, leaving Miranda to return to her Connecticut home, with Turner who has fallen for her, to follow close behind.

"It was my first Gothic film," recalled Vincent. "And it was also Joe Mankiewicz's first film (he was both writer and director). I played the part of an egomaniac who thought the world should be run his way. *Dragonwyck* came from a very good Gothic novel, but the film was hampered unfortunately, by censorship, because at that time the villain had to be apprehended by the law. It ruined the end of the picture, which showed this heroic thing he does, which was ridiculous. Censorship was a bastard. It was a killer, because it made things happen that shouldn't have happened. However, I think it was one of the best pictures I ever made!"

Kate Cameron of the *New York Daily News* agreed, calling "Vincent Price's characterization of a proud, cultured man disintegrating into a crazy drug fiend: the most arresting performance in the film.

"Nicholas Van Ryn was the ideal Aristotelian villain," Vincent continued. "He was arrogant, educated, rich and owned a marvelous piece on the Hudson River. He had everything in the world he wanted, but he had one added thing to Jack Manningham, to his ego, to his assurance of his own villainy. He had a belief in survival of the fittest. He thought that anything that wasn't right should be destroyed. And one of the things that wasn't right in his life was his wife. So he thought he should destroy her. She had given him a daughter. He needed a son to carry on his name, and so he had met Gene Tierney. And he thought that she would be a good mother for his son. So he had his wife, who was getting fat and drinking too much, and he baked her cake, and the frosting had ground-up oleander leaves, which are deadly poison, in it. She died, and he married Gene Tierney. And it was a lot better.

"The extraordinary thing now --- in trying to figure out where this man got this kind of arrogance, this kind of assurance because he was not just a villain, Jack Manningham --- he wasn't a murderer! He was an educated, marvelous human being who just had an edge of evil. I read the book over and over trying to discover where Anya Seaton had gotten this character. And then, finally I looked in that place that we never look in, called The Preface. And there it was! She said that she drew the character of Nicholas Van Ryn from a poem called 'Alone'."

'Alone.'
by Edgar Allen Poe

From childhood's hour I have not been
As others were; I have not seen
As others saw; I could not bring
My passions from a common spring.
From the same source I have not taken
My sorrow; I could not awaken
My heart to joy at the same tone;
And all I loved, I loved alone.
Then- in my childhood, in the dawn
Of a most stormy life- was drawn
From every depth of good and ill
The mystery which binds me still:
From the torrent, or the fountain,
From the red cliff of the mountain,

From the sun that round me rolled
In its autumn tint of gold,
From the lightning in the sky
As it passed me flying by,
From the thunder and the storm,
And the cloud that took the form
(When the rest of Heaven was blue)
Of a demon in my view.

"One of the great autobiographical poems of the world was written by Edgar Allen Poe who was indeed born with a demon in his view! Lots of people have been born with demons in their view. Poe's demon was genius, fortunately for us. But Hitler had a demon; Charles Manson had a demon; that's one kind of villain, that villain who is born with a demon in his view. Nicholas Van Ryn had a demon. He believed that anything that didn't couldn't survive, deserved to be destroyed or to die, and that is not humanity."

Upon completion of *Dragonwyck* Vincent's next film had him recreate his role of England's King Charles II from *Hudson's Bay* for the film *Forever Amber*, but after several weeks of filming, director John M. Stahl was replaced by Otto Preminger, who immediately re-shot the entire film with a new cast, which included George Sanders taking over the role of King Charles II.

During the 1940's it was common practice for the studios to produce radio adaptations of their current productions and Fox was no exception. Vincent's voice could be heard on such shows as *The Hollywood Star Time*, *Screen Guild Players*, *The Lux Radio Theater* and *This is Hollywood* in abridged versions of some of his own films. He also helped to create the Los Angeles Modern Institute of Art.

Vincent made one more film for Fox, *Moss Rose*, in which showgirl Belle Adair (Peggy Cummins) suspects rich gentleman Sir Alexander Sterling (Victor Mature) in the murder of fellow showgirl Daisy Arrow (Margo Woods), after she spots him leaving the scene, just after she discovered the body. Police inspector Clinner (Vincent Price) is called in to investigate and discovers a bible and a Moss Rose near the body. Belle accuses Sir Alex of the crime but when the Inspector calls him in for questioning, Belle refuses to identify him. Deciding to improve her life, she blackmails Sir Alex into taking back to his country estate for two weeks. As he is planning to marry society girl Audrey Ashton (Patricia Medina) in a few weeks, he decides to accept the offer instead of suffering a scandal.

Making herself at home, she befriends Sir Alex's society matron mother, Lady Sterling (Ethel Barrymore), and makes an enemy of Audrey, who is afraid she will lose her intended to Belle.

When Audrey is found murdered in the same way as Daisy, Inspector Clinner arrests Sir Alex, who quickly confesses to the crime. Lady Sterling, who is obsessed with her son, fears Belle is responsible for the loss of her son and tries to murder her in the same way as she murdered the others. But before she can kill again, Sir Alex, Clinner and the police arrive just in time to save her. The film also re-teamed Vincent with is former *Victoria Regina* costar George Zucco who appeared as the family butler.

"The New York Times," Bosley Crowther thought, "Vincent Price did very nicely as one of those polite but persistent Scotland Yard men."

After the film was completed, Vincent's contract with Fox was not renewed at his own request. "I was part of the Fox stock company along with Tyrone Power, Linda Darnell, Alice Faye, Don Ameche, Gene Tierney, Gregory Peck, Jack Oakie and John Payne. It was fun and I liked it for a time but I felt that I would make the giant step into real stardom if I left Fox studios and become a freelance actor, free to choose the roles I wanted and not forced to go into picture after picture where I was part of the wallpaper."

Chapter Eight

Vincent, the Saint
or
Abbott and Costello Meet the Freelance Villain

Now a freelance actor, Vincent found himself back at his old home, Universal, in as Otis L. Guernsey, Jr of the *New York Herald Tribune* put it: "another of his chilling portraits of suave villainy" in the routine whodunit aptly entitled *The Web*. When his former partner, Leopold Kroner (Fritz Leiber) is released from prison for a crime he did not commit, Andrew Colby (Vincent Price) hires brash lawyer, Bob Regan (Edmund O'Brien) as a body guard, as he fears Kroner will try to kill him. Needing the cash and having fallen for Colby's secretary and girl friend, Noel Farraday (Ella Raines), he takes the job.

Colby gives Regan a gun from his collection, who in turn pays a visit to family friend, Police Lieutenant Damico (William Bendix, future star of TV's *The Life of Riley*), to obtain a gun permit. Damico is suspicious but arranges for the permit. That night at Colby's home, Regan is alerted to trouble in the upstairs office and rushes in to find Kroner standing in front of him holding a gun. Believing himself in danger, Regan kills him. Although Regan is cleared of murder charges, Damico is still suspicious, which alerts him to the fact that he may have been set up by Colby, who swindled Kroner out of a million dollars.

When Regan begins to get too close to the truth, Colby kills his assistant Charles Murdock (John Abbott), who refused to go along with Colby's future plans and blames the murder on Regan and Farrady, who dumped Colby for Regan. Fortunately, Lt. Damico, having suspected Colby from the start, steps in to save the pair from Colby, who later tries to kill them.

Afterwards in the summer of 1947, he assumed the role of Simon Templar, the title character of *The Saint* radio series, a role he would later reincarnate from the summer of 1950 until the spring of 1951. "I thought radio was a very great training ground for actors," Vincent stated, "because you have to create everything with your voice: the atmosphere of the whole piece, the makeup, what the character looks like, etc. I loved radio. I really adored it."

Upon his return from the war, actor Henry Fonda joined producer/director Anatole Litvak for the independent feature (co-produced with RKO Pictures) *The Long Night* in which G.I. Joe Adams (Henry Fonda) returns home from the war and takes a job in a mill town on the Ohio-Pennsylvania border, where he falls for Jo Ann (Barbara Bel Geddes, later one of the stars of the *Dallas* television series). Shortly thereafter, second-rate magician Maximillion (Vincent Price) and his assistant Charlene (Ann Dvorak) arrive in town. Maximillion, who totally ignores the advances of Charlene, romances Jo Ann, which angers Joe, who comes gunning for the magician and in a fit of passion and kills him. Adams then barricades himself inside his room and holds an all-night shoot-out with the police but is finally killed in the end. The film, which was co-produced by Select Pictures, lost over one million dollars when it was first released. It has rarely been seen since.

Returning to Universal, Vincent won the unlikely role of Boss Tweed who, as the reviewer in *Cue Magazine* pointed out, "Vincent Price....tall, aristocratic and British-accented, is surely the strangest portrait of short, squat, bearded and grafting Boss Tweed ever offered to a bewildered citizenry," in the film version of the Broadway musical *Up in Central Park*. It was the story of *New York Times* reporter John Mathews (Dick Haymes) who joins forces with an Irish immigrant girl, Rosie Moore (Deanna Durbin), in exposing the corrupt dealings of crooked politician Boss Tweed (Vincent Price).

While at the studio, he also recreated his first horror role by providing the uncredited voice of the Invisible Man for the end sequence of *Abbott and Costello Meet Frankenstein*. It would be the only time Vincent and Bela Lugosi would appear (or in Vincent's case not appear) in the same film. Unfortunately, the film had already completed filming when Vincent was brought in to provide the invisible one's voice, so Vincent and Bela never met each other.

For his next venture, Vincent traveled back in time for the MGM Technicolor version of the classic tale of *The Three Musketeers* featuring Gene Kelly as D'Artagnan and Vincent as Cardinal Richelieu, whom a reviewer for *The New Yorker Magazine* pointed out, "appears in no clerical trappings and is never addressed by his ecclesiastical title. In fact, if it were not for his doublet and hose, you could hardly tell him from the standard Hollywood version of a Fifth Columnist or crooked used-car salesman."

It was during the making of this film that Vincent's marriage fell apart. On May 10, 1948, Edith Price was granted a divorce and in the subsequent settlement was given custody of their son. He wouldn't reconnect with his son for many years, and blamed himself for not being a good father.

Years later, he would father a daughter, with his second wife, Mary Grant, only to alienate himself (like he did with his son) from her when he divorced her mother and married his third wife, actress Coral Browne.

Finding himself alone for the first time in years, Vincent bought himself a dog which he named Joe. Until his death, Joe proved to be a faithful companion, so much so that Vincent would later write entire book about his best friend, aptly entitled *The Book of Joe: About a Dog and his Man* (1962).

He spent time with Joe shooting his new picture *Rogue's Regiment* at Universal, in which U.S. agent Whit Corbett (Dick Powell) joins the Foreign Legion and travels to Indochina to track down escaped Nazi official Carl Reicher (Stephen NcNally). Along the way, he meets up with German antique dealer and gun runner Mark Van Ratten (Vincent Price), who tries to blackmail Reicher by threatening to expose his identity. Vincent soon found himself preoccupied with his new girlfriend, costume designer Mary Grant. The couple would later marry on August 25, 1949, in Tijuana, Mexico.

For his next film, MGM's *The Bribe*, Vincent "leered with diabolic glee," or so Bosley Crowther of *The New York Times* believed, as a smuggler, dealing in war surplus aircraft parts. The cast, which was headed up by Robert Taylor and Charles Laughton, was a good one, but the film was a dull one. The story had Federal agent Rigby (Robert Taylor) arriving on a Caribbean island to break up a war surplus smuggling racket headed by Carwood (Vincent Price). Cafe singer Elizabeth Hintten (Ava Gardner) is sent by Carwood to lead him off their trail, as is beachcomber J.J. Bealler (Charles Laughton), who tries to bribe him to give up the chase. But in the end, Carwood and his gang are captured and Rigby winds up with Hintten, who leaves her drunken husband, Tug (John Hodiak) for him.

"The thing that made the picture really outstanding was that there were three villains, three entirely different kinds of villains. And of course, there was the hero and heroine. But first of all, there was John Hodiak. Now John Hodiak was the sleek, black-haired villain with flashing eyes and teeth that went all the way around his head. You know, wherever you looked at him, he had teeth. And then, there was Charles Laughton who was kind of chubby and cuddly and really sinister. And then, the third villain was the perfect, the suave, the debonair villain…..myself!"

"The whole thing about these three different kinds of villains, and very few films have three villains in them, was how they fitted into the story. And they fitted into the story through the leading lady, the star, Ava Gardner. Now, I have played with some of the biggest stars and sex symbols in the business, but the only one who seemed to me to be really sexy was Ava Gardner. In fact, every time I think about her, I just go limp! No, I don't mean that! That's not what I mean at all. I'll never forget for as long as I live that after the picture was over, the studio, which was MGM, kind of liked us. And so they gave a little party for us, and they had a little orchestra, and we all had a chance to dance with Ava Gardner. I'll never forget. My turn came, and I took her in my arms, and she fit! It was like dancing with a warm, wet towel. And if you haven't tried it, don't knock it; let me tell you---marvelous--what a wonderful woman!

"In the beginning of the story, Ava Gardner was going steady with or was crazy about John Hodiak. Now then, that's the one with the teeth. Then, Charles Laughton came along and knocked off John Hodiak, and she sort of palled along with Laughton for awhile. And then, I came along, and I knocked off Charles Laughton, and she and I went steady for awhile. And then, of course, what happens? Along comes the leading man, kills me, and what does she end up with? In what was probably the biggest anti-climax in the history of movies. From Charles Laughton, John Hodiak, and Vincent Price--she ends up with Robert Taylor. Can you believe it? What a bore!

"During the making of *The Bribe*, Laughton used to come up to me and ask, 'Am I doing too much?' Now, Laughton was this great star to me, so I avoided answering. Finally, one day I said, 'Yes, Charles, you are doing too much!' He was all over the place! Unless the director had enough weight and nerve to hold him back, he could go way overboard."

Vincent's last film of the decade was Universal's desert costume adventure *Bagdad*, which had Vincent portraying the corrupt Turkish Military Governor of Bagdad, complete with Fez and eye patch, "the studio thought it would make me look more menacing." They actually were trying to cover up the sty that Vincent was currently suffering from, in the belief his distorted eye, might be more than the audience could handle.

When Princess Marjan (Maureen O'Hara) returns from England to Bagdad, she finds her tribe homeless and her father murdered. Believing Prince Hassan (Paul Christian) to be the leader of an outlaw gang called the Black Robes and her father's murderer, and unaware that the evil Prince Raizul (John Sutton) and Turkish military governor Pasha Al Nadim (Vincent Price), are the true villains, she plans to take her revenge.

Masquerading as a camel driver and later a jewel merchant, Hassan hides his identity from the princess while trying to stave off attacks by Raizul and Nadim. Hassan finally convinces the Marjan of his innocence, and together they set out to defeat the villainous pair before they slaughter the Arab chieftains and take over the country.

The film teamed Vincent up with one of Hollywood's most glamorous leading ladies, Maureen O'Hara, who was a favorite of Vincent's. "I've always enjoyed the ladies who were sort of the sex objects. They were great fun because none of them really took themselves too seriously. Jane Russell was great fun. Lana Turner was a wonderful lady. Maureen O'Hara was really one of the most beautiful women I have ever known and one of the funniest!"

It was now 1950, some fifteen years since he made his Broadway debut, and Vincent's career, which had a promising start, was floundering. He had worked his way through numerous studio programmers and costume epics, but had yet to really make his mark in Hollywood. To most people, he was just another generic leading man who could easily play the hero or villain. However, the films of this new decade would prove to be the most influential on Vincent's career and would prepare him for the position of the Crown Prince of Horror and the subsequent successor to the King of Horror, Boris Karloff.

Chapter Nine

Vincent, the Soap Tycoon
or
A Devilish Good Time

Vincent's first film of the decade was *Champagne For Caesar*, a wonderful satire of the radio and television game shows (directed by Richard Whorf, a close friend of Vincent's and an accomplished painter, who nearly sold out his exhibition of 28 paintings, when it debuted at Vincent's gallery a few years earlier) which had out-of-work genius Beauregard Bottomley (Ronald Colman) applying for a job at mad soap tycoon Burnbridge Waters'(Vincent Price) company. He is turned away for being too intelligent, so Bottomley decides to take his revenge out on Waters. Learning that the soap company is worth forty million dollars and knowing the company sponsors a game show entitled *Masquerade For Money*, hosted by Happy Hogan (Art Linkletter) and believing the game show (which aired nationally on radio as well as locally on television) is a detriment to human intellect, Bottomley now plots to appear on the show and win enough money (the cash prize is doubled with each subsequent question) to take over the company, so he can cancel the program.

As Bottomley continues to win, Waters begins to get worried and tries everything he can to foul him up; he even sends Hogan over to Bottomley's house to take piano lessons from his sister, Gwenn (Barbara Britton), but Bottomley gets wise and sends him on his way.

As it appears Bottomley will make good on his threat to take over the company, Waters sends for Flame O'Neil (Celeste Holm) to vamp Bottomley. Finding himself falling for O'Neil, Bottomley begins to get suspicious and turns the tables on her and continues to win on the program. But when the time comes for the final question, Bottomley makes a deal with Waters and throws the contest in return for a big payoff so he can live happily ever after with O'Neill (as his sister has done with Hogan).

Vincent was hysterical in his first real over-the-top hammy performance as the mad soap tycoon, and in many ways outshined the film's star Ronald Colman. The reason for this was, as Vincent once speculated, because "Ronnie Colman took his work very seriously, but *he* didn't take himself terribly seriously." Vincent, by comparison, of course didn't take himself very seriously, but also never quite took his work that seriously as well, which gave him the opportunity to have fun with any part he played. And this particular film was no exception as co-star Art Linkletter remembered, "Vincent and I had a wonderful experience on *Champagne for Caesar*, because we were very compatible. I was a comparative newcomer to film, although I had done a couple of pictures, Vincent was very helpful, warm in fact. We developed such a rapport that we were like two cut-ups on the set.

"One of the most unusual things that ever happened to me in show business happened in the scene in the film where Vincent is sitting at this huge desk, as the head of the soap company and he is having one of his occasional trances and I pour a bottle of pills into his open mouth. We shot the scene and it seemed so funny to us we'd break up. We couldn't finish; and we shot it and we shot it.

"Now there were three cameras and a big crew and Dick Whorf, a wonderful guy, who was the director. Well, after about fifteen takes and unbeknownst to us, Dick told the crew, 'Look, if they break up this time, just leave the lights on and we'll go to lunch.' Of course, we broke up. Like a couple of idiots and after wiping the tears from our eyes, we turned around and said, 'Let's give it one more try.' The entire studio was empty! There we were all alone, and everyone else was gone. We felt like horse's tails. So, when we came back from lunch, there was no more laughter.

"Since then the film has become quite a cult film and it still plays quite often on late night TV. Interestingly enough, Vincent called me and said that they were going to do a retrospective of his films at the Screen Actor's Guild Theater in Hollywood and asked if I would come down and be with him on the stage afterwards and answer questions.

"Now, I hadn't seen the film in twenty-five years and I must tell you I went down there with a great deal of misgivings. I was going to see myself up there and I was not going to be happy because I've learned so much and done so many other things since then. Well, I went and sat there, and to my huge surprise and delight I thought it was great! I was really pleased with it. And I attribute part of that to the fact that Vincent and I had such a good relationship. Since then the only thing Vincent and I had in common was the same barber."

By contrast, Linkletter recalled that "Ronald Colman was an interesting man and much more reserved, but a good fellow and nice to work with, except when his wife appeared on the set. He was married to an English girl and it was one of the most amazing things because Ronald was kind of a 'regular' guy but the minute she came around the set, for lunch and so forth, he became very "British" and she became very "British." When they were together they spoke so "British" you could hardly understand what they were saying. Then, when she was gone, he just became an "American" again speaking with perfect diction."

Producer Harry M. Popkin paid his stars a flat fee when *Champagne for Caesar* went into production, and promised them a second installment after the film had been released. The film played briefly in the theaters and was quickly sold to television without the actors getting the additional payments they were promised. According to Ronald Colman's daughter, whenever her parents drove past Harry Popkin's home in Beverly Hills they would shake their fists and shout, ""That's where that son-of-a-bitch Harry Popkin with all my money used to live.""

Vincent followed his comedic success with *The Baron Of Arizona*, which not only was the second film (the first being, *I Shot Jesse James*) directed by Samuel Fuller, but it gave Vincent his first opportunity in years to play a complex and multi-dimensional character: a real life forger and con man who devised a scheme to take control of the territory of Arizona (it had not yet become a state) by creating a phony land grant to a mythical Mexican family by the King of Spain, knowing the United States government would honor his claim, should it prove to be true. He then finds a Mexican orphan girl and claiming she is the last descendant of this mythical family sets out to pass her off as the heir to the territory of Arizona.

Vincent recalled the film as being "the first film to be made by Sam Fuller, and it was a really extraordinary picture in that it is the story of a man who tries to forge the rights to the state of Arizona, and succeeds in taking the whole state away from the United States! Then he tried to sell it back to them for five million dollars and they began to get suspicious. But they offered him the five million dollars, and then he got very greedy and decided that if it was worth five million then it was worth more. He really started to believe in himself and finally ended up caught. But in a sense he really did get away with it, in that the United States deeded the state over to him."

Vincent next found himself playing the "ham" actor in a troupe of traveling performers in the seldom seen 1950 western comedy, *Curtain Call at Cactus Creek.* Also in the cast were Eve Arden, Gale Storm, Donald O'Connor and Walter Brennan.

Vincent also found time to add a new dimension to his career by making the first of hundreds of appearances in the new medium of television. "I happened to have been on the first transcontinental television show," Vincent reluctantly remembered. "There were six people in New York and six people in Los Angeles who had been on local television suddenly broadcasting across the country. The engineers explained it to us, we were the first people to be seen immediately by 50 million people, which frightened us all to such a degree that none of us could remember our lines and we shook a great deal. It was such a terrifying moment!"

Later that year, Vincent was honored by the Los Angeles County Museum by being elected to their board of directors, a position he would hold for many years.

His next performance was as a Narcissistic adventure movie idol in the now cult classic *His Kind of Woman*, a role that Vincent was "very fond of. It was a really funny film, because it is about a movie star who believed in himself and everything he did."

Professional gambler Dan Milner (Robert Mitchum) is offered fifty thousand dollars and a trip to a Mexican resort for an unknown purpose. Along the way he meets and falls for singer Lenore Brent (Jane Russell) who is romantically interested in swashbuckling ham actor Mark Cardigan (Vincent Price). Milner soon learns he was lured to Mexico so deported mobster Nick Ferraro (Raymond Burr) can kill him and assume his identity with plastic surgery.

Milner soon becomes wise to the plot but Ferraro, who is growing impatient, has Milner kidnapped and carried aboard his yacht for the needed surgery. Heroic ham Cardigan uses his vast gun collection to storm the yacht (with the help of the Mexican police) and frees Milner, who disposes of Ferraro.

"Producer Howard Hughes didn't direct the picture, but he fell in love with the character that I was playing. So, six months after we finished the film, he built a set that cost at that time around $250,000 and then he called me back for that scene where I and the policeman go down with the boat and all go underwater. There I am standing on the prow of the boat and I turn around and say, 'Stop mumbling and abandon ship!' and their heads pop out of the water. It cost him $250,000 to add that scene and he just loved it!"

Long-time friend and co-star Jane Russell remembers Vincent for his "outrageous sense of humor" which was in direct contrast to his "sophisticated, cool and removed" screen image. As an example of Vincent's true persona, she recalled the time that she and her then husband were going to throw a party. "My husband at the time was Robert Waterfield and we called him 'Old Stoneface,' because, while he was very bright and intelligent, he wasn't very gregarious at all. Well, one day I managed to get Robert and Vinnie together during the shooting and I told Vinnie that we were going to have a party and he said, 'You mean, HE's going to be the host!' and then he roared with laughter. Robert was always so quiet and stone-faced that Vinnie couldn't resist and that's all Robert needed and out came his nasty humor. They were friends from then on."

But aside from his sense of humor, Vincent was a warm and giving man, especially of his time, as Ms. Russell fondly remembers, "We used to hang out in Bob Mitchum's dressing room. His secretary at the time would just order in Cokes or whatever anybody wanted and we would just sit around on couches and on the floor. One day during filming when Vinnie wasn't shooting, we called him on the phone and he came down to the studio. By the time he went home, he was late for dinner, late for everything. Mary was mad as hell at him. It wasn't that he did that a lot but we just got him down there and got him into a lot of trouble.

"Vincent and Mary, Dorothy and Robert Mitchum and later Pat and Richard Egan were about the only people in the business who Robert and I saw, and then usually in each other's homes. Dorothy and Mitch had a comfortable sprawling home in Mandville Canyon, while Vincent and Mary had a museum in Benedict Canyon. When that wouldn't hold everything they'd collected, they had to buy a huge old Spanish house in Beverly Glen Canyon. There were shelves everywhere to hold Pre-Columbian Art and gold leaf church artifacts from Mexico. In fact, one day I dropped by there and Vinnie was gold leafing a carved door, all by himself. And of course, paintings were everywhere. They were both marvelous cooks and it was a joy to visit them to see what they had done since I had been there last.

"In 1968, when I got married to Roger, Vinnie and Mary loaned me their beach house for a honeymoon. Everything they did was so artistic and so interesting, as they did a lot of it themselves."

Upon completion of the film, Vincent spent three weeks at the Los Angeles Las Palmas Theater with Jane Wyatt in a production of *The Winslow Boy* before heading off to France to co-star opposite producer/writer Errol Flynn in *the Adventures of Captain Fabian.*

In 19th century New Orleans, Creole servant girl Lea Marriotte (MIcheline Prelle) is accused of murder by George Brissac (Vincent Price), but is rescued by Captan Fabian (Errol Flynn), who takes a liking to her. She plans to improve her station in life and when Fabian buys a tavern for her, she plots to marry former boyfriend Brissac.

Brissac eventually marries Marriotte, who convinces him to murder his rich uncle, Henri (Victor Francen). Brissac then pins the murder on Fabian, who, although is arrested for the deed, is helped to escape from jail by Jesbel (Agnes Moorehead). Fabian tries to make it back to his ship, but Brissac arranges for him to be ambushed by a gang of thugs. During the fight, a supply of ammunition explodes, killing Marriotte, whose body is carried away by Fabian. ("Errol walked off the picture before the final scene," remembered Vincent. "So, the person who's carrying Micheline away at the end isn't Errol at all; it's an extra.")

Legal problems later arose when Flynn paid Vincent only twenty thousand of the thirty-five thousand dollars salary he had been contracted for. Vincent sued Flynn for the balance and finally received payment three years later in 1954.

Taking a break from film work, Vincent and Mary traveled extensively throughout Central and South America, adding to their vast collection of Pre-Columbian art before they returned to Hollywood where Vincent signed a non-exclusive contract with Howard Hughes and R.K.O. Pictures; included in the contract was an option which allowed Vincent to direct a picture of his choice (an option he was never given the opportunity to exercise).

Vincent soon discovered a film he wanted to direct called *The Great Man Votes*, a story which had been filmed previously with John Barrymore in 1939. Unfortunately, the remake never came about as he was quickly cast as Jane Russell's husband in *The Las Vegas Story*. A part he soon found was not well thought-out, as Jane Russell remembers, "Vincent played the part of my husband, a man who didn't have any redeeming characteristics. And the way it was written in the script I managed to brush him off awfully fast, without Vincent's character making a real fuss about it. Vincent pointed this out to the producers but they didn't pick up on it. They wanted to go ahead with the script the way it was."

Married couple Linda and Lloyd Rollins (Jane Russell and Vincent Price) stop off in Las Vegas, where she used to work as a singer. While her husband goes off to gamble, Mrs. Rollins becomes reacquainted with her old flame, Dave Andrews (Victor Mature). When the gambler to whom he lost a bundle to is found murdered, Rollins is accused of the crime. Andrews, who has fallen once again in love with Mrs. Rollins, solves the crime and discovers the real murderer, Thomas Hubler (Brad Dexter), who kidnaps Mrs. Rollins and tries to flee the state. Andrews follows close behind in a helicopter and rescues her. Returning to Vegas, Mrs Rollins finds her husband being arrested for embezzlement, leaving her free to continue her romance with Andrews.

After filming was completed, Vincent returned to television to recreate his role of Mr. Manningham in the broadcast version of *Angel Street* along side his old co-stars Judith Evelyn and Leo G. Carroll.

Then on December 21, 1951, while appearing in a road show version of the play *The Cocktail Hour* in Tacoma, Washington, Vincent collapsed after the evening performance and was rushed to the hospital with what was later diagnosed as a perforated duodenal ulcer. A few days later he returned home to Los Angeles to recuperate.

Several weeks later with his health fully restored, he joined Charles Boyer, Cedric Hardwicke and Agnes Moorehead in a touring company of George Bernard Shaw's *Don Juan in Hell,* replacing the departing Charles Laughton in the role of the Devil, a part Vincent was thrilled (if not destined) to play. "I jumped at the chance to play the great part of the Devil. I loved Shaw's works, and the tour gave me the chance for long talks with those two art lovers, Boyer and Hardwicke. Every town we visited, all three of us went to the museums, to every place of interest. It was a fabulous experience."

After the tour was completed, he was told by Howard Hughes that he was going to play the male lead in the forthcoming Jane Russell film, *Topaz,* but the picture was never made. Instead, he found work in one of the first feature-length theatrical documentaries on the subject of art. It was entitled *Pictura: Adventures in Art.* Vincent redubbed the original French narration provided by Jean Servais for one of the film's multiple segments as well as appearing on screen as a guest lecturer to a college art history class. The film has not been seen since it was first released in 1952; the company that produced and distributed the film (aptly called Pictura Films) no longer exists, and the film prints are lost somewhere in limbo.

Also that year, Vincent narrated a documentary film entitled *The Ancient Maya,* produced by the United Fruit Company, which received a limited theatrical and television release.

Chapter Ten

Bela Lugosi Visits the House of Wax
or
Casanova's Disappearing Act

In 1953, Vincent was faced with the most difficult challenge of his already long career. Actor Jose Ferrer, who was producing a Broadway comedy entitled *My Three Angels* contacted Vincent and offered him one of the lead roles in the play. At the same time, Warner Brothers offered Vincent the lead role in the 3-D remake of the 1933 film *The Mystery of the Wax Museum* starring Lionel Atwill and Fay Wray. Vincent opted for the film (a wise choice as the play closed very quickly), which quickly became one of the top ten money making films of 1953, bringing in a box office gross of 5.5 million dollars.

House of Wax told the tale of Professor Henry Jarrod (Vincent Price), a gifted sculptor who is horribly scarred in both mind and body when he is trapped in his wax museum during a fire (set by his partner to collect the insurance), who must resort to murder to fill his wax museum with figures (he embalms the bodies of his victims in wax and displays them as historical figures, with the help of his deaf mute assistant, Igor (played by Charles Buchinsky (soon to be Charles Bronson, in one of his first film roles).

The film was being made in color, and in the 3-D process, which required the makeup to be as realistic as possible if it were to stand up to the scrutiny of the audience. George Bau created the special makeup for the film, which as Vincent recalled, "was one of the most elaborately real makeup ever done. Two doctors supervised it to be sure the burns were as real as possible. It took almost three hours to put it on and to take off, and both processes were very painful. Because the picture was scheduled for only thirty days, I sometimes had to wear makeup for ten hours. I couldn't eat because my mouth was partially 'scar tissue,' so I drank many liquids and because of the running around in the makeup, I fainted one day from lack of oxygen."

The makeup was so horrible, "I was banished from the studio commissary. This cold shoulder treatment started when I walked into the commissary for lunch the first time. The girl at the cash register turned green and almost fainted. Then the patrons got up and headed for the door. It was a bad day for business, to say nothing of the indigestion it must have caused a couple of hundred people. I'd seen strong men on the studio lot turn white and head for the nearest bar when I walked by in the makeup. The first time I looked at myself in the mirror I wanted to catch the first plane to Borneo.

"George Bau and I became great friends, not only because he was a wonderful man, but we spent six hours a day almost alone together getting to the studio before anyone else and checking out at night after everyone one else had already left. George, under the supervision of the two doctors, especially Dr. Gunzberg, an eye specialist who was credited with perfecting the process of 3-D took great pains, and I don't mean just mine, to study burnt scar tissues. These were then molded in rubber, applied with alcohol, or spirit gum or collodion, and then tinted with many colors of makeup.

"For the famous scene where Phyllis Kirk strikes my face and it cracks and falls off, showing the burnt face underneath, a wax cast of my own face was made, then another of my burnt face, the 'real' one enlarged to fit over the burnt one, and for one hour of horror, I wore two masks while the camera was set up and the director was satisfied everything was perfect for hopefully one perfect take, it worked and the scene is still remembered as one of the horror highlights of the history of the cinema."

Aside from its advances in makeup, *House of Wax* has the unique distinction of being the only 3-D film directed by Andre de Toth, a man who had only one eye, which made him the only one associated with the film who could not see the film in 3-D. But that did not stop him from making a cinema classic. As director Andre de Toth recalled, it could have turned out differently: "We were budgeted at a million and a half and had a sixty day shooting schedule, but I finished the picture for $650,000 and shot it in twenty-eight days. Vincent Price was a very talented actor and a gentleman. He was an absolutely superb. He never missed a minute. A real pro! I had great respect for the man as a human being and an actor. Our meticulous search for reality, credibility and understanding of the character is probably the reason that in something that could have been a phony hoax, and in particular the cardboard character of *The Mystery of the Wax Museum* came to real life, and the makeup was not only scars attached to his face, but something that scarred his inside, which made him into the character he played, and which I was finally able to put on the screen."

"3-D can combine all the forces, all the possibilities of the motion picture and the theater. It's not to throw things at you but to involve the audience. Instead of showing it to an audience, make them part of it; the feeling, experience."

One experience de Toth fortunately did not share with the audience was the time he set fire to the sound stage. "During the scene where we set fire to the museum, the fire became too real. A hole was burned into the roof of the stage and firemen were spraying water on the roof (and sets) while the cameras were rolling. And since the wax figures couldn't be readily replaced, once the fire was started we had to keep filming. We began with spot fires; one figure would begin to burn and would be shot, another would be ignited and filmed, with three bulky Natural Vision camera units being pulled around on huge dollies, trying not to run into each other in a traffic jam. Luckily, the only casualties of this adventure were the eyebrows of Vincent Price, which came away singed, and the stage roof."

When the film had its premiere at the Paramount Theater in New York, *Dracula* star Bela Lugosi arrived at the theater leading a man in a gorilla suit on a leash. It was an obvious publicity stunt, but it was Vincent who had the last laugh on the audience weeks later, "When *House of Wax* had been playing for about thirty weeks at the Paramount theater in New York, I was in town doing a play so, I used to sneak into the back of the theater and I would have fun watching the people with these silly glasses on. Since I was also wearing the silly glasses, no one could tell it was me.

"I chose to sit behind two teenage girls because I knew their reactions would be marvelous. Finally, towards the end of the film, these two girls who were really riveted to their seats started moving forward. Then finally after I am thrown into the vat of wax and burnt up. I leaned forward and asked, 'Did you like it?' They went right into orbit!

"After the picture was a success, the people who ran the Movieland Wax Museum decided to add a wax statue of me to the museum (recreating a scene from *House of Wax*). Pretty soon, I got a call from a columnist for the *Los Angeles Times*. He said, 'Do you want to do a gag?' We went to the museum and he took the figure out. Then they wheeled me in on a cart and put me up where the wax statue had been. I was holding a hypodermic syringe and did my best to look like a dummy. Pretty soon, people began crowding around, and the columnist informed them that 'This is a real animated statue of Vincent Price. In a minute it will start moving.' I then squirted water at them." Until it closed its doors for good, the statue of Vincent still remained on display in the museum's Chamber of Horrors for all to see.

The film almost instantaneously turned Vincent Price into a horror film star. But Vincent refused to allow himself to become typecast as another B-movie horror star like so many other actors he had known, by turning down the many horror film offers he subsequently received following the release of *House of Wax*. Instead he decided to return to Broadway in the role of the Duke of Buckingham in a limited run version of *Richard III*, staged by Jose Ferrer.

Vincent also found time to narrate a documentary for the British Film Institute entitled *Notes on the Port of St. Francis*. This was based on a text written by Robert Louis Stevenson.

For his next film *Casanova's Big Night*, an unbilled Vincent portrayed the 18th century Italian great lover Casanova, who skips town without paying his bills. So, when the Duchess of Castebello (Hope Emerson) arrives and offers to pay Casanova to see if her son's fiancée is truly in love with her son or only after his money, the local merchants try to pass off tailor's apprentice Pippo Popolino (Bob Hope) off as the real Casanova. Aided by merchant Francesca Bruni (Joan Fontaine) and Casanova's valet, Lucio (Basil Rathbone), Pippo gets in and out of trouble, leading to a double ending in which he is beheaded as well as becoming the hero and getting the girl. Also in the cast were John Carradine and Lon Chaney, Jr. (in a wonderful comic part).

Vincent returned to RKO to appear in the 3-D film *Dangerous Mission* produced by future disaster movie king, Irwin Allen.

Louise Graham (Piper Laurie) witnesses a mob murder at a nightclub and, knowing that both the cops and the mobsters will be after her, she flees to Glacier National Park and takes a job at a tourist hotel. When strangers Paul Adams (Vincent Price) and Matt Hallett (Victor Mature) arrive at the hotel, she is unable to tell which one is the cop and which one is the hired killer sent by the mob.

At the same time, forest ranger Joe Parker (William Bendix) tries to get Indian girl Mary Teller (Betta St. John, who would later star in the horror film classic *Horror Hotel with Christopher Lee*) to help her find her fugitive father, Kicking Bear (Trevor Bardette). Teller is also romantically involved with Adams.

Adams, of course, turns out to be the killer and Hallett the hero, who finally shoot it out on top of a glacier before Adams is buried beneath a wall of falling ice and snow, leaving Graham to return with Hallett and testify against the mob.

"Victor Mature always called himself 'The President of the Coward's Club of America.' When we did *Dangerous Mission* we had a fight scene together. They used doubles but when we got to the point where we had to do the close-ups. He was terrified!"

Vincent then ventured to Columbia Pictures for his third and final 3-D film, *The Mad Magician,* which reunited him with the producer, director of photography and screenwriter of *House of Wax* Bryan Foy, Bert Glennon and Crane Wilbur respectively.

When illusion inventor Gallico the Great (Vincent Price) is prevented from performing his own creations by his employer, Ross Ormond (Don Randolph), who years earlier stole Gallico's wife from him, he snaps and kills Ormond with his own buzz saw illusion. Using his talent for creating lifelike masks, Gallico creates a duplicate of Ormond's face and, donning the mask, sets himself up in the Prentiss' (Lenita Lane and Jay Novello) boarding house. Once there, he disposes of Ormond's body and eventually kills his ex-wife Clair (Eva Gabor), as well. With Ormond out of the way, Gallico plans to perform his newest creation, the Crematorium, but is blackmailed by magician Rinaldi (John Emory). Gallico soon does away with him. Meanwhile, Gallico's assistant Karen Lee's (Mary Murphy) boyfriend, police officer Bruce Allen (Patrick O'Neal) and Mrs. Prentiss, who writes mystery novels, discovers Gallico's secret. Gallico tries to do away with Allen but is rescued by Lee and Prentiss, while Gallico is destroyed in his own Crematorium.

Towards the end of the film, Vincent fights to the death with hero Patrick O'Neal (in one of his first films). As Vincent painfully remembers, the fight didn't quite go as planned.

"Patrick O'Neal had never done a screen fight before. But if you do what the stunt people tell you to do, you never get hurt. But Patrick was absolutely paralyzed, and didn't watch them. He thought he could fake it, but he couldn't. He picked up the wrong table, the one that was not made of balsa wood, and hit me over the head, just about smashed my nose all over my face. The damage was so bad, that I finally had to have plastic surgery, because I couldn't breathe."

Chapter Eleven

Vincent, the Master Builder
or
Scratch the End of the World

Late in 1954, Vincent decided to return to Broadway in the comedy *Black-Eyed Susan* which was directed by Gregory Ratoff. It also starred Everett Sloane, Kay Medford and Dana Wynter (soon to co-star in *Invasion of the Body Snatchers*). Unfortunately, the play was a total flop and closed after only four performances.

In 1955 Vincent returned to the screen in the RKO film *Son of Sinbad*, a film that was made in 1953, shelved for two years and then released with a huge publicity campaign promoting the film as "too hot to be released," due to the hundreds of scantily-clad woman dancing in and out of the film including famed stripper Lili St. Cyr. Although the film was intended to be an another Arabian Night adventure film, it was more of a tongue-in-cheek comedy with Dale Robertson as the womanizing son of Sinbad who teams up with Vincent's poetry-spouting Omar Khayham and the female descendants of Ali Baba's original forty thieves (which included a young Kim Novak) to save Bagdad from an invasion of Tartars.

Although he had done a number of pictures for RKO and had been a favorite of Howard Hughes since making *His Kind of Woman*, Vincent never met him face to face. "Working for Howard Hughes was like working for the Invisible Man. He used to call me up from Las Vegas. That's as close as I ever got to meeting him."

While making *Son of Sinbad*, Vincent found himself entrusted by Hughes with a rather bizarre task. "For some reason or other Hughes liked me. So, he would call and have me tell him all the dirty jokes told on the set every day. He loved to hear dirty jokes. The only problem I had was that Hughes was half deaf, so I had to scream the jokes into the phone."

At the time that the film was made, Howard Hughes had dozens and dozens of young starlets under contract and as Vincent pointed out, "It's illegal to put somebody under contract or give them a beauty contest prize without paying off. But Hughes would just say to his gopher, or pimp or whatever you want to call it, "I'd like to talk to that girl." They'd set her up in a wonderful apartment, then she'd never do anything, as he didn't make enough movies to use them all. Well, finally he had to pay off, and that's why there were over two hundred girls, they were being paid off. It was hysterical!"

Included among the girls were three winners of the Miss Universe contest, and Misses United States, Australia, New York, California, Michigan, Detroit and Beverly Hills.

"One day the producers called me down to their office and asked me, "What do you think of the script?" I said, "It's the worst script I've ever read in my life!" They said, "Isn't it the truth!" And they never changed a word! because they had to pay off on the contracts."

In order to help publicize the film, Howard Hughes had four beautiful girls dressed as Persian Harem maidens; he called them *The Sinbadettes* and they'd travel around the country on a personal appearance tour.

After the Broadway fiasco, Vincent made several television appearances as well as playing substitute host for friend Herbert Marshall's radio series, *Your Radio Theater*, while Marshall took a film role. Vincent also ventured to Australia to appear in a radio version of George Orwell's *1984*.

Also in 1955 Vincent appeared and narrated a thirty minute documentary for the American Petroleum Institute entitled *The Story of Colonel Drake.* It was a truth to life tale of the first man to successfully drill for oil in America.

Returning to feature films in 1956, Vincent provided the opening narration for Paramount's musical fiasco, *The Vagabond King*, followed by a supporting part as a concert booker in Warner Brothers *Serenade*, a soap opera musical starring tenor Mario Lanza and Joan Fontaine. Also in the cast was a young Vince Edwards, who would later star in the television series, *Ben Casey*.

"Mario was an experience," remembered Vincent. "He looked like a department store dummy. He had a hairpiece about a foot high and lifts (in his shoes) that were just as high. He was on a diet of garlic and whiskey and when they'd call Joan Fontaine for a scene with him, she'd panic! The picture was awful."

Vincent then ended his RKO contract with the Fritz Lang film *While the City Sleeps,* in which media mogul Amos Kyne (Robert Warwick) dies leaving his playboy son Walter Kyne, Jr. (Vincent Price) in charge of his empire. Kyne decides to create a new position at the company and sets up a contest between the three leading candidates for the job: John Day Griffith, Mark Loving and Harry Kritzer (Thomas Mitchell, George Sanders and James Craig). The one who uncovers the identity of a serial killer (John Barrymore,

Jr.) will win the job. Griffith asks reporter Edward Mobley (Dana Andrews) to help, who in turn uses his fiancée Nancy Leggett (Sally Forrest), as a decoy for the killer.

Loving uses Mildred Donner (Ida Lupino) to seduce Mobley into helping him instead, while Kritzer seduces Kyne's wife, Dorothy (Rhonda Fleming), in the hopes of blackmailing himself into the job.

The killer eventually tries to kill Leggett but instead nearly kills Mrs. Kyne. Mobley arrives in time and chases the killer into the subway, where he overpowers him and is soon captured by the police. Kyne finds out about his wife and Kritzer and sends him on a long trip to Europe and gives Griffith the job, who in turn gives Mobley his old job as newspaper editor as a wedding present.

Following the completion of the film, Vincent then took the featured role of Baka, the Master Builder of Egypt in the Cecil B. DeMille biblical epic *The Ten Commandments*, the story of Moses (Charlton Heston) and his rise to become Prince of Egypt. The prince discovers he is actually the son of Hebrew slaves and eventually becomes the savior of his people, as he is chosen by God to free them from the bondage of slavery under the Egyptian ruler, his former rival, Rameses (Yul Brynner).

Vincent portrayed Baka the Master Builder, the architect of Egypt who, together with Moses, build Pharaoh Sethi's (Sir Cedric Hardwicke) treasure city. When Baka takes Joshua's (John Derek) girlfriend, Lilia (Debra Paget, later to star with Vincent in the House of Usher), for his own, Joshua attempts to kill him but is captured instead. As Baka prepares to whip Joshua to death, Moses arrives to kill Baka and free Joshua, because having learned that he himself is Hebrew, he could not allow Baka to kill a fellow Hebrew. "There was a scene where I had to whip John Derek to death," laughed Vincent. "Well, he deserved to die; Anybody that pretty should be whipped. I took lessons on how to use the whip for about two months. I really had a man who came everyday and I took on the whip to the point I could do anything with it. Like whipping a cigarette out of people's mouths."

Vincent's part in the film was relatively small compared to some of his co-stars; so many people wondered why he even bothered to do the film. Vincent's answer was thus, "I was asked if I wanted to do it and I read the script and really I could have phoned in the part. I felt that if I hadn't worked in a DeMille picture, I really wasn't a movie actor. I know that Judith Anderson and Edward G. Robinson, all really felt the same way I did."

"DeMille was really quite an extraordinary man. He was a tremendous stickler; he would spend a million dollars on anything as long as it was seen on the screen. Nothing was worth anything that wasn't seen on the screen. There was always a scene in every DeMille picture where somebody discovered silk. It was in every picture you ever saw. A man would come in and say we just discovered silk, and then bolts of silk would be flying everywhere and the girls would dance and they would take baths in silk. It was marvelous!"

During the filming Vincent noticed the oddest thing, "If you had blue eyes or pale eyes, you had to wear contact lenses. Everyone had to wear contact lenses except me. I never could figure it out. I was the only person in the picture that didn't have dark eyes."

"Later on, I finally figured out that I must have been from the south of Egypt," joked Vincent. "There are blue-eyed Egyptians down there."

"One of the great moments on that film happened when DeMIlle called me one day, personally, and said 'Vincent, I have a very strange request; could you come down to the set tomorrow at eleven o'clock just as we break for lunch.' So, I went down and I was put through this makeup. I got all dressed up with all this jewelry and glorious clothes and body makeup and went down to the set and DeMille said, 'We are going to break for lunch and I want you to come with me, Vincent.' So he set me up on this marvelous sedan chair, one of those things that people pickup and carry. Where upon four of the largest black men I have ever known in my life, grabbed hold of this thing and heaved it up. I managed to retain my equilibrium and sat there very regally and sort of bowed. He said, 'that's it, I mean, that's the way it should be done.' They laid it down, I got out and he said, 'that's all Vincent.' I said, 'Mr. DeMille, I spent two hours in makeup to come down here and sit in a chair, why!' He said, 'two days ago, we had a scene with Anne Baxter and she got in the chair and she looked like a bottle of milk.' But he had a marvelous sense of humor. The old fellow, I loved him."

While on the subject of DeMille and his sense of humor, he recalled the following incident: "There was an enormous scene where poor Martha Scott was being crushed under hundreds of tons of granite. They had all these girls (who had been on the picture for months) in mud pits making bricks. DeMille really loved cranes. (Every picture you are ever on, they try to get a crane and a crane is terribly expensive to rent. In low budget pictures, you have a very small crane.) In a DeMille picture you had an enormous crane. It went thirty feet in the air. And he would ride around on it and he had a very big electric loud speaker (so he could talk to the cast and crew). Suddenly, at the top of his lungs he yelled over the loud speaker, 'You two girls over there,' (now remember, here were over 800 girls over in this mud pit), and he said "What are you talking about? If it is so important come over here and tell everybody.' So these two poor girls trudged over; they were covered with mud and they got over to where DeMille was and this great crane came down and DeMIlle thrust his loud speaker in their faces and said, "If it is so damn important, then tell everybody what you were saying.' One of the girls said, 'Well, Mr. DeMIlle, I just said to my girlfriend, I wonder when the old son-of-a-bitch is going to call lunch.' He then did the loveliest thing and turned around and said 'Lunch!'"

Unfortunately, many of Vincent's scenes were cut from the final theatrical version, including one in particular that gave Vincent a little bit of trouble. "I played Baka, the architect of Egypt and I had a scene with Cedric Hardwicke and Yul Brynner. We were standing there, looking out over this great achievement of mine, which was a blue cyclorama, that's all. There was nothing there at all and I had a line: *Yonder is the city of Sethi's glory.* Mr. DeMille said, 'Vincent, you don't read that line with much conviction.' I said, That's because I don't know what the hell I'm talking about!" So he said, 'You're right! Come along and see what I've put on the screen for you to talk about.' And we went into the projection room and saw 13,000 people carrying an obelisk up the Valley of the Kings. It was one of the most extraordinary shots ever photographed. And it changed my reading, I might add."

"I remember the scene and the line Vincent spoke of," Charlton Heston recalled. "It was in the original first cut of the film which was at least a half hour longer than the final theatrical version." (Unfortunately, both the video and television versions of the film are the theatrical cut of the film; until the film is restored, we will never get a chance to see "the city of Sethi's glory.")

While his screen time was limited, Vincent made the most of it. At times he even managed to outshine the star of the film, Charlton Heston, who thought Vincent was "extremely good in the role.

"The scene in which I break Vincent's neck is one of the many elements of the film based on Exodus. Vincent played the Egyptian that Moses slays, afterwhich he says, "If Pharaoh finds this out, Pharaoh will slay me, I must flee." The neck-breaking took place out of camera range. You heard a loud crunch, but they were a bit more fastidious then.

"Vincent was a wonderful actor, a fine professional and a gentleman, and a combination you don't find too often. And if you recall, in the film I referred to him as 'The Master Butcher,' which sort of anticipated the types of roles he would become famous for the horror genre.

"Aside from *The Ten Commandments*, I also did the first *Playhouse 90* with Vincent. It was called *Forbidden Area* and it also starred Tab Hunter, Charlie Bickford and Jackie Coogan. We all played Air Force officers in a story dealing with Soviet espionage with Tab Hunter playing the Soviet spy."

Years later when he was asked how he liked working with Charlton Heston on *The Ten Commandments*, Vincent responded (with his tongue firmly planted in his cheek), "I always loved Charlton Heston, because he was brand new to the screen and *HE* was telling DeMille how to direct the picture."

Following his demise at the hands of Charlton Heston's Moses, Vincent spent the rest of 1956 appearing in over thirty dramatic television shows including *Have Gun Will Travel* as (what else) a ham Shakespearean actor, *Climax*, *The Alcoa Hour*, and two episodes of *Science Fiction Theater*. He also went face-to-face with jockey Billy Pearson on the subject of art on the *$64,000 Challenge* quiz show. "It was before the quiz show scandals. The show had a very good premise: the contestant would be a person who was, say, an actor or a shoemaker, or whatever, who knew about some other subject, one other subject. Then, because it was so popular, there came shows where a guy knew about everything. Well, I never could believe that, I couldn't go along with that for a minute. Ours was very honest; at least, it was with me. I studied; I never put down books on art. I studied the whole time I was on it!" After several weeks the pair tied and subsequently split the $64,000 between them.

Vincent's only film role was as the Devil in 1957 all-star fiasco entitled, *The Story of Mankind*, a film which proved to be Ronald Colman's last film, as he passed away shortly after the film's release. "Ronald Colman was a marvelous gentleman, quiet and charming and with a delicious sense of humor," recalled Vincent. "We knew during the filming that the picture was heading downward, the script was bad to begin with and it worsened with daily changes. I remember one puzzled visitor asking Ronald if the picture was based on a book. He replied in that beautiful diction of his, "Yes, it is, but they are using only the notes on the dust jacket."

The plot (what little there was of it) has the inhabitants of the planet Earth discovering the power of the atomic bomb years before it was scheduled, so the ruling forces of Heaven decide to hold a trial to see if the people of the Earth should be allowed to use the bomb to destroy the planet, or if Heaven should intervene and prevent the use of the bomb.

Court is convened in outer space headed by a judge (played by Sir Cedric Hardwicke), with the prosecution headed by Mr. Scratch aka the Devil (Vincent Price in a role that the reviewer for "New Yorker" magazine thought "has, as usual, the suave and sinister air of a headwaiter in a backs-to-the-wall supper club"), and the defense by the Spirit of Man (Ronald Colman). Each brings forth witnesses from history to prove their case that either the Earth should be saved or destroyed. But in the end, the scales of justice prove to be equally balanced with the court unable to come to a definite conclusion either way. Therefore the court decides to wait allowing man to create his own future.

"Cedric Hardwicke, Ronald Coleman and I were in Heaven surrounded by fake clouds created from steam and mineral oil," Vincent remembered. "We had really humorous, very witty dialogue and it was kind of fun. What we didn't know was that Groucho Marx was playing Peter Minuit and that about half of the earthly stories were farce and the other half were straight. One of my favorites ones was with Dennis Hopper (who was five foot nine) playing Napoleon and Marie Windsor, who was about six foot six (actually five foot nine but she *was* twice Hopper's age) was playing Josephine. There really were the most terrible inconsistencies that we didn't know about. We didn't have anything to do with those scenes. They had us standing behind a tree on a different set making a comment without any idea what was really going on in the scene."

Producer Irwin Allen began his film career making documentaries and this film was just that. A hodgepodge of old film clips mixed in recreations from history by a collection of actors ranging from has been silent film stars (Francis X. Bushman), former leading ladies long past their prime (Hedy Lamarr), leading players fallen on hard times (Peter Lorre), old time comics (the Marx Brothers), dozens of familiar character actors (John Carradine, William Schallert, Edward Everett Horton, etc) and a then a relatively unknown Dennis Hopper as Napoleon.

The film was so bad even the film's screenwriter, Charles Bennett, thought it was "a dreadful picture. Irwin Allen implored me to work on that thing. I didn't realize quite how dreadful it was going to be. I didn't realize when I was starting off that it was really going to be just a collection of snippets from old pictures. It was dreadful. I hated the picture. But I'm the writer. I wrote it, I was being paid quite handsomely, so that was it. I never read the book it was reported to be based on, and I don't think Irwin Allen did either!

"Vincent was a very dear friend of mine. I was awfully fond of him. But I don't know that he enjoyed playing the Devil. I don't think anybody enjoyed any part of it. I know that Ronald Colman hated it. It was just a revolting picture and it should have never been made."

Despite his hatred of the film, Bennett did manage to get in a good-natured dig at his friend Vincent's reputation as an art expert. When the Spirit of Man chides Mr. Scratch about his dislike of Da Vinci's *The Last Supper,* Mr. Scratch admits, "I've never pretended to be an art expert!"

Producer Irwin Allen, who would later achieve fame by creating the disaster film craze in the 1970's as well as for his four science fiction series in the 1960's, *Voyage to the Bottom of the Sea*, *Lost in Space*, *The Time Tunnel* and *The Land of the Giants*, was notoriously cheap. His favorite axiom, "Time is money," is featured prominently in the film.

Groucho Marx, who portrays Peter Minuit in the film, was a close friend of producer Allen, and would later bankroll many of his later productions including *Lost in Space*. Groucho, in fact, went as far as to promote the film during several segments of his *You Bet Your Life* television series. And Groucho's daughter, Melinda, appears in the part of an early Christian child (although without dialogue) and Groucho's then-wife, Eden Hartford, and good friend Harry Ruby appeared as Indians during his segment in the film. The film also features brothers Harpo (as Issac Newton) and Chico (in a very short segment with very little dialogue) as a monk in whom Columbus confides. It was the last time the three brothers would appear (although not together) in the same film.

After traveling to Africa to conduct a charity benefit show, Vincent returned to the *$64,000 Challenge* to face off against fellow actor and art collector Edward G. Robinson. "Here we were, two actors, one known for playing gangsters, and the other known for being a fiend, answering questions about the fine arts. But the thrill of appearing on these shows was not so much the money as it was a wonderful exposure that they gave to the world of fine art.

"After I had been on the first show for a few weeks, I asked the producers if they would let me do one thing. I said, 'As long as I'm on, may I publicize the museums of America and the richness of American art?' They let me do it. And the result is that I received letters from almost every museum saying that their attendance had increased up to three hundred percent because of the TV show. That program was a sort of a soapbox for me to explain my lifelong interest in the arts." Once again a tie occurred and the pair split the prize money between them. His appearance on the quiz show soon established Vincent as a nationally recognized art expert and he soon found himself in demand as a lecturer all across the country. By 1959 he became the number one guest speaker in the country, even out-distancing the then popular Eleanor Roosevelt.

Chapter Twelve

My Brother, the Fly
or
Vincent, the Skeleton

In 1958, Vincent filmed the first of four films which would establish him as the new King of Horror Films, *The Fly* (the others are *House on Haunted Hill*, *The Tingler* and 1960's *House of Usher*). Although he played the brother of *The Fly* in this film and its sequel, *The Return of the Fly*, many uninformed members of the viewing public assumed he played the title role, causing his name to become synonymous with the title character.

Alerted by the death of a man in his family foundry, Francois Delambre (Vincent Price) discovers that the body belongs to his brother, Andre (Al "David" Hedison) and that his brother's wife, Helene (Patricia Owens) has admitted to crushing him in the metal press. Helene later tells Francois and Police Inspector Charas (Herbert Marshall) about her husband's experiments with teleportation, how he first experimented with inanimate objects, and then animals before experimenting on himself. Unfortunately, during one of his experiments, he accidentally transports himself through his machine together with a common house fly, which results in the transfer of his and arm with that of the fly.

Unable to speak and falling under the ever-increasing power of the fly head, Andre orders his wife to find the fly, with the white head, which is still in the area of the house, because without it he will not be able to return to normal. But after several attempts to capture it, it escapes. Having little choice, Andre wrecks his laboratory, burns his papers, and orders his wife to destroy his fly parts in the metal press at the foundry.

Francois and Charas believe Helene is insane and while they prepare to take her to the asylum, her son, Phillipe (Charles Herbert), arrives and informs his uncle Francois that he has found the fly in a spider web. Rallying Charas, they race off into the garden to find the fly. Spying the human-headed fly about to be devoured by a spider, a horrified Charas picks up a rock and kills both insects. Realizing that Helene's story was true, Charas and Francois cover up the evidence and create a story that Andre committed suicide; thus freeing his wife from the murder charge.

The most famous scene in the film occurs at the end when Vincent and Herbert Marshall find the human headed fly in a web being attacked by a spider. The fly is screaming "Help Me! Help Me! As intense as the scene seemed on the screen, it was quite a different situation when it was filmed, as Vincent remembered, "So here we were, Herbert Marshall and I co-starring with a talking fly, and trying to speak our lines while staring at a spider's web. It was supposed to be a philosophical scene as to whether to let nature take its course and the spider eat the fly, whether to throw a rock and hit him and put him out of his misery or whether to catch him and put him in a jar and study him for science. Well, we'd start to play the scene, and I'd say, 'Well, Inspector.'

"And the little voice would say, 'Help me!'

"Then, Herbert would say, 'Well, Monsieur, I think what we should....'

"Help me! Help me!

"Well, finally, Herbert Marshall said, 'help you? The Hell with you, Help us.'

"In the end, we had to film it standing back to back. We just couldn't look each other in the face.

"It took us four hours to get film the scene that should have taken us about ten minutes because Herbert and I kept ruining the takes by breaking up and laughing ourselves sick."

While Vincent was having a good time, actor David Hedison, who played the title character, was not quite as happy with the film as he recalled, "I had first read the story in *Playboy*, and I thought it was thrilling. Shortly after that, Fox got the rights, and several actors who were under contract turned it down; when they asked me if I wanted to do it. I was thrilled; I thought it could be a terrific picture. But when I saw the finished film, I was a little disappointed in it. When I read the story, I was really thrilled because I'd always loved that Dr. Jekyll and Mr. Hyde story, and this had something of that in it. So I said to Fox chief Buddy Adler, 'I think you're going to have a terrific picture here, but it must be done with progressive makeup. When she pulls the cloth off, there's got to be enough to frighten anyone, you know, like half a face.' But instead they used this mask, which I didn't like at all. Unfortunately, they wanted to use it and thought it was faster to use than makeup. As masks go, it wasn't bad, but it didn't scare me much. I think the mask could have been the final stage, but at the beginning it could have been wonderful, if they'd come up with something really frightening. However, I think I did my best work under the mask.

"As for the infamous "Help Me" scene, they had me in the net, and then they painted me white (the fly was supposed to be aging rapidly). I went to see the dailies and when I saw that scene I thought it was truly horror, you heard the sound of a man who's going to be eaten by a spider. But they chose to go with that effect of heightening my voice to make it sound like a chipmunk."

Looking back on the film, Vincent brought up an interesting observation, "There is one strange thing about the picture, the fly can speak, since he has the human brain. Since the man can plot his own suicide, he must have a human brain, too. What happened to the fly's brain?"

What is surprising is that the film has stood the test of time even after more than thirty-five years since it was made. Vincent believed that it was because "The film had a sense of suspense. You never knew what was going to happen. When you saw the *Fly*, you only saw him for a short while. I mean, there is such a thing as suggesting something. It's like nude women. Very few women should be caught nude.

"When I learned that they were going to remake *The Fly*, I thought they were going to call it *The Zipper!* So, when it came out, I received a lovely letter from Jeff Goldblum (who starred in the remake) saying, "I loved your fly, I hope you like mine!" So I went to see the film and I thought parts of it were marvelous except for the ending. He didn't turn into a fly, he turned into a glob and then there was nothing left of him! It lost all credibility. I believe that horror films must be logical. You must be able to believe some part of it, not all of it, but you must be able to believe it could happen, otherwise it is not frightening."

His next scheduled film was as the lead villain in a western opposite good guy Jimmy Stewart, but when Stewart took ill the studio replaced the tall actor with the much shorter Alan Ladd. Not wanting Vincent to tower over their new star, he was replaced by a shorter actor.

After losing the Jimmy Stewart film, Vincent was offered the *House on Haunted Hill* by showman/producer William Castle. The film was basically a murder mystery but Castle successfully enhanced the thrills with a process he called "Emergo," in which a glow-in-the-dark skeleton would appear to leave the movie screen and fly over the heads of the audience members.

After the success of his first independent film *Macabre,* producer William Castle was approached by Allied Artists to supply them with another film. Having decided to make *House on Haunted Hill*, he set out to find a star for his film and, according to Castle, he accidentally stumbled upon a depressed Vincent Price in a coffee shop on a rainy night. Price, upset over losing the western to 'a shorter actor,' told his tale to Castle, who, upon realizing that Price was perfect for the lead in his film, told him about the project and the part he wanted him to play. Intrigued by Castle's story, he agreed to do the film. The film would firmly establish Vincent Price's place as a horror star.

Millionaire Frederick Loren (Vincent Price) invites five strangers, Lance Schroeder (Richard Long, later star of *The Big Valley* and the *Nanny and the Professor* television series), Dr. David Trent (Alan Marshal), Nora Manning (Carolyn Craig), Watson Pritchard (Elisha Cook), and Ruth Bridgers (Julie Mitchum, sister of actor Robert Mitchum) to a haunted house for a party. If they agree to spend the night in the house they will receive ten thousand dollars each. When Schroeder is struck by an unseen force and Manning frightened by a ghost, (who turns out to be the blind wife of the caretaker), she decides not to stay, but the caretakers leave early locking them all inside the house.

When Loren's wife, Annabelle (Carol Ohmart), is later discovered hanged by the neck, the others, armed with guns, lock themselves in their rooms believing they may be next. Unaware that Mrs. Loren and Dr. Trent are lovers and faked the hanging as part of their plan to do away with husband, Manning is driven to the point of hysteria with the idea that Loren is trying to kill her. When she finds him in the cellar, she panics and shoots him dead. However, when Trent attempts to dump his lifeless body into a convenient vat of acid, Loren returns to life and pushes Trent into the vat instead. Later, when Mrs. Loren goes to the cellar to meet up with Trent, Frederick's skeleton rises out of the vat and frightens his wife into the vat herself. Loren later explains that he was aware of his wife's plan to kill him and turned the tables on her and her lover.

"William Castle was a good director," Vincent recalled. "He knew how to put this kind of film together. He had wonderful ideas, and in this film he had me invite people to a haunted house. Well, Bill couldn't find a haunted house that pleased him, so he took one of the most famous Frank Lloyd Wright houses in Hollywood and turned it into a haunted house."

"*House on Haunted Hill* was shot mostly at Allied Artists," added screenwriter Robb White. "The exterior was shot at Frank Lloyd Wright's Ennis House on Los Feliz, built during his Egyptian period. We were not allowed to shoot inside, but the guy who owned it let us look around. It was one weird house! The ceilings were 22 feet high! And in one room there was closet door that was 22 feet high and two feet wide with nothing in the closet to hold up clothes or anything else.

"The man who owned the house had furnished only one of the many rooms with a bed, a chair, a nightstand, and in the kitchen, a card table. He complained that the famous glass walls, which joined each other at the corner with only the edges of the glass panes meeting, leaked when it rained and made a weird screaming noise when the wind blew. And there was nothing you could do about it.

"The swimming pool was about three feet deep; ten feet wide and a hundred feet long and in the middle there was a statue of a horse! It was just ridiculous.

"As for the film, I liked the whole thing right from the beginning. I loved Vincent; he was a professional get-along-wither. He knew his lines, he knew what to do, he didn't need much direction and he gave nobody any trouble. However, I thought we could have had him for $12,000, but Bill Castle said, "No, we'll give him a piece of the movie." Vincent got a tremendous amount of money out of it. I went to a party at his house after the movie was out and he had just bought another painting for about $200,000. I told him, "I'm glad we could afford it!"

During the climax of the film, a life-sized skeleton (with Vincent's voice) rises out of an acid bath to pursue actress Carol Ohmart. It was at this point that the projectionist in the theater was to activate a glow in the dark skeleton positioned near the screen. The skeleton was rigged to fly over the heads of the audience. However, the skeleton didn't always work the way it was supposed to as Robb White recalls its first appearance at a private screening:

"The skeleton which appeared during the showing of the film was operated from a fishing reel in the projection booth. The projectionist's job was to pull the skeleton out from the stage and over the heads of the audience. We got the thing made and rigged it all up, rented an empty theater and got in about 22 big producers. I mean John Huston and people like that. We sat them down and ran the picture, and then this skeleton came out floating over them. Well, they thought that was great until the line snapped and the skeleton fell straight down on top of them. They all got up and walked out!"

After that fiasco, they redesigned the flying apparatus as "the government specified how much our skeleton could weigh and made us guarantee that they couldn't hurt anybody if it fell on them. We finally got it figured out so they worked all right, but then the kids shot them down and they'd come in with everything short of bazookas and kill our skeletons! They cost us more to make than the movie!"

According to a report in Variety, *House on Haunted Hill* became the second-highest grossing film for Allied Artists up until that time, pushing Billy Wilder's *Love in the Afternoon* into third place. *House* was second only to *Friendly Persuasion*. According to Vincent, "when the film opened in at a theater in San Francisco and the skeleton appeared, the audience knocked out the first eight rows of seats!

"A similar incident occurred in one theater down in Alabama that catered to primarily black audiences and they stampeded. They were really terrified; they knocked out the first six rows of seats. There really wasn't anything terrifying about it but the marvelous thing was that they finally found that they could run it for like twelve months because people loved to stampede. So, they just left the seats just idly lying there, waiting to be knocked over again."

In 1999, *House on Haunted Hill* was remade with actor Geoffrey Rush (doing his best to impersonate Vincent, complete with pencil thin mustache and suave voice) in the starring role of Stephen Price. Needless to say, it had little to do with the original story or film. It was a complete disaster.

After completing the film, Vincent filmed a television pilot film for a series that was to be called *Collector's Item*, in which he and co-star Peter Lorre portrayed art dealers who also solved crimes as they traveled the world searching for lost art treasures. The pilot episode *The Left Fist of David,* which also featured Eduard Franz and Thomas Gomez, failed to generate any interest. He was later offered the hosting job on a proposed series by actor/producer Mark Stevens, based on the old radio series *The Mysterious Traveler*, but it never got off the ground.

Deciding to try his hand at selling a series to television, Vincent offered the networks a weekly series on art which combined information and entertainment, but the networks weren't interested and the Public Broadcasting System which might have jumped at such a series was still years away from its creation.

Vincent eventually did host a series called *ESP*, on July 11, 1958. It started as a game show in which contestants tried to see if they possessed extra-sensory perception, but it was canned after three episodes. The series continued for a few more weeks under the title *Tales of ESP*, (also hosted by Vincent) in which fictional stories were presented showing people with the powers the producers hoped to find among its game show contestants. The series left the air on August 22, 1958.

Vincent would not host another regular series until April 1979 when both he and his then-wife Coral Browne hosted the short lived series *Time Express*, which ran for total of four episodes before being derailed by the network.

On November 15, 1958, about three months after the cancellation of his ESP series, Vincent encountered "0ne of my most perplexing experiences in the mysterious realm of extrasensory perception (or whatever you want to call the super sensitivity of the human mind that picks up news before it happens) involves someone who enjoyed a colorful and successful life. This occurred on a plane, which was coming into the New York Airport.

"I am an avid viewer of the panoramas which present themselves beneath a plane, especially those coming into a city such as New York. You really feel you are momentarily a master of the world and that perhaps some of the secret hopes of those swarming millions down there might come up to you for inspection, at least, if not for fulfillment.

"That day, a heavy fog hung in the air, and I felt disappointed at being cheated of my 'view.' The air was so thick that it was really impossible to see anything, so I picked up a magazine by way of diversion. I casually thumbed through it until my eye chanced on a picture of a handsome actor engaged in filming a Biblical spectacle in Spain. I never knew this actor very well. I'd done one picture with him years before, but the few times we had encountered each other since, we felt we might like to know each other better. Unfortunately, nothing ever came of it.

"Now, as I looked down at the magazine and gazed at the clear-cut features of Tyrone Power, I felt extremely depressed. The magazine fell from my hand and I could not bring myself to retrieve it. I glanced out the window. Somewhere out there in the shifting clouds, something was trying to spell itself to me. I swear this is true! I saw huge letters emblazoned across a cloud bank which said TYRONE POWER IS DEAD!"

"It was a tremendous shock of course, and I thought that I was seeing things at first. I looked around and couldn't see anybody else acting as though they'd seen the words. But I had definitely seen these words which were like giant teletype that were lit up with brilliant light that came from within the clouds.

"After circling the shrouded sky for a while, the plane finally landed. I hurried to the baggage shed where I claimed my bags and turned to go for a taxi. As I went past the newsstand, my eyes were diverted—and stopped—by the latest headlines. In big, black type they proclaimed: TYRONE POWER DEAD.

"Tyrone Power had died in Spain where he was making *Solomon and Sheba.* He'd had a heart attack on the set while I was in the clouds. There was no way I could have known he was going to die so I didn't just imagine the words. Yet I think the words were somehow formed only for me, perhaps in my mind, like a message sent by Ty.

"At various times I have wondered why I, who liked but scarcely knew this popular actor, should have had an intuition about his death. Could it be that what Tyrone and I had suspected—that we should have been friends—was granted to us both when it was no longer possible?"

Even though news traveled much slower in 1958 than the news of today, the news of Power's death in Spain and Vincent seeing the headlines of the NY papers proclaiming his death on the same day is quite possible if you keep in mind that Vincent was flying from Los Angeles to New York and Tyrone Power was in Spain, if you factor the time difference between California and Spain and add in the much-slower travel time it took to fly coast to coast in 1958, there should have been plenty of time for the news to reach the east coast papers, in time for Vincent to learn of his death when he landed in New York. As to having a heart attack while Vincent was in the clouds, it's hard to prove as he would have needed to know what time Power died and to determine where he was at that same time, and in what time zone he was flying through. More than likely, Power was already dead when Vincent was headed to New York but arrived just as the newspapers reached the airport newsstands.

1959 brought Vincent a mixed bag of projects, the first re-teamed him with producer Irwin Allen, Victor Mature and friend Peter Lorre in the superficial but entertaining film *The Big Circus*, in which circus owner Henry Jasper Whirling (Victor Mature), having separated from his former business partner, applies for a bank loan to keep his circus afloat. The bank agrees to give him the loan but insists on sending Randy Sherman (Red Buttons) along to keep an eye on the books. As the circus prepares to tour the country, Whirling's former partner hires former mental patient Tommy Gordon (David Nelson, son of Ozzie Nelson) to sabotage the circus, thus eliminating the competition for his *own* circus. After several tragedies including a fire, an escaped lion, and a train crash which kills Zach Colino's (Gilbert Roland) wife "Mama" (Adele Mara), Gordon is discovered and falls to his death from the trapeze. The publicity gained from Colino's crossing of Niagara Falls on a tightrope helps the circus stay in business.

Vincent portrayed the circus ringmaster Hans Hagenfeld, a role which gave him very little to do but occasionally play straight man to Peter Lorre's circus clown, as Vincent recalled: "Peter Lorre was a joker. He just loved to make remarks and jokes and things. He was wonderful." As for cowardly Victor Mature, Vincent recalled "When we did the *Big Circus*, the lions were so elderly that they could hardly walk, but Victor didn't want to take any chances."

Despite the limited role, Vincent was always in good spirits and did his best keep everyone happy as co-star Red Buttons recalls, "All I remember about the film was the smile Vincent had on his face for all of us on the shoot. He was a charming, generous person."

Vincent's next project was a film version of an old play entitled *The Circular Staircase* It had been filmed twice before as *The Bat Whispers* first as a silent in 1926 and then four years later as a talkie and now re-titled *The Bat*, by screenwriter Crane Wilbur, who had written both *House of Wax* and *The Mad Magician*.

Mystery writer Cornelia Van Gorder (Agnes Moorehead, a few years away from her role as Endora, the witch, on the television series, *Bewitched*) and her maid, the cowardly Lizzie Allen (Lenita Lane, in a role far removed from the one she had in *The Mad Magician*) move into an old mansion owned by bank president Carter Fleming (Harvey Stephens), unaware that he has hidden the million dollars he stole from the bank somewhere in the house. Fleming, who is away on a hunting trip with Dr. Malcom Wells (Vincent Price), offers to give the good doctor half the money if he will help him fake his own death, thus escaping suspicion. Wells agrees but instead shoots Fleming once he is told the location of the hidden money.

Meanwhile, the Bat, a homicidal murderer who tears his victims throats open with a razor sharp claw, is also after the money and tries to frighten Van Gorder out of the house.

When she refuses to be frightened, the Bat murders a number of her friends and acquaintances including Wells, (whom the local police inspector Lt. "Andy" Anderson, (Gavin Gordon), believes is the Bat).

Having discovered the location of Fleming's hidden treasure room, Van Gorder decides to set a trap for the Bat. However, when they are overpowered by the Bat and are about to be murdered, Van Gorder's butler, Warner (John Sutton), arrives to shoot the Bat, aka Lt Anderson, dead. Van Gorder later turns the entire story into another one of her murder mysteries. Unfortunately, the film did not achieve much success as Vincent remembered, "It was a wonderful story but this was not a good version. When I decided to do it, I thought they would revise it and bring it up to date. When I was a little kid, I saw *The Bat* on the stage and it frightened me to death. I thought it could have that kind of hold on the audience again, but it didn't, because it wasn't a good script."

In between features, Vincent co-scripted and narrated *Revolution of the Eye*, an art documentary produced by the Metropolitan Museum of Art, which eventually aired on the CBS Network after a successful run in the museum's theater.

Chapter Thirteen

My Nephew, the Fly
or
Vincent and the Spine-Tingling Experience

After the success of *The Fly*, 20th Century-Fox brought Vincent back for *The Return of the Fly* as Francois Delambre, the brother of the *Fly*, only this time it's his now-grown nephew Phillipe who becomes the *Fly*. But as with most sequels it did not live up to the original, at least not in the final version as Vincent recalls, "It was not a bad film, in fact, it was quite exciting. When I first read the script, I was very excited about the possibilities as it was one of those rare cases when the sequel proved to be better than the original. Unfortunately, the producers, in obvious bad judgment, proceeded to put in a lot of gimmicks in the belief that films need gimmicks to be popular. I also thought it was ridiculous to shoot it in black and white. I love black and white, but you do two pictures in black and white….not *one* in color and the *other* in black and white. In the end, they lessened, if not nearly ruined, the dramatic effect that could have made it a truly superior picture."

After the funeral of his mother, Phillipe Delambre (Brett Halsey) the now-grown son of the original *Fly*, forces his uncle, Francois (Vincent Price, who despite supposed time passage since the last film, hasn't aged a day), to tell him the truth about his father's death. Francois reluctantly agrees and takes him back to his father's lab where he tells him the story of his father's accident and his subsequent death in the foundry. Phillipe, now a scientist himself vows to complete his father's work despite protests from uncle.

Using his inheritance, he and his assistant Alan Hinds (David Frankham) set out to duplicate his father's teleportation machine. Phillipe is unaware however that Hinds is actually a conman and murderer who plans to steal the plans for the machine, and with the help of corrupt mortician and part-time fence Max Berthold (Dan Seymour), to sell the plans to the highest bidder.

When Alan is discovered by Phillipe just after murdering a detective, he knocks Phillipe out cold and locks him and a fly in the teleportation machine. Turning on the machine before leaving, he fails to see the ill-fated

Phillipe reappear with a giant fly head, hand and leg. When Francois tries to stop Alan but is shot for his trouble, he stumbles into the house and Alan escapes in Francois' car with Phillipe trailing close behind. Phillipe tracks Alan to Max's mortuary where he proceeds to kill both of them.

Meanwhile, Police inspector Beacham (John Sutton, in the last of his many film appearances with Vincent; Sutton would die suddenly in 1963, at the age of 51) manages to capture the fly in the lab and, together with Francois's help, is able to restore Phillipe to normal once he returns home.

"Robert Lippert was supposed to produce the original *Fly*," recalled producer Bernard Glasser. "Regal purchased the short story by George Langelaan that appeared in *Playboy* magazine. Lippert felt that he had something special with this project, and he requested and received additional funds to produce the picture. But he did not receive production credit.

"Our budget on the sequel was increased to $275,000. The production department of the Fox studio asked Lippert to move *Return of the Fly* to the studio instead of our shooting it at an independent lot. Of course, this meant an increase in production costs and no controls. Because of the inefficiency of the slower Fox crews and the added charges and surcharges for set operation and construction, it was impossible for me to lock in any expenditures. Most of our money was being spent unproductively. The net result was that Lippert had to obtain additional production funds. But shooting on the Fox lot greatly enhanced the production values of the picture.

"We were surprised when Lippert approved Vincent Price and his salary. Perhaps Price had been a good luck omen for Lippert. It began with Price appearing in Lippert's *Baron of Arizona.* Or perhaps Lippert was playing on a hunch. At any rate he approved the additional expenditure for Price, $25,000. Price was always a gentleman, always ready and prepared, but as I recall he was not overly enthusiastic about the screenplay!

"Vincent Price liked my script for *Return of the Fly*," remembers screenwriter Edward Bernds. "He wouldn't sign to do the film until he read a script, so as soon as I had a draft ready, I sent it to him. Then, after he'd read it, I visited him in his palatial home; that's a funny word but believe me, his place was palatial, and he said he liked the script. We discussed it at considerable length, and he said he'd sign and he did. Sometime later a problem came up; what Vincent read was a first draft, and, like many first drafts, it was a little overlong, and some cuts were made to trim it down and some changes were made to bring about budget economics. Vincent liked some of the scenes we had cut, and he objected. If I recall correctly, they were mostly scenes with Danielle De Metz, scenes of warmth and charm, but, when you're pressed for footage, anything not truly essential to the progression of the story is usually cut out. But I conferred with Vincent from time to time, and I made changes that satisfied him."

Aside from his screenwriting duties, Edward Bernds was also the film's director and from that standpoint, he found that "Vincent was a delight to work with. Thoroughly professional, always prepared, and gave his best in every scene. He didn't even have the biggest part in the film, but his star status and the strength he brought to his performance lifted it out of the B category it might have fallen into. The whole cast was good to work with; Brett Halsey was excellent, as always. I guess the number of times that Brett and I worked together attests to the fact that I liked his work. David Frankham, who played the villainous Alan, was new to me, but he was everything I wanted as the charming, plausible, good-looking young Englishman who turns out to be a despicable double-crosser and killer. I wanted the contrast between the charming, pleasant Alan and the killer Alan to be a startling one, and David was everything I hoped for when I wrote his scenes. Danielle De Metz was very young, very pretty; practically no experience, but her youth and beauty were a plus. Maybe the fact that she wasn't an experienced actress made her performance seem more innocent and more real.

"I have still got a copy of the script I used to shoot *Return of the Fly*," continued Bernds, "and glancing at it reminds me that we tried to cast Herbert Marshall to repeat his role as Inspector Charas from the original. I must have written with Marshall in mind because the role in my script is referred to as Charas throughout, but in the dialogue the character played by John Sutton was named Inspector Beacham. I'm not sure why we didn't get Marshall; John Sutton was very good, but Marshall would have added stature to the part, and another link to the first *Fly*, would have been a definite plus. I was given to understand that Marshall was not well enough to take the part, but he made a half dozen more pictures before his death in 1966, so I suspect that maybe his price was a factor in not hiring him. I wasn't told that; I'd have fought to have him; even if we had to strain the budget, if I'd known it was a matter of money.

"Ed Wolff, the man who played the giant *Fly*, was a circus giant and he had very low endurance. With that head on and that heavy costume, we had to be very careful with him; we were afraid he'd have a heart attack and die! When we required him to run or anything, we'd have to give him several minutes to rest up. Like many giants, he was very weak." (Wolff also played the part of the giant robot in the film *The Colossus of New York*).

Vincent re-teamed with producer William Castle for his last film of the 1950's, the now-camp classic *The Tingler,* in which, during a post mortem at the state prison, pathologist Dr. William Chapin (Vincent Price) befriends next of kin Ollie Higgins (Phillip Coolidge), who takes him back to his house to meet his wife (Judith Evelyn), a deaf-mute who owns a silent movie theater. Chapin, who has been experimenting in the cause and effect of human fear, has discovered a strange parasitic creature that grows along the base of the human spinal column at moments of great fear and eventually crushes it unless the frightened person screams, releasing the tension and destroying the creature.

When Chapin speculates what would happen to Mrs Higgins (since she is unable to scream) if she were to receive a great fright, Ollie, believing he has found the perfect way to get away with murdering his wife, scares her to death (in the film's only color sequence).

"Bill Castle was wonderful," Vincent recalled. "Who else could do a black and white movie and have one scene in color, in which the woman turns on the faucet in the bathroom and instead of water, it's blood! He was a nutty fellow, but great fun to work with and very inventive."

After she dies, Ollie takes his wife's body to Chapin's house, where he removes a lobster-like creature from the dead woman's back, *the Tingler*. Chapin then begins to experiment with the creature and discovers it's indestructible and contains great strength.

After his wife tries to kill him with the Tingler, Chapin decides the creature is too dangerous to keep around so he locks it in a box and returns to Ollie's house in order to return the creature to the dead woman's body in the hopes it will eventually die.

Learning Ollie is planning to leave town, Chapin soon finds the ghoulish props he used to frighten his wife to death. But while Chapin confronts Ollie, the Tingler escapes from the box and disappears through a hole in the floorboard and into the theater below where it runs amok in the theater. It was one of the film's best-remembered sequences because it was where William Castle introduced his latest theatrical gimmick, a process he called Percepto. Chapin soon discovers it is missing and together with Ollie they search the theater for the creature.

The idea for the film came from the mind of screenwriter Robb White, who recalled that he got the idea from "the makeup guy that we had on *House on Haunted Hill*, Jack Dusick. Well, one day he showed me this rubber worm he had made, a horrible-looking thing, about a foot long. Now in those days we didn't have the violent makeup and special effects they have today, but this worm, it haunted you, it scared you! I began thinking about that, and I told Bill, "Let's find out where fear comes from and we'll use this worm!"

According to Castle, he invented the Percepto process one night when the bulb in his reading lamp went out. While attempting to change the bulb, he received an electric shock from a damaged cord. Suddenly, he came up with the idea of shocking the seats of his audience with electric motors during the film.

After the collapse of his flying skeleton during the preview, Castle thought it best to try out the electric motors on a test audience just in case something went wrong. And as screenwriter Robb White recalls, something did: "Bill Castle had the idea that if we take the motors out of thousands of vibrators and screw them under the theater seats, then rig the wiring so that at crucial moments in the film the audience would suddenly begin vibrating in waves, six rows at a time. We didn't want to buy thousands of vibrators without knowing whether they would really work out, so we scouted around until we found a theater in the Valley that was running *The Nun's Story*. The film was going to close on Sunday night and *The Tingler* was going to preview on Monday. We got in a huge crew of people to spend the day attaching the vibrators to the seats. But that night, just at the most tragic moment of *The Nun's Story*, somebody touched the master switch and the seats began vibrating in, wave after wave. There was absolute pandemonium!"

Weeks later when the film opened nationwide, the producers discovered another problem: kids. "They came and unscrewed the motors, broke them off and stole them. And they cost a lot of money."

One of the unique aspects of the film was its depiction of drug usage. In an attempt to experience the effects of the *Tingler*, Vincent induces fear by taking an injection of LSD. But as Robb White remembers, the screen version of the acid trip was not what he had wanted. "I wanted something different from the typical shot that you see in movie 'trips.' Author Aldous Huxley told me about a doctor at UCLA who was running an experiment on Lysurigic Acid (LSD). So I went up there to see this man, Dr. Cohen, and he gave me some of it. He took me into a nice little room with a cot and a radio and he got something out of his refrigerator and gave me a shot. It was all legal then. I watched the grain in the wood writhing around and listened to the music. It was very pleasant, although I didn't ever want to do it again.

"I went back and told Vincent about it, what the real reaction would be. I just wondered if it wasn't something that Vincent could be dramatic about without falling around and all that stuff. He said, 'Forget it.' And when he took the shot, he jumped around and did the same damned thing he always did! Whenever you killed Vincent Price in a movie, he was always so dramatic about it, he'd writhe around and scream and holler and carry on. I remember I told Vincent, when he got shot in *House on Haunted Hill*, "When someone gets hit with a .45 caliber bullet, they fall backwards. You always fall *forwards* when you get hit."

Vincent said, "My boy, no actor falls *away* from the camera!"

Chapter Fourteen

Vincent Price Meets Edgar Allan Poe
or
Vincent, the Conqueror

Following the success of *The Tingler*, Vincent's career was to take an unexpected upswing when he was chosen to star in American International Pictures' first color feature film (in Cinemascope) entitled *The Fall of the House of Usher*. Based on the infamous Edgar Allen Poe short story and directed by Roger Corman on a fifteen day shooting schedule, the film was an immediate success and soon led to a series of films based on Poe stories. Vincent starred in all but one of the Poe-based features (*The Premature Burial* starring Ray Milland is the exception) which were produced by AIP over the next ten years.

Until 1960, AIP had been producing low budget feature films for the teenage/drive-in market, when sudden changes in the film business made them take a gamble on Vincent, as Executive Producer and Co-Founder of AIP Samuel Z. Arkoff recalled: "We had been making less expensive pictures, all in black and white, since 1954 and we would release them in a double feature combination. Films like: *The Beast with a 1,000,000 Eyes*, *The Day the World Ended*, *The She Creature* and *It Conquered the World*. Then after a number of years, a number of imitators surfaced and began to move in on our territory. Until then, we were the only major independent film company. Now the question really was how to make our pictures scary enough so that we could replace the old rubber suit monsters we had been using and still be able to advertise them in such a way that we would not lose our audience. So, we decided we needed a horror star.

"We went down the list and found that there was a couple at Hammer in England, (Peter Cushing and Christopher Lee) which we later used in our films. Unfortunately Lon Chaney, Sr. was dead and Lon Chaney, Jr., whom we later used in *The Haunted Palace,* was not what we wanted. We decided on Vincent Price because he was the most prominent actor in the field. So, it was really a clear-cut decision.

"I had been a Poe aficionado for many years and so to a lesser degree was Jim Nicholson (co-founder of AIP). So, it was I who brought up the subject of using the Poe books."

Having decided on *The Fall of the House of Usher*, it was up to screenwriter Richard Matheson to turn the short story into a full-length feature, something he believes Poe would have been proud of: "Except for some of the short Poe stories I adapted for *Tales of Terror*, *House of Usher* probably comes the closest to the original. I tried to stay close, but even at that I added romance to it. Other people have made it exactly the way Poe wrote it, and it's a pretty moody piece. I really worked on it. I tried very hard to get the whole flavor. I did a long, complex outline and American International was very pleased with it and Vincent Price was delighted. I think he really outdid himself in *House of Usher*."

Vincent portrayed Roderick Usher, a strange white-haired man who suffers from a bizarre malady that makes him overly sensitive to any loud noise. He lives with his sister Madeline (portrayed by Myrna Fahey) and the family butler, Bristol (Harry Ellerbe), in a decaying old mansion in the middle of a swamp.

The scenes which feature Mark Damon riding through the desolate countryside on his approach to the Usher home were filmed in Hollywood Hills the day after a forest fire had burned through the area.

When Madeline's fiancé Philip Winthrop (Mark Damon) comes to visit, he is at first turned away by the butler and then by her brother claiming she is too ill to see him. When he is unable to get the young man to leave, Roderick finally admits that both he and his sister suffer the curse of the Usher family: inherited madness, and cannot marry him.

Late that night, Madeline apparently dies in her sleep and is then immediately buried in the family tomb. After paying his respects to his fiancée, Philip prepares to leave but quickly changes his plans when he learns that Madeline suffered from catatonic fits. Believing she could have been buried alive, Philip forces the disbelieving Roderick to open her coffin.

Finding a bloody trail leading away from the empty coffin to a hidden stairway, Philip searches for the now-mad Madeline but when he finally locates her, she attacks him. As the ancient house begins to crumble under the force of an occurring thunderstorm, Madeline finds her brother and proceeds to strangle him to death as the house crumbles around them. Philip manages to escape as the House of Usher burns to the ground and sinks into the swamp.

The final sequence of the film, in which the house burns to the ground, was in fact a huge barn Roger Corman had found which was scheduled for demolition. Deciding to take advantage of the situation, Corman offered the owner fifty dollars and set fire to the building at night and filmed the entire destruction of the building with two cameras. The results turned out so well, Corman reused the barn-burning sequence in almost all of his subsequent Poe films that required a burning building. Unfortunately, on the day they filmed the burning of the interior of the house, the crew accidentally set fire to the roof of the soundstage.

Years later, Vincent recalled fond memories about the making of the *House of Usher* and director Roger Corman, "the film was made in a mere fifteen days, but I loved every minute of it. Where else would I have been given the opportunity to bury a beautiful young girl alive and then die a sickening death by having a burning building collapse on me? I still think it was the best of all the Poe films. Now Roger is a marvelous person, and I owe him a lot. His energy, talent and drive amaze me. Besides, he let me pick the artist to do the portraits of the members of the Usher family that were used in the film."

Unlike his fondness for Corman, Vincent's memories of co-star Mark Damon were another matter. "Mark Damon was a method actor and on the first day I worked with him I recall I had a scene where we were kneeling in front of a coffin and the tears were streaming down the his face. He said, 'Isn't it wonderful. I've learned to control my emotions at the drop of a hat." I asked, "You do know where the camera is, don't you, Mark?' He said, 'What do you mean?' and I pointed out that the camera was on our backs, about twenty feet away, and that it would be two and a half hours before they got around to a frontal shot. So, when they finally got to a close-up of him, he had to have menthol blown into his eyes."

Screenwriter Richard Matheson happened to be visiting the set (which was located at the old Charlie Chaplin studio) one day when he happened to come upon a very rare occurrence: "I saw Vincent Price get angry. They were shooting a scene where Mark Damon comes in and he's about to strike Vincent with an axe, he flings the axe down, and it bounces right off Vincent's shin!

"Vincent uttered the only profanity I ever heard him say. He left the stage, and walked around the whole thing. And then when he came back, he was himself again. He was an incredibly nice man. You never met a nicer man than Vincent Price."

Over the many years since the *House of Usher* was filmed, there has been a famous (or in this case) an infamous story as to how the film actually came about, that has been told by producer Roger Corman concerning the lack of monsters in the film. "I remember Sam Arkoff saying at our final preproduction meeting, 'There's no monster in this story.' I really had no retort, but said, 'The House---the House is the monster.' I don't know if Sam really went along with that, but he agreed to make the picture.

"During the filming of the picture, Vincent questioned the line 'The House Lives, the House breathes.' He said, 'This doesn't make any sense. Why do I have to say this?' I said, 'That line is in there so we can make this picture,' and then related the story about Sam. Vincent said, 'Fine, I'll bring life to that line.'"

What makes this story so infamous is that there is no such line as "The House Lives, the House breathes" in the film. The closest the dialogue gets is when Vincent tells Mark Damon how the house became evil by association with its evil inhabitants. So, the basis for the entire story is nonexistent, something to which executive producer Samuel Z. Arkoff agreed, "Roger has been telling that 'House' story so long, I think he believes it. In reality it was not Roger that brought up the whole subject of the Poe books anyway. It was actually me. But my question was how we were going to make them scary enough to replace the monsters that we featured in our earlier pictures. That was basically the whole thing, and I think Roger was going a bit far at that point. But you are absolutely right; the dialogue that Roger talks about is not in the film!"

House of Usher was both a financial and a critical success. The film was budgeted (depending on different reports) at between $270,000 and $350,000 and, according to the *New York Herald Tribune,* was one of the five top moneymakers of 1960. Incidentally, Vincent Price was given the Herald Tribune Award for the best performance of that year.

Shortly after portraying the hypersensitive Roderick Usher, Vincent, (who previously told us the story about his paternal grandmother and his deceased uncle) recalled another encounter with the supernatural, this time with someone very special in his life. "A friend, whose strength not only guided me in life, but whose presence I have often felt since her death, my maternal grandmother. The power of our love for each other has come to me many times 'out of nowhere' to set me straight whenever I've been stumbling about, trying to find my way in life.

"Before I tell my story, I'd like to preface it with one which bears out the extraordinary perceptiveness of human senses. It's a classic story about the Empress Eugenie. Her young son was killed in Africa on an expedition and, though his body was returned to France for burial, the Empress Mother was obsessed by the desire to see the place where he had died.

"Several years later, the British Government arranged for her to visit the spot. It was known that a rock mound had been built at the actual spot where he'd been killed, but it was in the jungle and long since forgotten.

"The Empress was taken to a place which was in the approximate vicinity of the mound of rocks. From that indefinite location, she fought her way through the almost impenetrable undergrowth. Finally, she came to the exact place, led there by the overpowering scent of violets—the young Prince's favorite scent.

"I was reminded of this uncanny experience when I played Roderick Usher. Usher was a man so sensitive, the slightest sound almost deafened him and the faintest odor caused him to be ill. I'm a pretty hard-boiled character by now, having had my share of bruises and having been in some pretty smelly places. Noise doesn't really affect me very much and I guess I'm pretty average as far as all my senses are concerned. But a personal happening some years back proved, perhaps, I am more sensitive to smells than I'd imagined.

"I awoke one morning with a very definite odor in my nostrils. It was not an odor that I could connect with any special food or perfume or usual household occurrence—such as newly waxed furniture, creosoted lumber or fresh paint.

"It was an antique fragrance that made me think of my youth and, strangely enough, of a king and queen sitting on a throne; and all these odd memories—the king, the queen, the odor—all made me think of my mother's mother to whom I had been deeply devoted and who had passed away some twenty years before.

"But back to my strange and still familiar odor which would not leave me that morning long ago nor for several days.....oh, surely the odor was overcome temporarily by such lovely smells as coffee, bacon and the like, but it persisted for many days thereafter, it was a period of confusion in my life. I really wasn't sure that I could make it in my chosen work, the theatre, and I had been for many months on the point of trying a new vocation. Still, I adored the whole atmosphere of theatre life, and I was looking desperately for some solution to my problem.

"Somehow, I began to feel the odor had something to do with its resolution. I took off for a fishing trip to San Diego. Quite honestly in the hope that being alone on the road and in a boat would help me solve my indecision. I hadn't been there since I'd visited my grandmother many years before.

"When I arrived, I could find no place to stay. All the motels were filled and, desperate for a place to sleep, I vaguely remembered the funny old hotel when Granny used to live. I didn't even know if it was still there but I thought I'd try. It was there alright, and outwardly it hadn't changed a bit. I registered and was shown to my room. As I turned the corner to the stairs, an ancient odor hit my senses like a swig of oxygen. The odors of an ancient building, long lived in and long loved, almost knocked me down. All the sweet scents the dear old ladies wore, the years of waxing and polishing, of good foods and carpets deep with people-dust all surrounded me, and there was no mistake this was the odor of my waking several days before. When I recovered enough to climb the stairs, I almost passed out, for on the second landing were a king and queen, seated majestically on their tapestry thrones. These tapestry majesties were hanging on that wall when I had been a boy and took my granny's arm to help her every evening down to dinner.

"I sat in my room that night and breathed her presence. I drew in all the love she'd lavished on me and, most of all, I renewed for myself her belief in me, for it was to her alone I had confided my young ambitions to be an actor and she alone had understood and told me I must live my life and 'let my light so shine.'"

Following the success of the *House of Usher*, AIP and Vincent re-teamed for what was to become the most successful of all the Poe pictures, *The Pit and the Pendulum*. In the film Vincent portrayed Nicholas Medina, the son of the Spanish Inquisition's grand inquisitor who, while still a young boy, witnessed his father torture his mother and uncle to death for adultery. Years later, when his own wife Elizabeth (Barbara Steele) mysteriously dies, he begins to believe that he buried her alive.

Suspecting foul play, Elizabeth's brother, Francis Barnard (John Kerr), arrives at Medina castle to learn the truth, only to find that Nicholas is being slowly driven mad by Charles Leon, the family doctor (Anthony Carbone) and the still very-much-alive Elizabeth, who plan to drive Nicholas insane so they can make off with the family fortune.

Nicholas eventually snaps and assumes the identity of his dead father. He then throws Dr. Leon to his death in a deep pit located in the torture chamber beneath the castle and then ties, gags and locks Elizabeth up in inside an iron box.

Believing Francis to be his late uncle, Nicholas binds him beneath an ever-descending blade. In the nick of time, Nicholas' sister, Catherine (Luana Anders) and the butler, Maximillian (Patrick Westwood), arrive to rescue him, as Nicholas falls to his death in the pit. Catherine then orders the torture chamber sealed forever, unaware that Elizabeth is still alive in the iron box.

The film was shot on a sixteen-day shooting schedule at a cost of $1,000,000, but despite its short production time it was not without its problems. During filming of the final sequence Vincent, who insisted on doing his own stunts, unintentionally landed on his head when he fell into the pit; fortunately he wasn't seriously hurt.

Another problem arose when the pendulum did not perform as planned, as executive producer Samuel Z. Arkoff recalls: "John Kerr was chained beneath the eighteen-foot 'Pendulum of Fate' that inched closer to him with each swing. The pendulum set filled a complete soundstage; Danny Haller did a wonderful job designing the pendulum itself, although he had to do some improvising when problems developed with the original model. It initially had a rubberized blade which would graze Kerr's chest as it swung from side to side, sometimes even getting stuck against his body. That's when Danny made a suggestion, 'Let's try using a sharp, metal blade instead,' he said. 'It will look remarkably realistic in the close-ups.'

"The trick, of course, was to have the blade swing close enough to slice Kerr's shirt, without drawing blood. I had nightmares of trying to explain this one to our Blue Cross insurance agent."

"'Don't worry', Roger told John, 'We have this steel band you can wear around your midsection. Even if the pendulum drops a little too low, you're not going to get hurt.' As the pendulum swung, of course, Roger was at least fifteen feet away, securely positioned behind the camera, out of the line of the pendulum's swing. Despite the heavy makeup, John seemed to be sweating a little more than usual during that scene. After five takes, he had perspired enough to melt away a few pounds.

"With its blade in place, the pendulum was eighteen feet long, and it took four men to operate it. Even so, they could never get it moving fast enough to satisfy Roger. 'The pendulum has gotta swing quicker,' he would say with exasperation. 'What's wrong? Why is it going so slow?' Finally in the cutting room, Roger came up with a solution. He spliced out every second frame of the pendulum scenes thus giving the appearance that the blade was moving at twice its actual speed."

The Pit and the Pendulum was the first of AIP's many horror star team-ups, this time pitting Vincent against the reigning queen of European horror films (most notably *Black Sunday*) Barbara Steele, who recalled Vincent as "a completely charming and a fabulous actor but very protective and kind to his fellow actors. He was very compassionate and also wickedly funny."

While Roger Corman was editing *Pit and the Pendulum*, AIP hired director William Witney to take the helm on their next Price film, *Master of the World*. The story was based not on Poe but on the Jules Verne stories *Robur the Conqueror* and its sequel *Master of the World*. Witney, who had been directing Saturday matinee movie serials for decades, was ill-suited for the project and, according to screenwriter Richard Matheson, knew it: "He had a demeaning attitude about the whole project –'Well, if you really want to do this stupid thing, I'll see if I can pull it together.'"

Witney was not the only one who felt out of place. Matheson continues, "Charles Bronson was miscast, and he knew it, he was very unhappy. Testy is more the word. I remember a real strange day on the set. The first day I went in to watch them shoot. I walked up to him and said, 'Hello, Mr. Bronson, I'm the writer of this picture.' And he said, 'Oh, don't talk to me,' and he walked away! This really pissed me off!

"Later on, he came back, I guess feeling a little guilty about it, and said, 'Hey, I hear you're a very good writer.' I said, 'I am,' then walked away from him. Then after lunch, I went back to him and said, 'Can we start all over again?' We chatted awhile, and then he said, 'I hope you don't mind me playing it like a coal miner.' And then the next morning he walked by me and never said a word.

"Vincent, who could make friends with a dead man and very often has, in his movies, said, 'I can't get through to this guy, I cannot make friends with him.' I guess Bronson's always been that way. Very strange."

But even if Witney and Bronson didn't care for the film, Vincent did. "I loved *Master of the World* because it had a marvelous moralizing philosophy. I adored it. It was of a man who saw evil and wanted to destroy it. And if that meant the whole world, then it had to go! It was the great Jules Verne concept, that evil must be destroyed. I loved doing that also because I love movies that are trick movies."

When strange sounds and voices are heard coming from inside a Pennsylvania mountain, government agent John Strock (played by Charles Bronson who last worked with Vincent in *House of Wax*) is called in to investigate. Using a hot air balloon, Strock, ammunitions manufacturer (and owner of the balloon) Prudence (Henry Hull, star of the early horror classic *The Werewolf of London*), Prudence's daughter Dorothy (Mary Webster) and her fiancé Philip Evans (David Frankham, last seen in *Return of the Fly*) fly up to examine the hollow mountain. Moments after they reach the crater, they are shot down and then kidnapped by Robur and carried off in his flying machine. Robur, who has a hatred of war, intends to use his invincible flying ship to put an end to war by destroying the weapons of war.

Strock and the others eventually make their escape, but not before setting fire to the Robur's ammunition stockpile, causing the ship to crash and subsequently explode in the ocean.

The film, which cost approximately one-half million dollars, brought in over two million dollars at the box office.

~Intermission~

Photo Gallery of Fear

VICTORIA REGINA

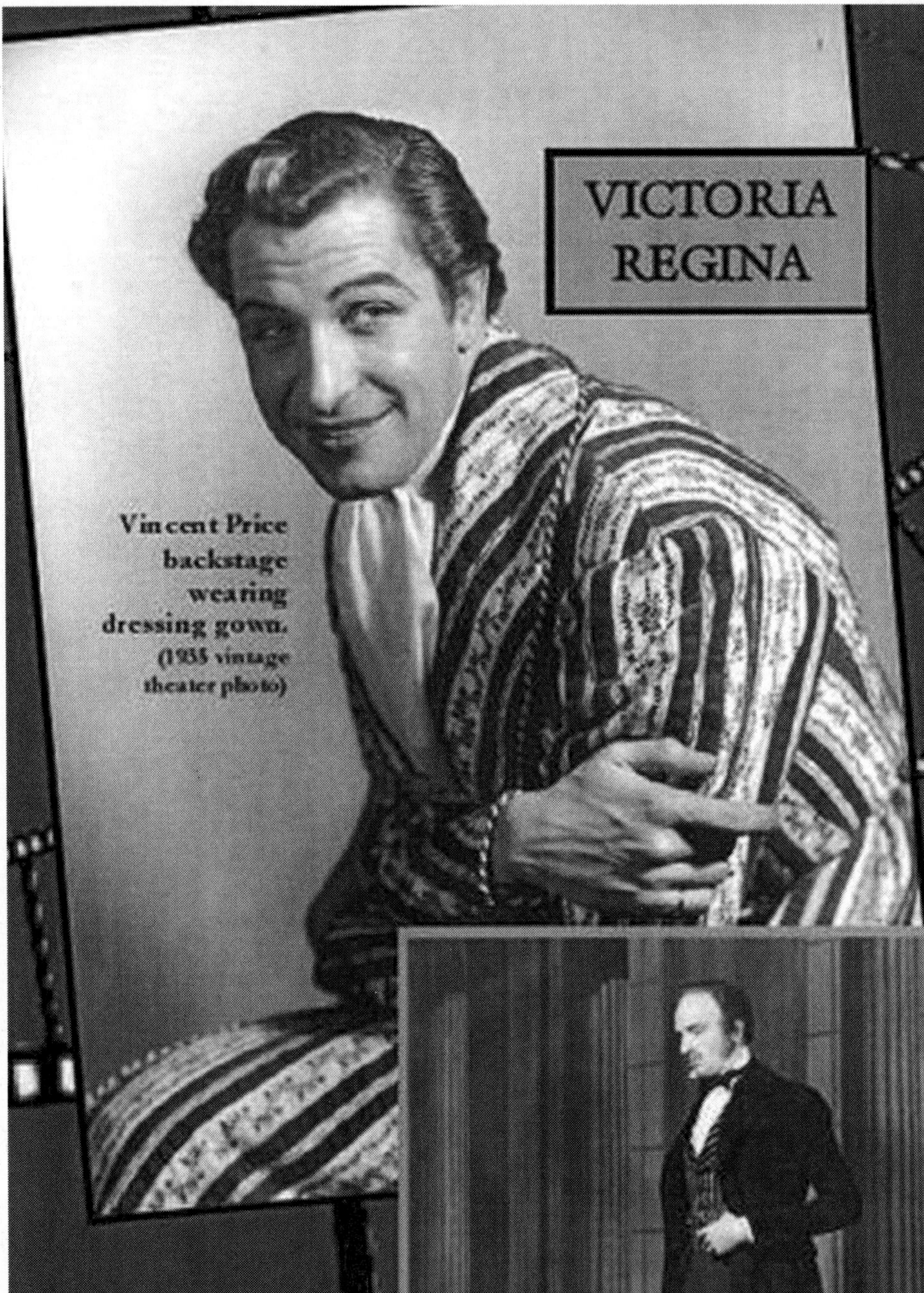

Vincent Price backstage wearing dressing gown. (1935 vintage theater photo)

Vincent Price as Duke of Clarence (1939 Universal Pictures)

Constance Bennett as Helen Murphy & Vincent Price as Robert Wade (1938 Universal Pictures)

Vincent Price as Prince Albert (1935 vintage theater photo)

Nan Grey as Helen Manson & Vincent Price as Geoffrey Radcliffe, the Invisible Man (1940 Universal Pictures)

ANGEL STREET

Vincent Price & Judith Evelyn as Mr. & Mrs. Manningham (1941 vintage theater photo)

SONG OF BERNADETTE

Vincent Price as Dutour the prosecutor (1941 20th Century Fox)

DRAGONWYCK COSTUME TEST

Vincent Price as Nicholas Van Ryn in a costume test pose (1946 20th Century Fox)

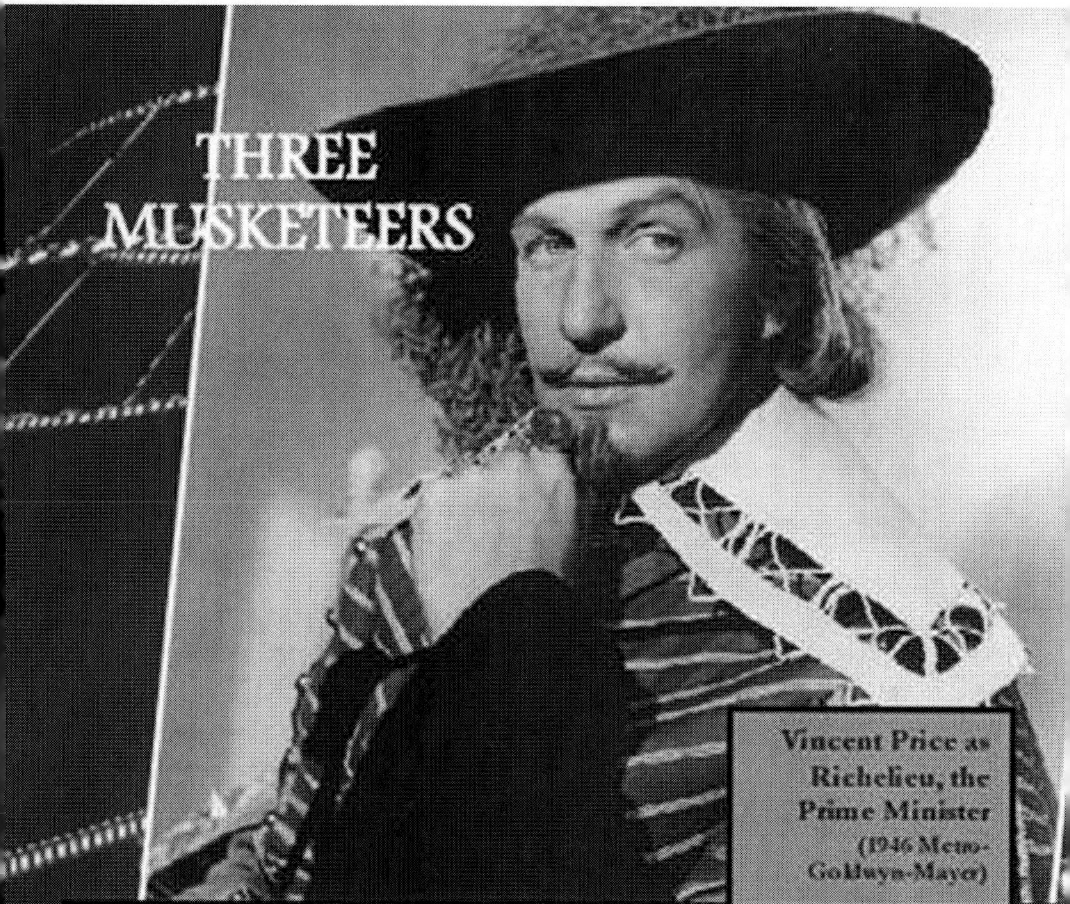

Vincent Price as Richelieu, the Prime Minister (1946 Metro-Goldwyn-Mayer)

Art Linkletter as Happy Hogan & Vincent Price as Bumbridge Waters
(1950 United Artists)

HOUSE OF WAX

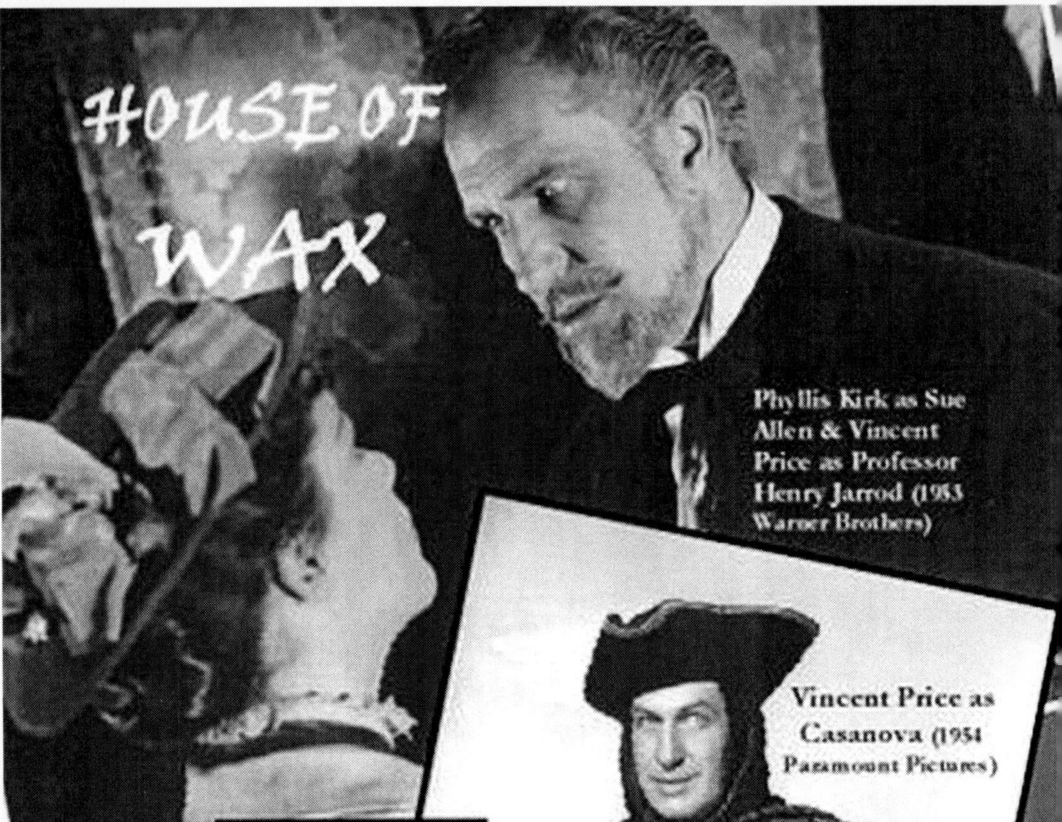

Phyllis Kirk as Sue Allen & Vincent Price as Professor Henry Jarrod (1953 Warner Brothers)

CASANOVA'S BIG NIGHT

Vincent Price as Casanova (1954 Paramount Pictures)

TEN COMMANDMENTS

Vincent Price as Baka the Master Builder (1956 Paramount Pictures)

Vincent Price as Mr. Scratch, the Devil & John Carradine as Khufu (1957 Warner Brothers)

Vincent Price as Francois Delambre & Charles Herbert as Phillipe Delambre (1958 20th Century Fox)

HOUSE ON HAUNTED HILL

Vincent Price as Frederick Loren behind the scenes with the skeleton (1958 Allied Artists)

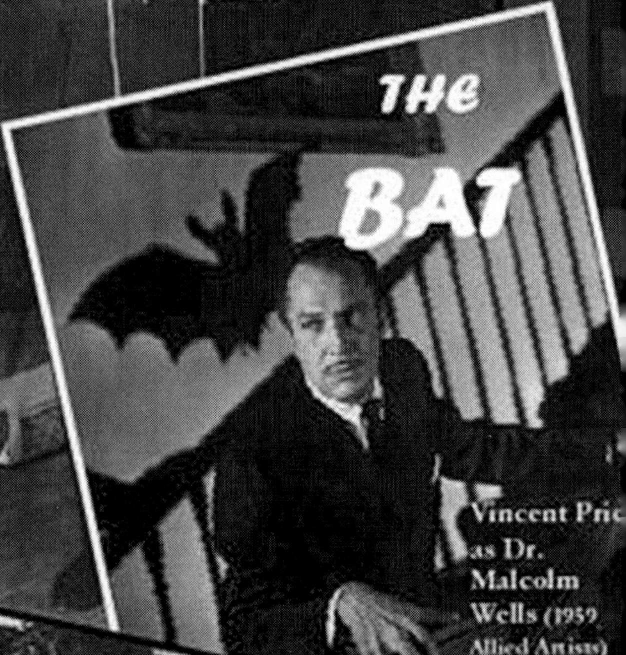

THE BAT

Vincent Price as Dr. Malcolm Wells (1959 Allied Artists)

THE RETURN OF THE FLY

Vincent Price as Francois Delambre behind the scenes with the giant Fly (Ed Wolff) (1959 20th Century Fox)

Vincent Price as Dr. William Chapin, Darryl Hickman as David Morris and Pamela Lincoln as Lucy Stevens with the Tingler (1959 Columbia Pictures)

Vincent Price as Roderick Usher (1960 American International Pictures)

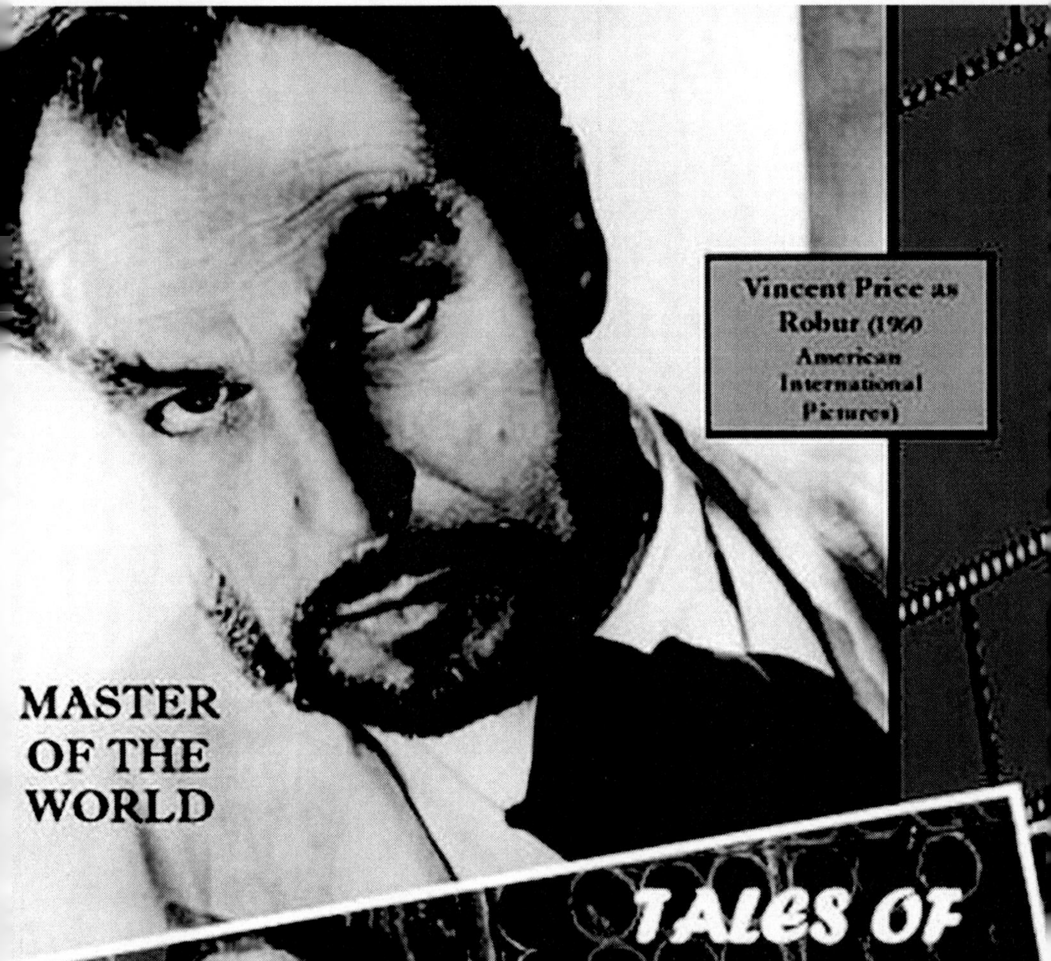

Vincent Price as Robur (1960 American International Pictures)

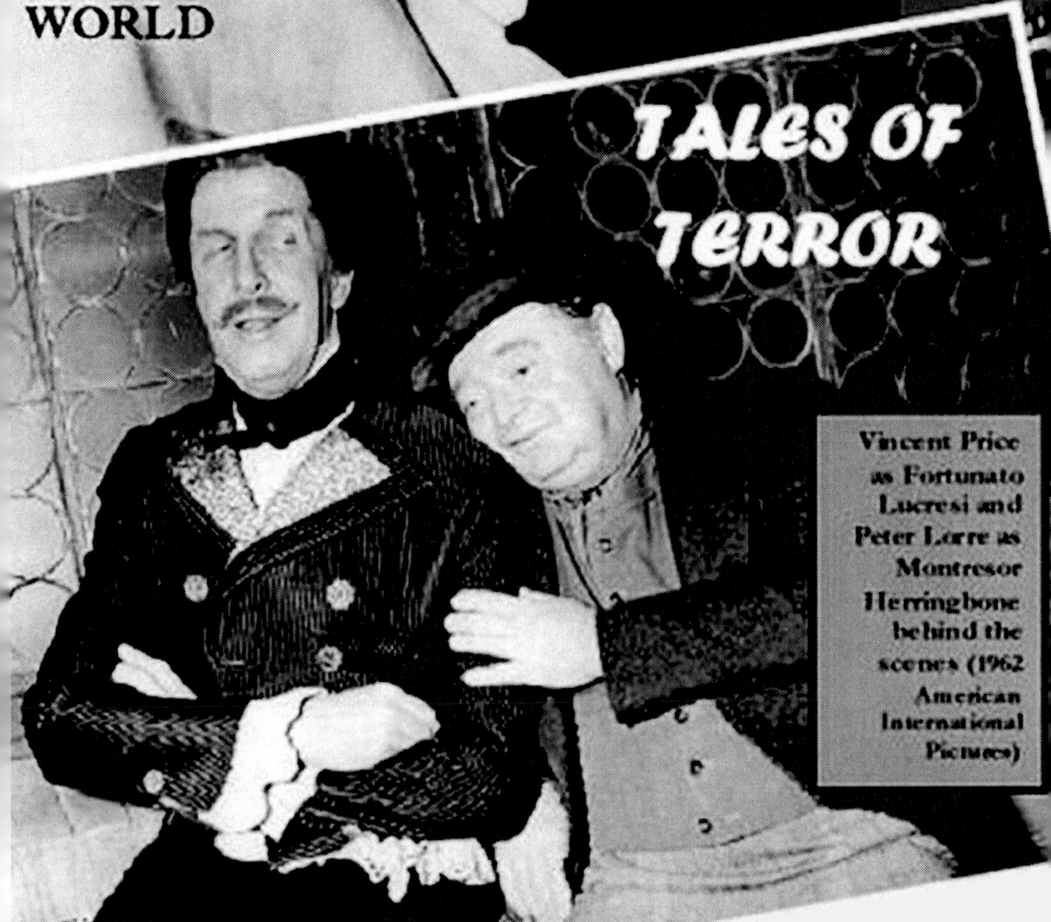

Vincent Price as Fortunato Lucresi and Peter Lorre as Montresor Herringbone behind the scenes (1962 American International Pictures)

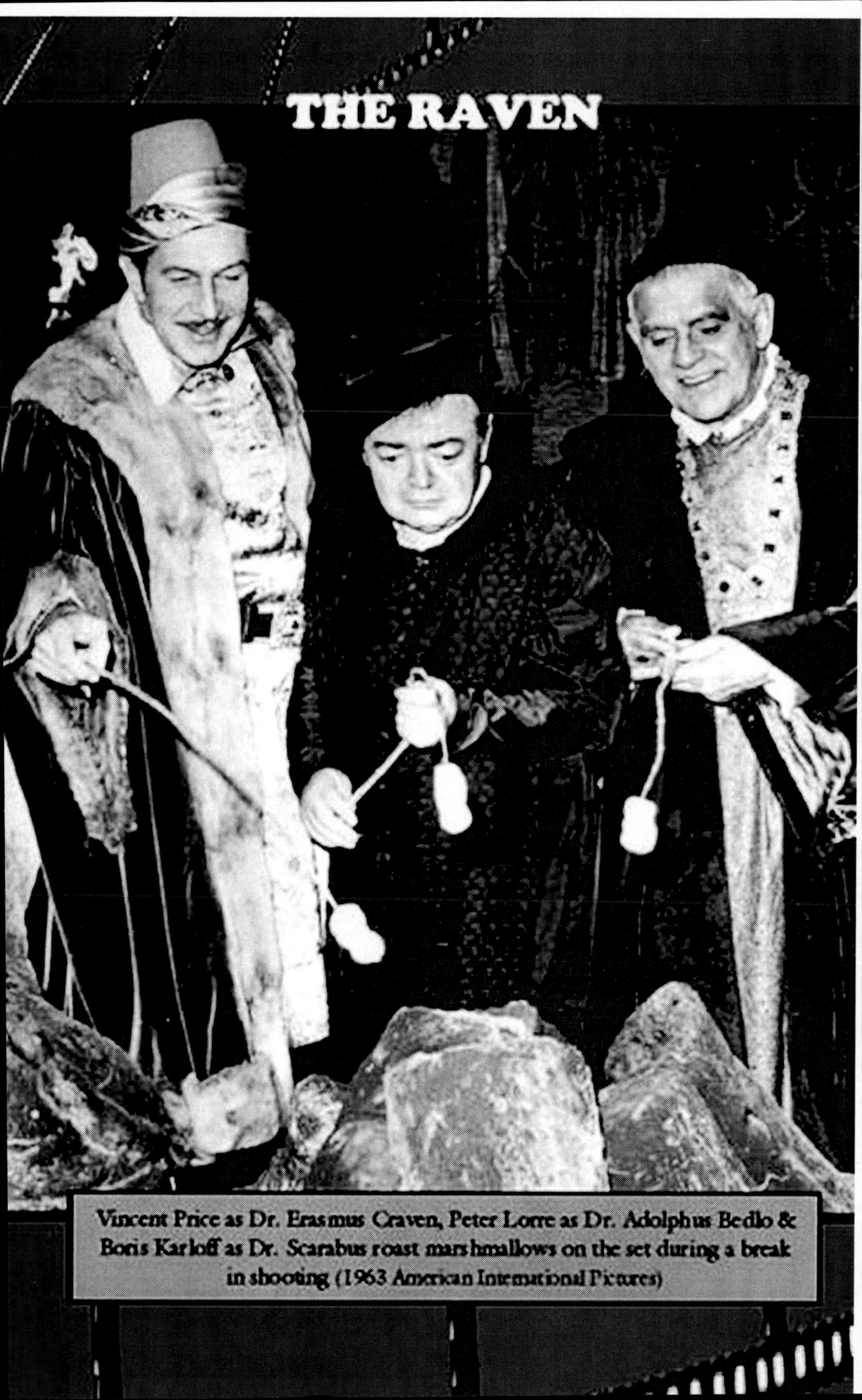

Vincent Price as Dr. Erasmus Craven, Peter Lorre as Dr. Adolphus Bedlo & Boris Karloff as Dr. Scarabus roast marshmallows on the set during a break in shooting (1963 American International Pictures)

Basil Rathbone as John F. Black, Peter Lorre as Felix Gillie, Boris Karloff as Amos Hinchley and Vincent Price as William Trumbull in coffins between scenes (1964 American International Pictures)

COMEDY OF TERRORS

Giacomo Rossi-Stuart as the undead Ben Cortman and Vincent Price as Dr. Robert Morgan (1964 American International Pictures)

THE LAST MAN ON EARTH

MASQUE OF THE RED DEATH

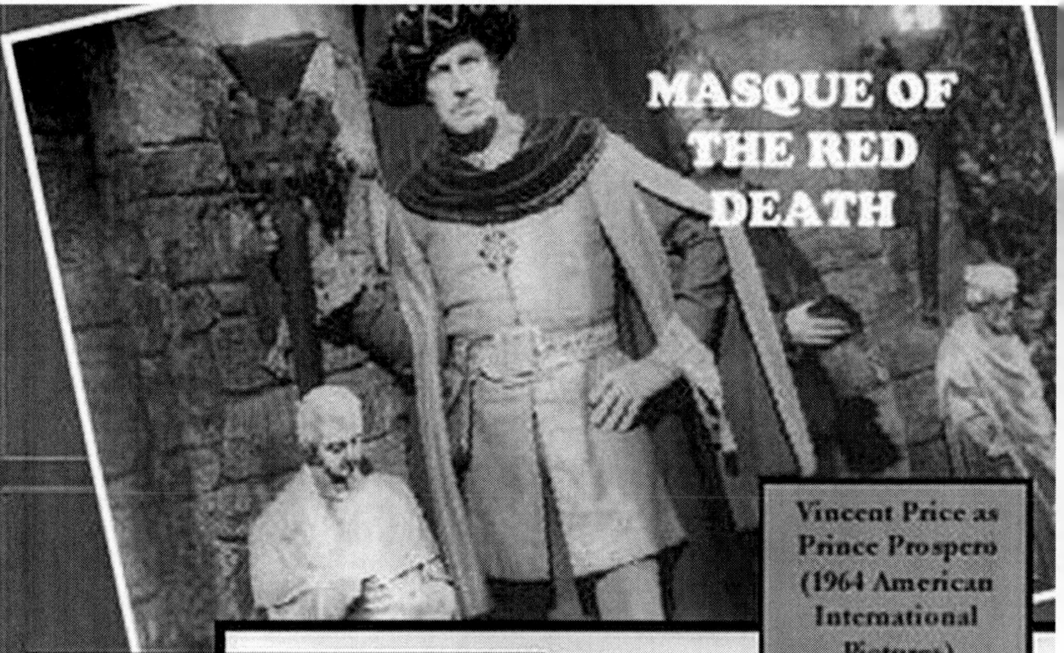

Vincent Price as Prince Prospero (1964 American International Pictures)

War Gods of the Deep

Vincent Price as Sir Hugh, the Captain (1965 American International Pictures)

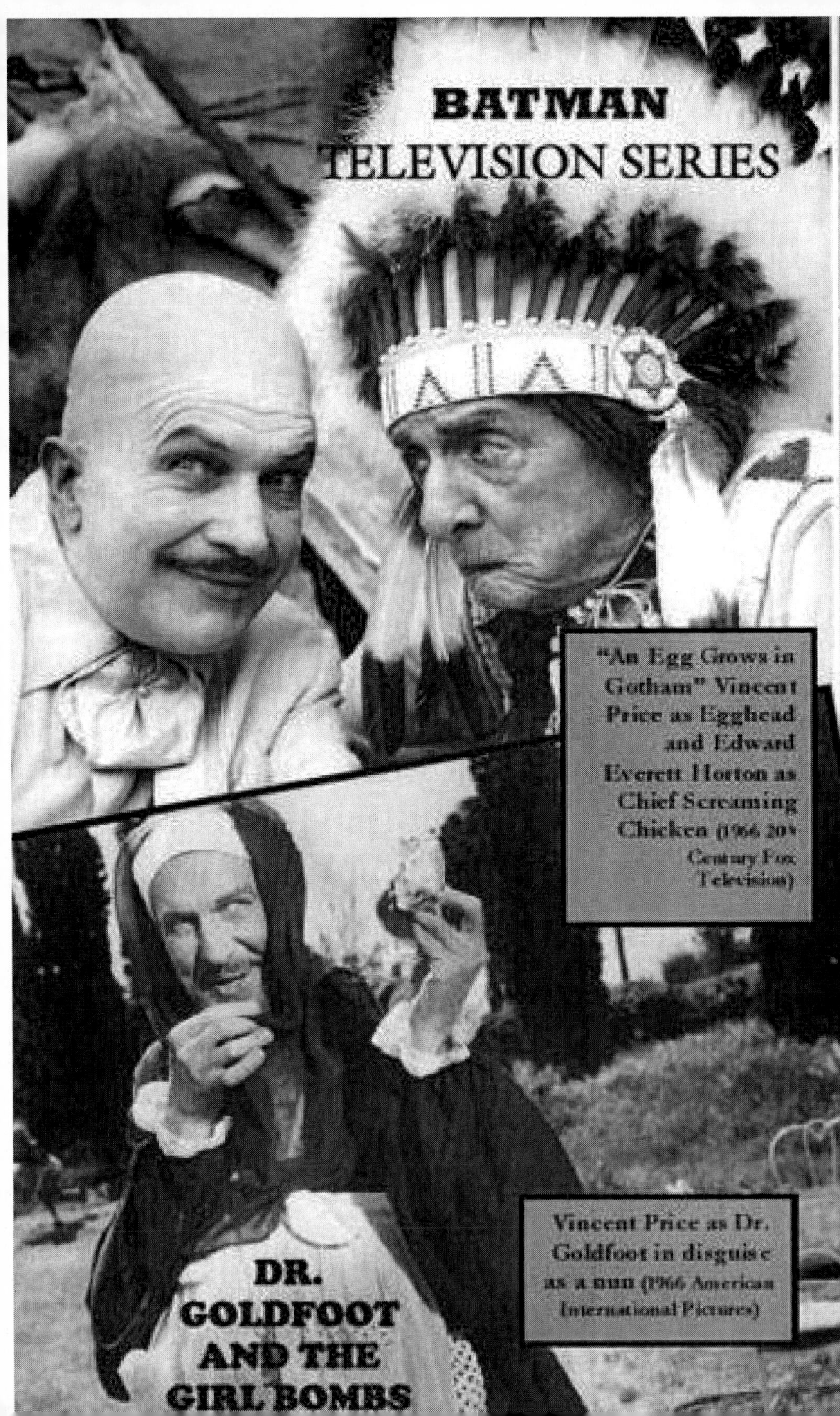

BATMAN TELEVISION SERIES

"An Egg Grows in Gotham" Vincent Price as Egghead and Edward Everett Horton as Chief Screaming Chicken (1966 20th Century Fox Television)

Vincent Price as Dr. Goldfoot in disguise as a nun (1966 American International Pictures)

DR. GOLDFOOT AND THE GIRL BOMBS

F-TROOP TELEVISION SERIES

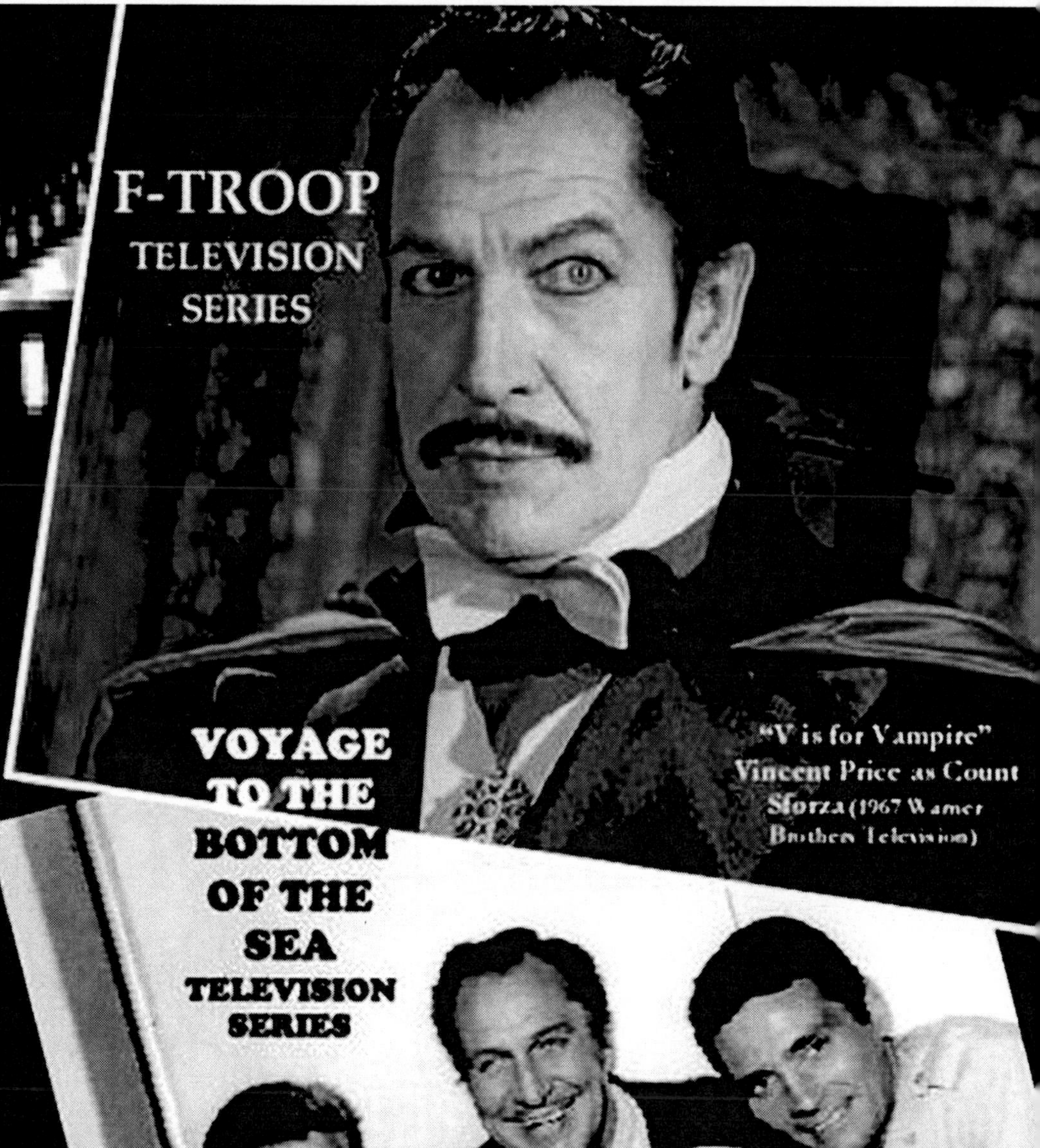

"V is for Vampire" Vincent Price as Count Sforza (1967 Warner Brothers Television)

VOYAGE TO THE BOTTOM OF THE SEA TELEVISION SERIES

"The Deadly Dolls" Vincent Price as Professor Multiple behind the scenes with Richard Basehart as Admiral Nelson and David Hedison as Captain Crane and their alien puppet look-alikes (1967 20th Century Fox Television)

Vincent Price as Matthew Hopkins, the Witchfinder General (1968 American International Pictures)

Vincent Price as Dr. Browning (1970 American International Pictures)

Vincent Price as Dr. Anton Phibes (1971 American International Pictures)

THE ABOMINABLE DR. PHIBES

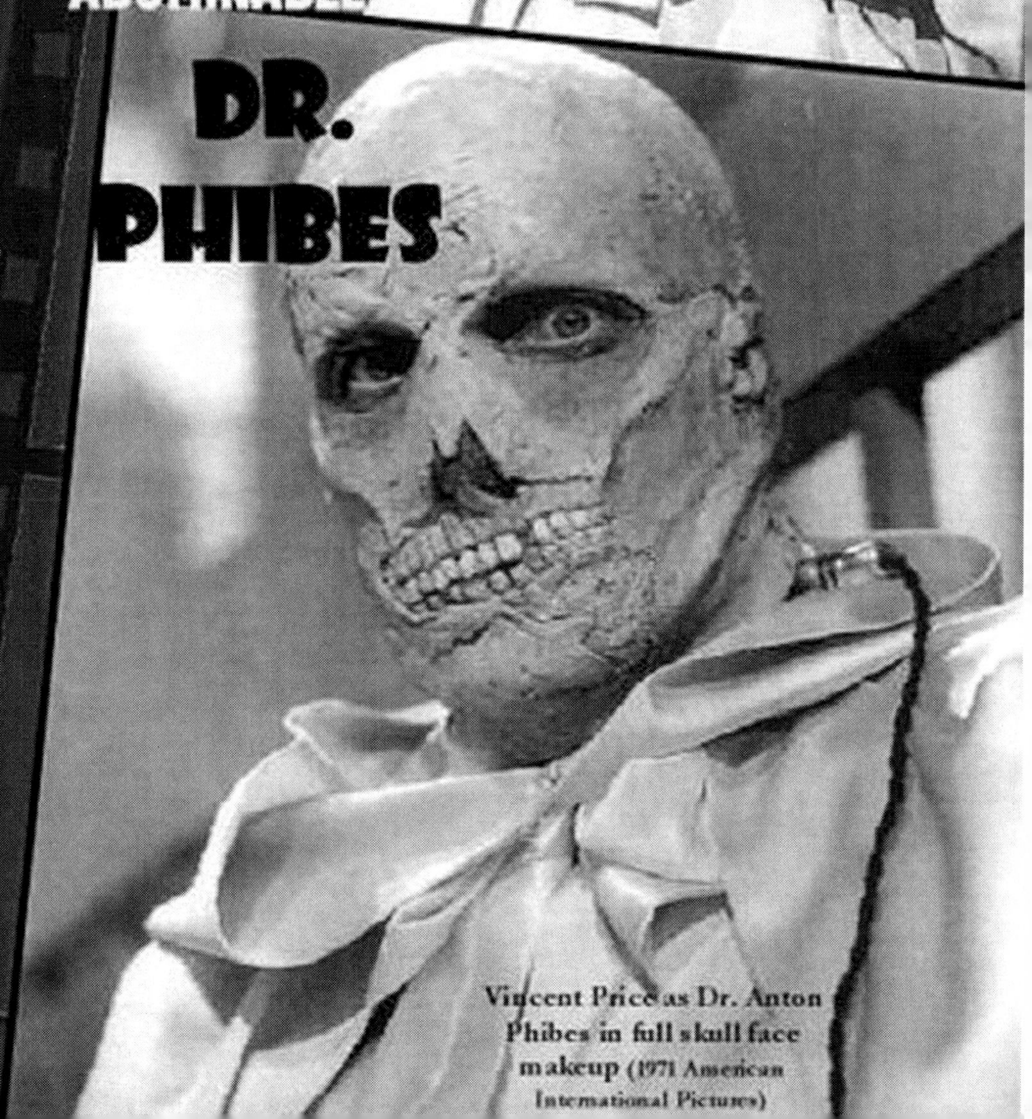

Vincent Price as Dr. Anton Phibes in full skull face makeup (1971 American International Pictures)

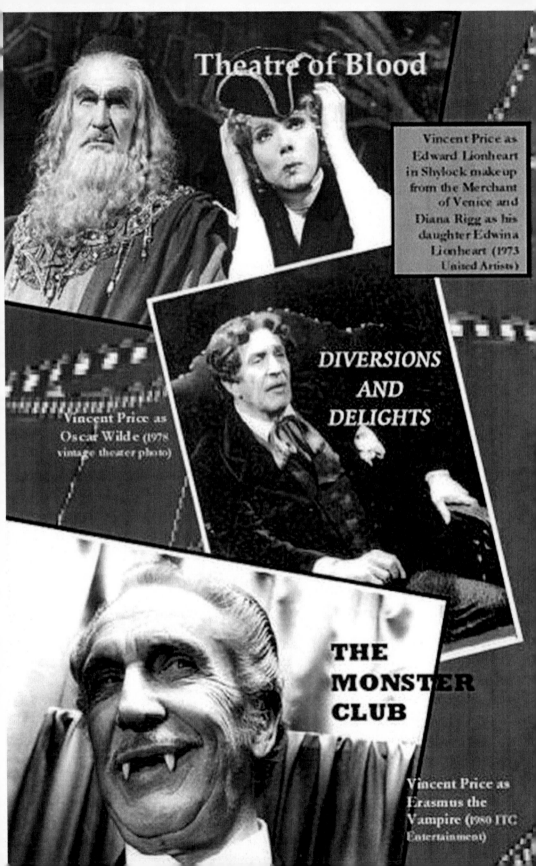

Vincent Price as Edward Lionheart in Shylock makeup from the Merchant of Venice and Diana Rigg as his daughter Edwina Lionheart (1973 United Artists)

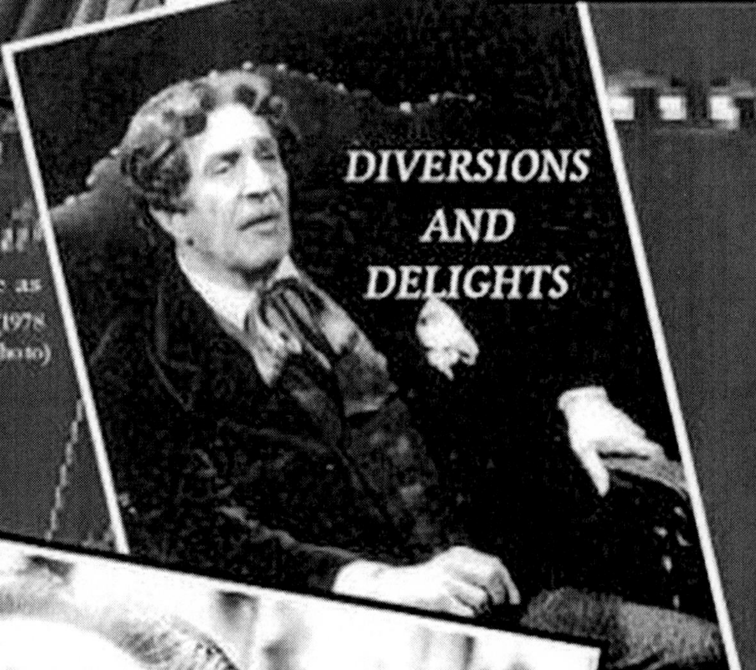

Vincent Price as Oscar Wilde (1978 vintage theater photo)

Vincent Price as Erasmus the Vampire (1980 ITC Entertainment)

THE HOUSE OF THE LONG SHADOWS

Christopher Lee as Corrigan, Vincent Price as Lionel Grisbane, John Carradine as Lord Grisbane & Peter Cushing as Sebastian Grisbane (1982 Cannon Pictures)

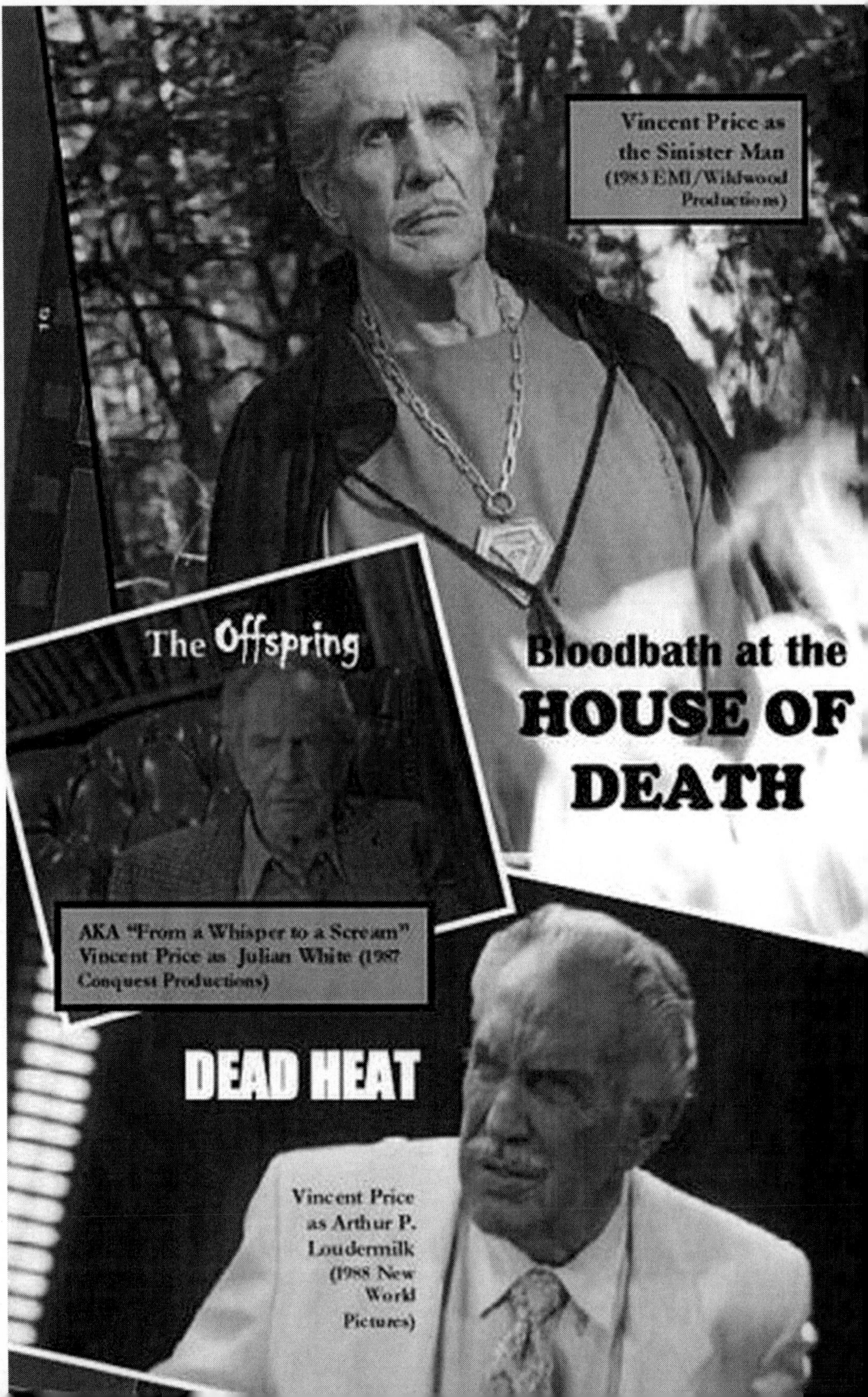
Vincent Price as the Sinister Man (1983 EMI/Wildwood Productions)
Bloodbath at the HOUSE OF DEATH
The Offspring
AKA "From a Whisper to a Scream" Vincent Price as Julian White (1987 Conquest Productions)
DEAD HEAT
Vincent Price as Arthur P. Loudermilk (1988 New World Pictures)

EDWARD SCISSORHANDS

Vincent Price as Reggie Shaw
(1993 Turner Network Television/Amblin Productions)

Chapter Fifteen

Vincent's Roman Adventure
or
Vincent meets the Spaghetti Vampires

After completing *Master of the World*, Vincent was hired by exploitation producer Joseph Brenner to narrate a Shockumentary entitled *Naked Terror*. The film, which hasn't been seen since its release in 1961, dealt with the ancient tribal rites and rituals of the African Zulu nation.

A short time later, Vincent and wife Mary left for Rome to star in three Spaghetti films to be shot back to back. The first film, *Nefertiti, Queen of the Nile*, reunited Vincent with Jeanne Crain, who had co-starred with him years earlier in *Leaver Her to Heaven*. Also in the cast was British actor and former Hollywood leading man Edmund Purdom, who returned to Europe to star in low budget action thrillers and horror films such as *Pieces* and *Don't Open until Christmas*. The completed film was an unintelligible mishmash of several genres including biblical epic, sword and sandal and romantic soap opera, with Vincent playing Benakon, an Egyptian high priest who is in love with vestal virgin Tanit (Jeanne Crain), who is in love with sculptor Tumos (Edmund Purdom). The film had a very limited release some three years later before it was quickly shunted to late night television in a package of Italian sword and sandal films.

For his second film, Vincent teamed with Ricardo Montalban for a swashbuckler called *Gordon, the Black Pirate*. "Why Gordon?" Vincent asked the producers, "It's such a terrible name." But he eventually found out "that it was Byron, who was Lord Gordon and had lived in Italy and he was the great romantic."

The plot was a simple one. Gordon (Ricardo Montalban) is an ex-slave who vows to wipe out the slave trade on the island of San Salvador. While masquerading as a wealthy Cuban plantation owner he is captured by his old nemesis Tortuga (Mario Feliciani) who is working for Romero (Vincent Price), the governor's secretary, who is also the leader of the slave traders. With the help of the governor's daughter, Gordon escapes from jail and overthrows Romero.

The film was made with a multi-national cast encompassing many languages so, like most Italian films of the period, it was dubbed into English. However, a major problem arose when it came time to dub it, as Vincent remembers, "They lost the soundtrack and the script, so we had to dub it using lip-readers. We had so many nationalities in that film, they had to hire lip readers in everything but Watusi. It was impossible and I don't believe anyone ever saw it."

Despite Vincent's belief that no one saw the film it did have a short theatrical release in 1962 under the title *Rage of the Buccaneers* before it was released to television under the title *The Pirate Warrior*.

Vincent's third and final Spaghetti film, *The Last Man on Earth,* is considered by many to be a cult classic. Based on the Richard Matheson novel *I am Legend*, Vincent plays scientist Robert Morgan, the last living survivor of an unknown plague which covered the world. Every night he barricades himself inside his home (which is covered with mirrors and garlic) while the living dead, victims of the plague including his former best friend Ben Cortman (Giacomo Rossi-Stuart), rise from their daytime hiding places to batter down his door. Weak and dying, the human vampires are no match for Morgan, who scours the city by day driving wooden stakes through their hearts.

Living from day to day and having watched his friends and family die and return from the grave as vampires has taken its toil on Morgan, so when he spots a puppy while out on one of his daily missions, he is overjoyed, but when he discovers it has the plague, he is heartbroken when it soon dies. Deciding to bury the dog in a grassy area, he encounters Ruth (Franca Bettoia}, who he believes will be the salvation of his empty life. Convincing her to return to his home, he tells her his life story and how he believes he is immune to the plague.

Learning she is infected with the plague, he plans to cure her with a blood transfusion until he learns she has a serum which allows her to live with the disease. Confronting her, she tells him that she was sent to spy on him by the community of contaminated people from which she comes. Believing him to be a danger to their new way of life, but feeling sorry for him, she tells him that they are planning to execute him that very night. Before they arrive he cures Ruth with a transfusion before managing to escape just as the execution squad arrives. Arming himself with gas grenades from a local armory, he eludes his attackers until they trap him in a nearby church where he meets his end surrounded by his attackers and their families.

The film, which did not get a release until 1964, had a very interesting history as screenwriter Richard Matheson explains: "In 1957 I went over to England for about six weeks adapting *I Am Legend* into a screenplay for Hammer films. I was working for Tony Hinds, who was going to be the producer. It turned out very well, and then later he told me that the censor wouldn't pass it. They finally ended up selling it to some guy in the United States, Robert Lippert.

"I remember going to Lippert's house and having him tell me, 'We're gonna get Fritz Lang to direct this thing.' And I thought, 'Oh Jesus, how wonderful!' Then later I got a call, and they told me that we're going with Sidney Salkow. And I thought, 'Well, there's a bit of a drop!'

"The last I heard of him, Salkow was teaching at some college in the Valley (he has since passed away), and he regards *The Last Man on Earth* as one of his masterpieces. While *The Last Man on Earth* closely followed the book, I thought it was so inept that I put my pen name, Logan Swanson, on it."

Despite its low budget, the film did have an eerie quality to it and together with a haunting musical score (lifted and reworked from the *Return of the Fly*), it still holds up as one of Vincent's more memorable foreign film projects. However, as Vincent once painfully pointed out, "The problem with *The Last Man on Earth* was that it was supposed to take place in Los Angeles and if there is a city in the world that doesn't look like Los Angeles, it's Rome. We would get up and drive out at five o'clock in the morning to beat the police and try to find something that didn't look like Rome!

"I was also never as cold in my life as I was in that picture. I had a driver and I used to tip him a big sum to keep the car running so I could change my clothes in the back seat."

The film was later remade in 1971 as the *Omega Man* with Charlton Heston in the starring role. It was remade for a third time as *I Am Legend*, Will Smith in the lead. Of the three versions, Vincent's is the most true to the original book.

Chapter Sixteen

Vincent, the Art Buyer
or
The Proper Way to Taste Wine

Returning to the to the US in 1962, Vincent soon found himself selected for a post on President Kennedy's White House Fine Arts Committee, where he spent the next two years restocking the White House with art treasures, to replace those taken by former White House residents.

"The White House was a ruin until Truman had it rebuilt," Vincent declared. "Former presidents simply pillaged it, Theodore Roosevelt even took out the lovely Georgian mantelpieces and replaced them with ones with buffalo heads, and it wasn't until the Truman piano went through the floor one day that anyone started caring. Did you know that Jackie once found a magnificent head of Washington in the men's room in the basement?"

And while on the subject of art, he was also hired by the Sears Roebuck Department Store chain as their official art buyer for their proposed Sears Art Gallery. Their plan was to offer affordable art works to the general public. Vincent continued in this successful and profitable position for many years.

And hoping to continue their profitable relationship, AIP signed Vincent to an exclusive contract to make horror pictures. In other words, he could not make a horror film for anyone except AIP. But in signing Vincent to an exclusive contract, AIP, being a small company with limited capital, found itself with a cash flow problem. Thinking quickly, Sam Arkoff came up with a plan that could guarantee him Vincent's services and yet let them hold onto their limited funds. "We paid Vincent $50,000 for *House of Usher* and by his last Poe movie he was making $80,000 per picture. That was a lot of money for AIP, and I wasn't sure that we could afford Vincent. But I sat down with him and we negotiated an agreement that we both could live with.

"'Here's my offer, Vincent,' I told him. 'You've already been doing quite well financially, not only from your movies, but from your art lectures and from your contract with Sears to help them choose art for their department stores. But what about *your* future? Why not let us hold onto the money we're paying you for the AIP pictures, and we'll give it to you sometime down the road? It will be like an annuity that will come due in a few years.'

"Vincent agreed to my proposal. I guaranteed him a series of AIP pictures, and we deferred his payments. That made him affordable to us and we clearly got our money's worth. Vincent was the consummate professional who had his own fans, a built-in audience he brought to AIP with him and that was the kind of actor we liked."

Vincent's first project under his new contract was *Tales of Terror*, an anthology film based on three Edgar Allen Poe stories. In the first tale, *Morella,* Lenora (Maggie Pierce) returns home after 20 years of exile to find her crazed father Locke (Vincent Price) living with the embalmed body of her dead mother, Morella (Leona Gage), who died in childbirth. Locke, who blames Lenora for the death his wife, soon regrets sending his daughter away when he learns she has a short time to live. That night, however, the spirit of Morella takes possession of Lenora and kills Locke as the house burns to the ground.

Morella was the weakest of the three tales and at times quite hard to follow. "It just didn't work," recalled screenwriter Richard Matheson, "because they cut a lot out of it. The casting also bugged me which is why I always refer to that first segment as *Shirley Temple in the Haunted House.* In my script it was a really great character relationship between the two of them (Locke and Lenora). Vincent was up to it, but this girl that they got, Maggie Pierce, was terrible. I visualized someone like Nina Foch playing the dying daughter."

The second tale, *The Black Cat,* has an ever-out-of-work Montresor Herringbone (Peter Lorre), while off on his usual drinking binge, stumble upon a wine merchant's convention where he challenges champion wine-taster Fortunato Lucresi (Vincent Price) to a contest. In the end, the contest is a draw and the now-drunken pair are the best of friends. Montresor takes Fortunato home for another round of drinks, where he falls for Montresor's beautiful wife, Annabel (Joyce Jameson).

Weeks later, Montresor returns home early and spots Fortunato leaving his house. Realizing his wife has a new lover; he flies into a rage and kills her. Chaining her lifeless body to a wall in the basement, he invites Fortunato over for a drink and after drugging him chains him next to Annabel's corpse. Fortunato finally awakens he finds Montresor in the process of entombing him behind a wall of bricks.

With his wife out of the way, Montresor goes on a spending spree at the local pub, which alerts the local police, who insist on searching the house for his wife. When horrible screams are heard coming from behind the basement wall, the police remove the bricks and find the bodies of Fortunato and Annabel, and Annabel's still-living cat, which was unknowingly sealed behind the wall.

The Black Cat was played mostly for laughs with a hilarious wine-tasting scene between Peter Lorre and Vincent, setting the pace for the entire segment. And as Vincent recalled, "a professional wine taster showed us the whole thing about testing the wine and breathing it in and doing all that stuff, then Peter and I just went a little further. I was trying to do it in an exaggerated fashion, which made it so funny. To this day, people still talk about that scene. I was doing it the way wine tasters do it, and Peter was doing it the way they *didn't* do it. But here was an example again where I think Roger (Corman) was so bright, he had two actors who were very inventive, who had this opportunity to see how it was actually done, and we were allowed to 'comedy' it up."

Peter Lorre was a notorious ad-libber, something screenwriter Richard Matheson learned first-hand. "Everyone in the film except Peter Lorre read my lines word for word; that dialogue was very well written, and they relished the way it fell off their tongues. Lorre just sort of gave the basic essence. Usually that kind of thing really bugged me, but he was such a nice man, I couldn't really get fired up. He used to tell me that he drove Sidney Greenstreet out of his mind like that. Greenstreet came from the theater, and would do every line down to the last semi-colon, and then Lorre would just sort of spew out some general reaction to it and Greenstreet would get all bent out of shape! And they were in a lot of pictures together."

In the third and final tale, *The Case of M. Valdemar*, Ernest Valdemar (Vincent Price), knowing he is dying a slow death, agrees to allow hypnotist Carmichael (Basil Rathbone) to hypnotize him just at the moment of death in return for using his skills to minimize his pain during the final days of his life.

Months pass and Carmichael, who has moved into Valdemar's mansion and has taken a fancy to Valdemar's wife Helene (Debra Paget), refuses to release Valdemar from his torment, even as his body slowly decays. Helene, who is in love with Dr. James (David Frankham), pleads with Carmichael to release her husband. He will agree but only if she will marry him. He then threatens her with the knowledge that Valdemar's spirit will never find rest until she complies. As the doctor rushes to her rescue, Carmichael locks the door to the bedroom. As Helene screams for help, Valdemar's body rises out of bed and attacks Carmichael. When the doctor finally breaks down the door, he finds Carmichael lying dead beneath the dissolving corpse of Valdemar, leaving him free to marry Helene.

For the part of Valdemar, Vincent went from a dying old man to a putrefying corpse, but the question was how to do it on AIP's limited budget. "I played an old man who is killed physically but kept alive in his mind," Vincent recounted. "The question was: what would a man look like in this state? We settled for an old-fashioned mud pack, it dries and draws the skin up and then crack open. It worked beautifully. But the hardest job was the part where the dead man actually comes back to life. They decided on a mixture of glue, glycerin, corn starch, and make-up paint, which was boiled and poured all over my head. Hot, mind you, I could stand it for only one shot, and then I'd have to run. It came out beautifully because it gave the impression of the old man's face melting away."

For his next film, Vincent went from playing a decaying corpse to a renowned art critic. *Convicts 4* was based on the true story of John Resko (played by Ben Gazarra), who was convicted of murder and sentenced to life in prison, where he develops his skills as an artist and painter which eventually wins him his release from prison after 20 years. Vincent portrayed real-life art critic Carl Carmer, who was responsible for helping Resko develop his artistic talents and arranged for him to get his work shown outside the prison. The part was basically a one day job but it gave him the opportunity to get away from horror films if only for a short time.

On April 27, 1962, Vincent and Mary celebrated the birth of their daughter Mary Victoria Price. The then-51-year-old Vincent used to joke that "she was the child of his middle age."

In *Confessions of an Opium Eater*, Vincent plays Gil DeQuincey, a soldier of fortune who arrives in San Francisco to help his old friend George Wah (played by veteran movie villain Richard Loo) end the slavery/wife auctions still being held in Chinatown. The film, which took place in 1902, had rich Chinese men trade large quantities of opium for beautiful young women kidnapped from China to make them their wives. Aided by a Chinese dwarf (Yvonne Moray, the non-Asian female lead of the all-midget western *The Terror of Tiny Town*) and a kidnapped girl named Lotus (June Kim), DeQuincey attempts to end the slave auctions run by the evil Ruby Low (Linda Ho) masquerading as an ancient Chinese mandarin. After several attempts on his life, including one while he is under the influence of opium, Vincent successfully ends the slave auctions and destroys Low's horde of treasure, before dying with her in the sewers beneath Chinatown.

The film had a short release before being released to television under the title *Souls for Sale*. There is one rather interesting sequence in the film in which Vincent's character experiences opium-induced hallucinations and as the reviewer for *Film Comment Magazine* pointed out, "Price has probably consumed more drugs onscreen than anyone except Bela Lugosi, and his "trip" sequence here tops them all. Everything and anything is included, from stock-footage of alligators with hiccups on the soundtrack to some of the dreamiest slow-motion imagery I've ever seen--rich, shadowy black and white stuff by Joe Biroc." Some of the stock footage used came from various scenes in the film itself plus clips from the following AIP films: the disembodied crawling hand from *Invasion of the Saucermen*, the human skull from *The Screaming Skull*, the face of the monster from *Voodoo Woman*, the giant spider from *The Earth vs. The Spider*, the sea monster from *The Viking Women vs. the Sea Serpent* plus various ghostly screams borrowed from *House on Haunted Hill*.

"I have a great sympathy with the characters I play, I really do. I think you have to have that in order to play them. But on this film, I found I had no sympathy for the character at all. I didn't understand him, I didn't find him interesting, I found him dull. Then I realized that I had better put on my bootstraps and try to figure out a way of making him not dull. I just struggled; it was agony to think of something, because he was just a dull man."

Vincent was terribly miscast and it showed (he seemed totally bored throughout the film), but as he pointed out, "I think the challenge of doing trash is trying to make the trash a little better than it is.

"Clunkers, however," he added, "everybody has done. I mean, you can do Hamlet and it can still be a clunker, too."

Chapter Seventeen

Return to the Tower of London
or
Vincent, the Sorcerer

Vincent returned to the costume drama in the remake of his old film *Tower of London*, only this time assuming the Basil Rathbone role of Richard, Duke of Glouster. The plot differed in that he is aided not by a club-footed executioner but by royal henchman, Sir Radcliffe (played by movie villain Michael Pate), and in an interesting plot twist succeeds in reaching the throne but finds himself haunted by the spirits of those he has killed until he himself is finally killed in battle.

The film was produced by independent producer Edward Small, who was notorious for being cheap as director Roger Corman learned, "My brother Gene knew an independent producer named Eddie Small, and Eddie liked the Poe films and wanted to bankroll a similar picture. He figured the *Tower of London* story would be fine. I said sure, as I wasn't doing anything at that time.

"I had a fifteen day shooting schedule and my old crew, so I thought that everything would run smoothly, but to my great surprise I found that I was supposed to shoot the picture in black and white. Somehow, nobody had bothered to tell me that, I was flabbergasted, this was 1962. I shot the movie but I think that it suffered from the lack of color. It was of the Poe style but I found myself working on a movie with a script that was weak. The film didn't have the impact it could have had."

Roger wasn't the only one who thought the film suffered from a weak script, as co-star Michael Pate remembers, "I enjoyed working with Vincent Price, because he was a larger than life person. I had seen him of course in many, many films prior to working with him. I enjoyed his work very, very much over a long period of time. So I was totally delighted to have worked with him. He had a great style.

"However, the script written by actor Leo Gordon was not the greatest version of the story about Richard the Third, but it was technically well mounted and enjoyable to do. Vincent and I had a great deal of fun doing that film. He somewhat often voiced humorous asides on what was going on in the scene, which were well worth the price of admission. He was a very witty and a very funny person who had the wonderful ability to laugh at himself."

And there was no better film for Vincent to poke fun at himself than AIP's version of *The Raven*, in which he portrayed 15th Century magician Dr. Erasmus Craven who helps bumbling magician Dr. Adolphus Bedlo (Peter Lorre) return to human form after being transformed into a raven by evil magician Dr. Scarabus (Boris Karloff). When Bedlo tells Craven he has seen his long-dead wife Lenore (Hazel Court) at Scarabus' castle, Craven sets off with his daughter, Estelle (Olive Sturgess), Dr. Bedlo and Bedlo's son, Rexford (Jack Nicholson in an early film role) to Scarabus' castle to see for himself.

Once at the castle, Bedlo is changed once again into a raven while Craven and Estelle are taken prisoner. Lenore, it seems, is very much alive, having faked her death so she could run off with the more powerful Scarabus.

Threatening Estelle with torture, Scarabus tries to force Craven into showing him the secret of his powerful hand gesture magic. Craven refuses, and with Bedlo's help almost escapes from the castle. However, before he can escape, Scarabus bars the exit and then challenges Craven to a duel to the death. After a fierce battle, Scarabus is defeated and Craven returns home the victor.

"The original script of *The Raven* was supposed to have comedic overtones: that is, it was a lot straighter than it finally finished up," Vincent disclosed. "Boris, Peter and I got together and read through it and decided that it didn't make any sense at all. So then we all sort of dreamed up the broader laughs."

"I told Roger we must tip the audience right away that there is something very different about this picture. So, I decided that every time I walk across my study, I would hit myself on the end of the telescope. Of course, this immediately set the mood."

"But you know, the thing of playing these pictures is really extraordinary because you walk a tightrope right down the middle between comedy and terror. It's fine if we make somebody scream, and then, they giggle. But God help us of they giggle and then scream! Some of them are really difficult to play. And we were very serious. Boris and I, particularly, we had a marvelous time because we'd say 'How can we scare them? What can we do? What's new?'

"Then one day, during the filming of *The Raven*, I had to walk down this long corridor, and I said, 'Boris, I'm doing nothing.' I said, 'We've done all that a million times.'

"He said, 'I've got an idea. We'll scare the men.'

"And I said, 'What? --- scare the men. What do you mean?'

"He said, 'There's one thing men are afraid of --- cobwebs.'

"And I said, 'What do you mean -- cobwebs?'

"He said, 'Men hate cobwebs. Women just think you're a bad housekeeper, but men hate them. They stick. You know. They're awful.'

"So we rigged up this great big cobweb, and as I came down this corridor, I suddenly walked into this cobweb. I looked like I had pantyhose over my boots.

"Well, sure enough, when I went to see the movie, when that scene came on, and the cobwebs went all over me, every man in the house went 'Aghh-ghh-ghh!'

"And the women said, 'Oh, why doesn't he keep the place clean?'"

"Vincent Price, Peter Lorre and Boris Karloff were just wonderful to work with, and each a little bit different in the way which he worked," Roger Corman recalled. "Boris Karloff was a very meticulous actor who would learn his lines to the letter; he would come in prepared to do them just so. Peter Lorre would more or less know his lines but was very creative and would improvise on the set and come up with wonderful stuff, which I would try to integrate into the script as much as I could. Vincent was more or less in between. He would come in as well prepared as Boris, but he would be prepared to improvise and play around a little bit with Peter. They all got along very well, but it did drive Boris a little crazy, because he would have done all this preparation and they would be changing scenes at the last minute."

"Peter loved to rewrite the script," Vincent revealed. "One time there was a scene where we went from one place to the other. There was an exposition there and I always knew my lines and Peter was sort of vaguely saying something else.

"So I said, 'For Christ's sake, Peter, say the lines!'

"He said, 'You mean that, old boy? You don't like my lines better?'

"I said, 'No.'

"So, he said all of the lines. He knew every line in the script, but he didn't like to say them!"

Peter Lorre received most of his training in Germany where improvisation was a major part of his studies. This often showed as in another particular scene that Vincent recalled, "Peter and I had a scene together in which I said 'Shall I ever see Lenore again?' and Peter said, 'How the hell should I know? What am I--a fortune teller?'

"It was a marvelous ad-lib. He was a very funny man, but because of typecasting, he was unhappy at the end of his career.

"However, the greatest imitation I ever saw of Peter Lorre in my life was by Peter Lorre. He would hold his nose and just talk and it sounded just like Peter Lorre. I read the obituary address at his funeral because all of his friends (Greenstreet, Bogart, etc.) were dead. He called himself a 'Face-maker.' He always delegated actors, but he was really a very bright man. But he always put them down, saying they were Facemakers."

Co-star Hazel Court recalled that "Peter never quite got the lines right, he'd just do his version and the rest of us would just muddle along. But, then there were three of them at it, Vincent and the others. It was wonderful to be with them, because one would tell a story, then that would spark another one, and then that would spark Vincent, and on and on. This round of stories would keep going, and you'd just sit there fascinated and your eyes would go from side to side.

"Boris Karloff was a great gentleman, but the raconteur, of course, was Peter Lorre, who had great sex appeal, and great charm for the ladies. You always felt that you were the only one in the world he was talking to. He used to make me laugh, a highly intelligent man. Peter Lorre was not well at all on that picture, I think his heart was bad, he perspired all the time, and his eyes were always teary. But nothing would hold him back, he was a wonderful pro. And I remember, too, that Karloff's leg was hurting him, very badly.

"Between shots Vincent often chatted with a young man, an unknown actor named Jack Nicholson, who played the son of Peter Lorre," recalled executive producer Samuel Z. Arkoff. "The name Nicholson really hit home with Vincent, and he and Boris figured that Jack Nicholson must be Jim Nicholson's (co-founder of AIP) son. They eventually found out that the two weren't related, but for awhile they just assumed that Jack had gotten the part because of family ties. Vincent and Boris used to joke among themselves, "Nepotism!, Nepotism!," and roar with laughter."

Looking back on his role in *The Raven*, Jack Nicholson recalled that "Roger gave me one direction on that picture: 'Try to be as funny as Lorre, Karloff and Price!' I loved those guys. I sat around with Peter all the time. I was mad about him. They were wonderful. It was a comedy and Roger gave us a little more time to improvise on the set."

"James Whale (the director of *Frankenstein*) was used to directing actors while Roger Corman expects the actor to get on with it himself," Boris

Karloff commented during the making of the film. "Vincent Price and Peter Lorre and I had to find our own way because he had all he wanted. He said, 'You're experienced actors, get on with it. I've got the camera, my lighting, the angles...I know how I'm going to put this together.' But if you asked him about advice on a scene, he'd say that's your pigeon."

One of the running gags in the film was when Jack would constantly adjust and try to straighten out Peter's cloak. But as Jack Nicholson remembered, "The business with Peter's cloak was just an actor's device. I grabbed his cloak, actually I grabbed a lot of other things that aren't visible in the frame, just to keep him alive to the fact that I was trying to get him out of there. Of course, the good actor that he was, he just reacted to it spontaneously, by slapping me and lashing out."

"The filming of the duel between Boris and myself was a frightening experience," Vincent vividly remembered. "I don't like snakes. Boris was supposed to throw a scarf at me which turns into a snake and wraps itself around my neck. When we were planning the scene, I said to Roger, 'That's nice. How are you going to do that?'

He said, 'We have this man, who is a snake trainer,' and he introduced me to him. 'Okay,' I said, 'I've met you, now I want to meet your snake.' He brought out this boa constrictor and told me not to worry. 'It's a very tame snake.' 'I'm tame too,' I pointed out, 'but strange things can happen.'

"He wrapped the thing around my neck and said, 'You know a boa constrictor doesn't bite.' But I screamed, 'Get it off of me, until the camera starts to shoot.'

"The scene began with that snake around my neck. Roger wanted the boa's head facing the camera, but the snake didn't want to turn that way, so we fussed for about an hour and a half with the snake around me. The snake must then have thought that I was his dinner or something. He started squeezing me and it took a little prying to get him to release me.

"Our horror pictures were tremendously successful. Oh, it's great to make *Mutiny on the Bounty*; but when I went to see it, there were only fifteen people in the theater, while next door, *The Raven* was playing to a full house.

"I really don't think my films made a moral judgment. I did a film with Bob Mitchum (*His Kind of Woman*) in which there was a line, 'I made a picture the other day with a message that even a pigeon wouldn't carry,' that is what I really and truly feel they mostly are. I don't think they attempt to point out a moral other than the kind of immolation at the end, especially in the funny ones.

"I've been asked a thousand times and I've written a thousand articles about horror films for *Ladies Home Journal* and those kinds of publications,"

Vincent declared. "I went to rabbis and priests and school administrators, and child psychologists and found that the films they worried about were the ones that pretended to reflect reality. They made the distinction and I think the films I did had an 'other world' quality that even children recognized as make-believe. On the other hand, I thought *Taxi Driver* was absolutely terrifying. It was too close to home."

Chapter Eighteen

When the Sleeper Never Wakes
or
Vincent Saves his Dying Business

Pleased with his work on *Tower of London,* producer Edward Small hired Vincent to star in his final film (Small died after the film was completed) *Diary of a Madman*, which was based on a short story by French author Guy de Maupassant called *The Horla*. The film, which was written and produced by Small's resident producer Robert Kent, starred Vincent as French Magistrate Simon Cordier, who accidentally kills a condemned prisoner in self defense, unaware that the man was haunted by an evil (and invisible) creature called the Horla (voiced by actor Joseph Ruskin).

Cordier, who has spent years in solitude since the accidental drowning of his wife and son, decides to revive his interest in sculpting after he meets up with the beautiful model, Odette (Nancy Kovack). Cordier eventually falls in love with Odette who, enticed by Simon's money and position, agrees to run away with him despite being married to struggling artist Paul Duclasse (Chris Warfield).

But when Simon prepares to leave with Odette, he is visited by the Horla, who takes possession of his body and forces him to kill Odette and blame the murder on Paul, who is subsequently convicted and sentenced to death (ironically by magistrate Cordier, who is completely unaware that he is the guilty party).

The eventual realization that he has sentenced an innocent man to death gives Simon the emotional power to overcome the Horla's evil influence. Discovering the Horla is afraid of fire; Simon traps the creature inside his house and then sets the place ablaze. Simon soon finds himself trapped as well and dies with the creature in the burning house. Fortunately, Simon detailed his encounter with the Horla and his murder of Odette in his diary, thus absolving Paul of the crime.

"I enjoyed working with Vincent Price," recalled actress Nancy Kovack. "He was very respectful and I found that unusual. He knew that I wasn't well known, and yet he was very respectful of me and kindly, he didn't have to be. He was a professional, and I appreciated that."

"I remember that just before the scene where he kills me with the knife, Vincent started tickling me. I began to laugh, and I couldn't stop laughing after that!"

Many years after the making of the film, director Reginald LeBorg recalled how the project came about: "Producer Robert Kent liked the story, *The Horla* by Guy de Maupassant, and he sold Eddie Small on the idea of making the film. Kent wrote the script, and I got the assignment.

"The budget was about three hundred or three hundred fifty thousand, and all of it was shot at the Goldwyn Studios. The film was very well received, had good reviews and did very well. I felt that the story was a good one and it came out very well, except for the voice of the Horla, which I wanted to distort quite a bit. We made a test of the voice, the way I wanted it, and Eddie Small said, 'I can't understand a word!' He wanted the Horla to speak normally, which was wrong.

"The film was just another job for Vincent Price," continued LeBorg. "But he did become conscious that I was holding him down. I had looked at some of his other pictures, and I thought he overacted in some. On *Diary of a Madman*, he started to gesticulate and raise his voice in some scenes, and so I took him aside and whispered, 'Tone it down. It'll be much more effective that way. The story is strong enough so that you come through, and your face is strong enough, and your whole attitude is strong enough. You don't have to go and grimace. So whenever he did this, I gestured him to slow down and he did, and he thanked me very much afterward. Even the producer Eddie Small said afterward that this was the best performance he'd seen Price give.

"I found Vincent to be entirely professional and very, very nice, and I enjoyed working with him very much. I was surprised how brave he was in the fire scene. I was scared for him, because he was surrounded by fire in that scene. I asked him if he wanted a double, and he said no. I said, 'Well, it might get really hot, so be careful.' He said, 'Don't worry, I've done things like this before.' He was a brave guy."

After a cameo appearance at the end of the Frankie Avalon/Annette Funicello comedy *Beach Party*, Vincent re-teamed with producer Robert Kent and *Last Man on Earth* director Sidney Salkow for an oddly-titled anthology film called *Twice Told Tales*, featuring three stories based on the writings of Nathaniel Hawthorne, in which Vincent (according to *Variety*) "has a chance to display the virtuosity which has made him master of the hounds of hell."

In *Dr. Heidegger's Experiment*, Dr. Carl Heidegger (Sebastian Cabot) and his friend Alex Medbourne (Vincent Price) find the body of Heidegger's long-dead fiancée Sylvia (Mari Blanchard) which has been preserved by fluid dripping into her tomb. Deciding to experiment with the mysterious fluid, Heidegger manages to restores both himself and Medbourne's youth as well as reviving Sylvia to life, but the miracle is cut short when he soon learns Medbourne originally poisoned Sylvia on the day of her wedding because she dumped him for Heidegger.

In *Rappaccini's Daughter*, Giovanni Guastconti (Brett Halsey, last seen with Vincent in *Return of the Fly*) discovers the girl who lives in the house next door, Beatrice Rappaccini (Joyce Taylor), is a prisoner of her crazy scientist father (Vincent Price). He soon learns that Dr. Rappaccini was dumped by his wife, and so to keep his daughter from being hurt by love, changes the blood in his daughter's body to poison. It's a poison so strong that one touch from her can kill instantly. So, with the aide of Professor Baglioni (Abraham Sofaer), Giovanni attempts to find an antidote so he can run away with her.

Abraham Sofaer was no stranger to Vincent as he had replaced George Zucco in the role of Disraeli in the play *Victoria Regina* many years earlier. The final tale is an abridged remake of Vincent's earlier film, *The House of the Seven Gables*, in which Gerald Pyncheon (Vincent Price) returns home with his new bride, Alice (Beverly Garland) to the House of the Seven Gables to find the valuable land deed hidden somewhere in the house and only to fall prey to the curse of Matthew Maule.

Veteran of such films as *It Conquered the World* and *The Alligator People*, actress Beverly Garland was no stranger to genre films, and while she did not remember much about working on the film, she did have fond memories of Vincent. "I loved working on that film," she recalled, "because I loved Vincent Price. He was the most wonderful, sweet, adorable man! I don't remember much about that movie but I do remember how wonderful Vinnie was!"

Looking back on his career, Vincent recalled how often people asked him how he could lecture about art and then come back to Hollywood and do thriller pictures. His answer was a simple one, "Baloney! Culture and terror films have a lot in common. Some of my terror films were taken from classic stories by such authors as Edgar Allan Poe, Jules Verne, Guy de Maupasant and Nathaniel Hawthorne. These pictures go on forever because they can't become dated. They're like fairy tales, and fantasy has been one of our greatest exports for years."

Late in 1963 Vincent underwent minor surgery for treatment of a new ulcer problem. While he recovered, AIP offered him a new project to be directed by Roger Corman and co-starring Martha Hyer. Based on the H.G. Wells story *When the Sleeper Wakes,* it dealt with a man who wakes from a long sleep in suspended animation to find a new futuristic world. The film was never made, Vincent explained, because "The trouble was, it was written so long ago that science had caught up with many of the wonders in the book and we were waiting for someone to concoct a whole new set of miracles."

After a string of film successes, Vincent was offered the opportunity to play Prospero opposite Katherine Hepburn in Shakespeare's *The Tempest*, but turned it down because the money wasn't enough. Vincent cited his monthly expense of alimony to his ex-wife plus the support of his current family as the reason he turned down the five hundred dollars he would have received for the entire eight weeks' work.

Over the years Vincent had been associated with many documentaries, but he was never prouder than to have narrated *Chagall*, a twenty-six minute film about the life of the Russian artist Marc Chagall. The film was directed by Lauro Venturi and was released theatrically as part of a double bill with the film *Tokapi*. The film won the Academy Award for the best short subject of 1963.

Although filmed in late 1963, *The Comedy of Terrors* was not released until early 1964. While it was not written by Shakespeare, it did feature a number of passages from his plays, performed with delightful relish by Basil Rathbone, in what was the best film of his declining career (Rathbone died in 1967 at the age of 75).

Playing opposite Rathbone were old friends Peter Lorre (who died a few months after the film's release), Boris Karloff, who had not worked with Rathbone since the *Son of Frankenstein* in 1939, and of course Vincent Price.

Vincent played mortician William Trumbull who, along with his bumbling assistant Felix Gillie (Peter Lorre), run a failing funeral parlor. So, when landlord John F. Black (Basil Rathbone) calls for the rent, they decide it is time to commit murder in order to create a few new clients. However, when the young widow of their latest victim runs off with her dead husband's money, Trumbull, who lives with his tone-deaf opera singing wife, Amaryllis (Joyce Jameson) and her senile father Amos Hinchley (Boris Karloff), decides to kill Black and end their money problems as well as their rent trouble.

Unbeknownst to Trumbull and Gillie, Black suffers from catalepsy which, although it causes the appearance of death, the sufferer is in fact very much alive. So, when Black (who is a devote Shakespeare fanatic), suffers a fatal attack while chasing Gillie around his house, Trumbull innocently moves the body back to his mortuary where Black revives.

Thinking quickly, Trumbull and Gillie chain Black inside a coffin until he apparently dies. Black is later entombed but once again returns from the dead, this time in a crazed state. Arming himself with an axe and babbling endless lines of dialogue from Macbeth he sets off to take his revenge on Trumbull.

After a series of misadventures, Gillie runs away with Amaryllis, Black is shot dead by Trumbull (several times) and Amos unknowingly poisons Trumbull with what he thinks is a bottle of medicine leaving Cleopatra, Amaryllis' pet cat, to see Black revive once more from the dead.

The Comedy of Terrors marked the last time Vincent would work with Basil Rathbone, whom Vincent recalled as "an extraordinary man. A very intelligent and wonderful man, but rather bitter at the end of his life, about having been stuck in the Sherlock Holmes films. However, I think he would have been pleased now to see the revival of them, but he was a brilliant actor. When movies changed and we were all sort of edged out by the Brandos, the Jimmy Deans and the people who didn't speak English anymore, suddenly, we had to go into other areas of the business, like the costume pictures and places where we would be understood."

"I hadn't seen Basil for some time and was shocked at how much he had aged. But he was still marvelous in the picture and we had a lot of fun. I remember that he hated lying in that coffin. He was almost violent about getting out of it after every set-up and he fought like hell to avoid retakes. I guess that thing made him nervous."

Ironically, "Karloff was originally supposed to play the part Rathbone eventually got," recalled Richard Matheson. "And Rathbone was going to play the father. They were approximately the same age, but Rathbone was really sprightly whereas Karloff by that time was really having pains. So, Karloff requested that they switch parts, which was fine with Basil."

Despite his advancing years, "Basil did virtually all his own stunts," remembered Matheson. Peter Lorre however was another story. "There were scenes calling for Lorre to climb up on the roof and run around and drive the carriage, and he could do none of it. So, they got this famous old stuntman, Harvey Patty, to stand in for him, because he couldn't do any of this stuff."

While the film was successful, a planned follow-up never materialized as Richard Matheson explains. "I wrote a script called *Sweethearts and Horrors* which AIP never got around to filming. It was going to follow up *The Comedy of Terrors*, and it had all of them: Karloff, Price, Lorre, and Rathbone, plus Tallulah Bankhead. It was about a family called the Sweethearts. Boris Karloff played the host of a kiddy show, a very irascible host, and always muttering curses under his breath; Basil Rathbone was to play an aging musical comedy star; Peter Lorre was to be a very inept magician whose specialty was a fire act, and every theater he worked in burned down. Tallulah Bankhead was an aging Hollywood actress; and Vincent Price was a ventriloquist. They're all called back to their father's home after he dies for a reading of the will; the father manufactured gags, and the whole house is booby-trapped with gags. Then they start getting murdered off, one by one. It would have been a ball, because it was a very funny script."

AIP followed *The Comedy of Terrors* with *The Last Man on Earth*, the Italian film made three years earlier, it was to be Vincent's last black and white feature film.

Chapter Nineteen

Vincent Meets the Wolfman
or
Poe Invades England

For his next film, Vincent was to re-team with Boris Karloff for a pseudo Poe film entitled *The Haunted Palace.* In actuality it was based on the H.P. Lovecraft tale, *The Case of Charles Dexter Ward.* But in order to sell it as a Poe film, AIP had Vincent recite the Poe poem *The Haunted Palace* during the opening credits. As for Karloff, he took ill and was replaced by horror veteran Lon Chaney, Jr. (whose health was also in a state of decline).

Vincent played warlock Joseph Curwen who was burned at the stake by the local townspeople, but not before putting a curse on the people of Arkham and their descendants. Over 100 years later, look-a-like descendant Charles Dexter Ward and his wife, Ann (Debra Paget) move into the warlock's old mansion.

The townspeople, who have suffered disfigurements from the warlock's curse, want nothing to do with the visitors; the only exception is the town doctor, Marinus Willet (Frank Maxwell). Upon reaching the mansion, they meet caretaker Simon Orne (Lon Chaney Jr.), a green tinged individual who unknown to them is well over 100 years old.

Soon, Charles begins to find himself being taken over by the spirit of his ancestor and together with warlocks Simon and Jabez Hutchinson (Milton Parsons) revive his dead lover, Hester Tillinghast (Cathy Merchant), in the hopes of carrying out their original plan, to create a new race of beings by mating human females with ancient demon gods.

Unable to get Ann to leave, Charles (under the control of Curwen) decides to mate her with the demon who resides in a pit beneath the house. Deciding to put an end to Curwen once and for all, the angry townspeople set fire to the mansion, but not before Dr. Willet rescues Ann and Charles from the burning house and moments before it comes crashing to the ground.

"It was a good idea and a good film, but was seen by practically nobody in the United States," recalled Vincent. "However in Australia it was the highest-grossing film ever to appear at that time. Figure that out!

"A wonderful thing happened during the making of the film," recalled Vincent. "Our director, Roger Corman, decided that every time I looked at a portrait of my grandfather, I should turn green. Well, that's easy enough to talk about, it meant that every time I looked at the portrait, I had to run out and put a little more green make-up on. Then, I'd look at the portrait and go back and put a little more green make-up on. Well, he forgot to tell the lab that developed the film, about the green make-up. And one day, the rushes were about four days late, and he called up, and they said, 'We can't send this film back. Vincent Price keeps turning green all the time!'"

Lon Chaney was the only actor ever to portray four of Hollywood's legendary monsters: the Wolfman, Dracula, the Frankenstein monster and the Mummy. He was the son of Hollywood's most famous silent horror film star. He worked with everyone from Boris Karloff and Bela Lugosi to Bob Hope and Abbott and Costello and while he and Vincent did appear in *Casanova's Big Night*, they had no scenes together. *The Haunted Palace* proved to be the first and last time the two great horror stars would ever work together. Chaney, who had a severe drinking problem, would die less than ten years later after several years of deteriorating health.

"Lon Chaney was one of the most talented actors in films. He had none of the high class attitude of today's stars. In fact, he was undoubtedly one of the most unassuming men I have ever had the pleasure of working with," remembered Vincent.

"However, Chaney was very ill at that time, I had admired him and always wanted to meet him but he was not very happy or very well and I really didn't get to know him well. I spent a lot of time trying to talk to him and make him cheer up but I couldn't do it. He was too sick."

Due to rising production costs, AIP and Roger Corman moved the location of their Poe films from Los Angeles to England's Elstree Studios, where Vincent was given the role of Prince Prospero, an 12th Century devil worshipper, in the film *The Masque of the Red Death*, who gathers his royal friends in his castle to await the passing of the Red Death, which is currently devastating the surrounding towns.

Believing that Satan will protect them from the horrors of the plague, Prospero holds a masquerade ball in Satan's honor, while his wife Juliana (Hazel Court) offers herself up to the devil, but is soon killed by her husband's pet falcon.

As the noblemen entertain themselves at the party, dwarf jester Hop-Toad (Skip Martin) takes his revenge on Alfredo (Patrick Magee) for humiliating his beloved, Esmeralda (Verina Greenlaw), by dressing him up in an ape costume and then setting him on fire.

Soon, the messenger of death arrives at the castle; Prospero, believing him to be a messenger of Satan, welcomes him into the castle, but soon everyone including the prince dies of the plague, leaving only a few select villagers to escape the Red Death.

While Vincent enjoyed working on the film there was one moment when he was up on a dais reciting a long speech, after which he came down off the dais and tripped over his long flowing cape. He fell down and knocked himself out absolutely cold.

Actress Hazel Court recalls that, "Much more money was spent on the film (than the previous Poe films) as it was a more opulent production. It was a big production, lots of costumes and a wonderful cameraman, Nicholas Roeg, who photographed me beautifully in that. I think I was like two or three months pregnant when I was doing the film."

While Roger Corman was filming *The Masque of the Red Death*, screenwriter Charles B. Griffith wrote a script for a film based on the Poe story *The Gold Bug*. It was written as a comedy and it was supposed to star Vincent Price, Peter Lorre and Basil Rathbone. And as Griffith remembers, "Basil was to be a visiting English carpetbagger who, after the Civil War, comes to call on Vincent, the owner of a burned-out mansion which has been turned into a hock shop. Vincent has two servants, one of them with squeaky feet.

"'Sometimes I squeaks and sometimes I doesn't,' the woman remarks after Vincent discovers the problem is not with her shoes. Peter is Vincent's other servant, a little guy who carries a gold bug around in a matchbox. At night Peter lets the little critter out to play the gold bug rag on the harpsichord in the front room. Anyone bitten by the bug turns to gold. Vincent tries to melt one of the victims, but in doing so breaks the spell and the gold returns to flesh. So, he simply sells the victims as gold statues."

Unfortunately, Peter Lorre died before the script was completed. So, when Griffith finally turned the finished script (which was over 300 pages long) over to AIP, they were reluctant to film it, as producer Samuel Z. Arkoff recalled, "We never did *The Gold Bug* because in my opinion, and although it is a well known story, it's not in the genre. I didn't think it would be successful frankly, because I didn't know who the audience was for it."

The Tomb of Ligeia had Vincent as widower Verdon Fell, a man who lives in a ruined abbey not far from the grave of his long-dead wife, Ligeia. Rowena (Elizabeth Shepherd, in a dual role) a look-a-like for Ligeia, soon falls for Fell and marries him. However, she begins to find strange events happening in the old abbey.

Together with Christopher Gough (John Westbrook, last seen as the Red Death in the previous film), Rowena finds Fell completely entranced, in a hidden tower room that also contains the body of Ligeia. It seems that Ligeia hypnotized Fell and never released him from her control before she died, causing him to revert to a trancelike state every night. Believing Rowena is Ligeia come to life, Fell tries to kill her. When he is finally brought out of his trance, he disposes of Ligeia's body with fire. But he is soon attacked by a cat which contains Ligeia's spirit and together they die in the now flaming tower as Rowena and Christopher escape.

"I had always wanted to shoot a film inside a real ruin," remarked Vincent, "so Roger Corman went to England and found a ruined abbey and had a film written around it. We shot most of the film in this 12th Century British abbey. It was fascinating place but we weren't allowed to move any furniture into the interior, however, because it was a national monument.

"So, the interiors were filmed at Shepperton Studios, where they painted the set with highly flammable liquid rubber cement. Of course, there were signs up all over the set warning of this, because it gives off a gas when ignited. Elizabeth Shepherd and I were positioned under some heavy timber that was supposed to have fallen on us. Of course, somebody walked on to the set and lit a match and the whole thing exploded before the camera was rolling. Poor Roger got set back a day, and on those pictures you didn't get set back a day. The whole set had to be cooled and repainted and then we had to start all over again."

"It was really terrifying---reality carried a little too far. Elizabeth and I had to drag ourselves out from under the timber. I grabbed poor Elizabeth by the hair and dragged her off the set so quick!"

"We had five whole weeks," remembered Elizabeth Shepherd. "This was a luxuriant schedule, for a Corman movie. The first week we were location in Norfolk, filming at Castle Acre, which is a ruined abbey, beautifully kept by the National Trust. Five weeks meant Corman could be, visually, more ambitious than usual, which certainly enhanced the movie. But not a minute was wasted.

"I can remember arriving on location in time to start shooting the next day. We were all settling into the hotel when word came:

"'Roger says there's enough light to start now---be there as soon as possible!' Pandemonium! The hairstyle hadn't been decided, the dress didn't fit, and John Westbrook and I were desperately learning our lines in the car. It was the scene in which Rowena tells Christopher that she feels that Ligeia is haunting the abbey. Notice the unique hairdo! Fortunately, the scene looks good, but the sound quality was poor, so I had the chance to add a more confident vocal quality to the scene in post-sync.

"The only time I sensed Roger being relentless was in the sequence in which Rowena is releasing Verden from the spell, in the 'Ligeia turret' near the end. I was standing looking up at Vincent, so close to that blazing brazier at my back that I was not only boiling hot, I was scorching! I had to stop. But the set-up was exactly what Roger wanted. 'Never mind, keep going,' he said. So I did. It certainly added to the intensity of the situation.

"Aside from having the most eloquent voice on earth, Vincent had enormous personal charm and charisma. I loved working with him; he made everything seem easy. He was such a superb actor, and extraordinarily generous. He was very open to working on our scenes together, which certainly put me at ease. I remember watching him create that moment at Ligeia's funeral when he reads from Glanville, and the priest says, 'Blasphemy!' and Verden snaps the book closed in his face and declares, 'Benediction!' It is daring, it is full of panache and utterly believable---passion and high style combined. But, I must say, for all of his intensity in the film, off-screen he had a wickedly witty sense of humor. He kept us laughing."

Many years later Vincent fondly remembered his roles in the Poe films. "Some of the Poe villains have been fascinating," remarked Vincent. "They were loosely based on Edgar Allan Poe, who doesn't write villains, he writes about men who are put upon by life. There is a great difference between a Horror villain and a man who has been put upon by life. *Frankenstein*, the doctor not the monster was a man who tampered with God's work. This is what the moral of that piece is: that he created man, who only God can create, because if man tampers around with it, he creates a monster. The evil is fiddling around with what you shouldn't be fiddling around with. There are certain things I think are very sacred. I don't mean that man can not attempt to do everything to preserve life, to enrich it, to make it better, but to create it; I agree with Mary Shelley, that you shouldn't fool around with that. You shouldn't hurt people either. The evil consists of the supreme act of ingratitude. Lack of gratitude is the number one sin in the world!

"To not be grateful for your life," continued Vincent. "Not to be grateful for your love, for your sharing with people your ideas and accepting from them their ideas. If I confess my sins, it is my sin of ingratitude and I try to be grateful. Gratitude makes me curious, more curious all the time."

Vincent's sense of humor came in quite handy for his next film *War Gods of the Deep*, which Vincent recalled as, "a disaster!"

The film which was supposedly based on the poem by Edgar Allen Poe, entitled *The City Beneath the Sea,* has Jill Tegelis (Susan Hart) kidnapped and taken to an underwater city populated by century-old smugglers lead by the Captain (Vincent Price).

Ben Harris (Tab Hunter), Harold Tufell Jones (David Tomlinson) and his pet rooster Herbert comes to her rescue. Knowing the underwater city is doomed to be destroyed by an active volcano, the Captain spares the intruders when he is lead to believe Ben can help quiet the volcano. When they try to escape, the Captain plans to sacrifice them to the amphibious Gillmen which inhabit the waters surrounding the ancient city.

With the help of an aging minister captured years earlier and primitive diving suits, they try to make their way out of the city to an ancient temple to find the passage back to the surface. Unfortunately, just as they make it to the temple, the volcano erupts, bringing the ancient structure down around them, and blocking off the passage to the surface.

As they try to find another exit, the Captain arrives, but before they can be recaptured the volcano erupts again, trapping the Captain beneath a giant stone hand and killing his men.

Unable to find another way out, Ben and the others don their diving suits again and walk towards the nearest land. The Captain manages to free himself and using the now unblocked passageway heads up towards the surface, knowing that the ultra violet rays of the sun will destroy him. As the others finally reach land, the Captain tries to follow but dies of rapid aging before he can reach them.

"It was a badly-produced picture," remembered Vincent. "Nobody knew what it was about. Jacques Tourneur was a marvelous director but he just couldn't get around the bad script."

The script was written by film veteran Charles Bennett, who recalled that *War Gods of the Deep* was "a dreadful, dreadful picture which I should never have had anything to do with. It was simply horrid, the worst thing I was ever involved in. I think Jacques, the poor devil, got the blame for it, but actually he was not to blame at all. I had written a good script, and (while it was in production) I was asked to go to England to make alterations. The wretched American International Pictures came up with a lousy offer which my agent turned down, so they put on some other writer who completely annihilated the thing. Their idea of money was absolutely so trivial that it would have cost me money to go.

"The film was supposed to be based on a tiny Poe poem; they said, 'Can you take this and make it into a story?' Which I did-I did a pretty good story, as a matter of fact. And it was completely ruined when it came to a matter of my not going to England and protecting my own screenplay. Jacques Tourneur did a good job himself with an impossible script. The writer who did rework it put a chicken into the movie, as one of the main characters. That was stolen directly from *Journey to the Center of the Earth*, which was made at 20th Century-Fox. In Journey, it was a duck. But the chicken in *War-Gods* that had nothing to do with me, thank you!"

When Charles Bennett refused to handle the rewrites, producer Louis "Deke" Heyward was called into help, "I was here in the United States while *War Gods* was being shot in England," recalled Heyward. "When they ran into problems with the then-producer, I don't remember his name, but he was English and he was causing some sort of problem. I called, and he said, 'Dear lad, the script is impossible.' I said, 'Most of our scripts are impossible!' He said, 'I cannot possibly shoot.' So, I went to Sam Arkoff and I said, 'Sam, we are having genuine trouble.' Sam clutched his breast and said, 'It's gonna cost money!' And I said, 'Yes, they don't like the script.' He said, 'Well, dictate something over the phone.' I said, 'Sam, that isn't the way you do scripts. I've got to see what they've shot, see how I can blend whatever it is that I'm going to write into it, find out what's lacking.'

"So I went to England and found there was a war between Co-Producer Daniel Haller and the English Producer, which is always very, very destructive. And they were getting nowhere. Dan Haller had been a scenic designer prior to this, and a protégé of Jim Nicholson's. Dan was an extremely good scenic designer, and he came up with some awfully good sets on *War Gods*.

"I wound up reworking the screenplay. The one thing that I felt was missing was humor, and that's where the chicken appeared. There was no chicken in the script, so I wrote it in along with the David Tomlinson character. Tomlinson was enjoying great vogue at that time because he had just done *Mary Poppins* for Disney. At the point when the English producer saw that I had written in a chicken, and knew that whatever I wrote was going in, he quit. He said, 'I don't do chicken pictures!' and Dan Haller took over the reins.

"But there were continuous problems there, because Dan at that time did not really know how to do what Sam used to refer to as 'take over the power.' I called Sam and said, 'Okay, I've completed the rewrite, but I think I better stay here 'til the picture is finished.' Again, I had a mental picture of him clutching his breast and thinking in terms of dollars, but I did stay, because there had to be someone backing up Dan. Dan turned into a very good producer later, but he couldn't do it alone in the face of an English crew who probably resented the fact that the other producer had walked off.

"There were a lot of things that I found satisfying about the film. However, the worst thing in it was my own contribution. The chicken didn't belong in a diver's helmet; not really. It was insanity, but that's the way we were doing things. There never was any time, there always was a crisis.

"Vincent and I had a thing for art, so we started talking art. I also enjoy cooking, and Vincent was well known for that. So, Vincent and I had a community of interests to keep us busy talking between takes. Occasionally, he would read a line, then look at me and say, 'Deke, dear, sweet Deke; You are screwing my career into the ground!' And indeed, I may have! But I appreciated his frankness about it. He was a delight to work with."

Taboos of the World is a film which hasn't seen the light of day since it was first released in 1965. It was made in Italy, purchased by AIP and then dubbed by Vincent Price in order to sell it to the horror film market. At the time these types of shockumentaries were very popular but since the subsequent television shows such as *Ripley's Believe It or Not* and other similar shows, this film as well as many others have become obsolete and dated. And as Samuel Z. Arkoff recalled, "We horsed around with many different things, but *Taboos of the World* was not a big grosser." The original Italian version later surfaced during the 1980's on video tape but without Vincent's velvet tones doing the narration, instead an uncredited British actor was heard on the soundtrack.

In between pictures for AIP and numerous television appearances, Vincent took time out to receive an award from the George Washington Carver Institute for his outstanding contributions to Art, Science, Education and Betterment of race relations.

It was also in 1965 that Vincent and wife Mary published the best selling *A Treasury of Great Recipes.* They would later publish *The National Treasury of Cooking* in 1967 and *The Come into the Kitchen Cookbook* in 1969.

Chapter Twenty

Vincent's EGGcellent Experience
or
Abe Lincoln Visits a Whorehouse

Vincent's next film, *Dr. Goldfoot and the Bikini Machine,* returned him to the world of broad farce. Vincent played the evil Dr. Goldfoot who, aided by his idiot assistant Igor (Jack Mullaney, co-star of the short lived television series *It's About Time*), uses female robots to seduce rich and powerful businessmen into turning their riches over to him. Enter bumbling secret agent Craig Gamble (singer Frankie Avalon) who, together with wealthy playboy Todd Armstrong (Dwayne Hickman, TV's Dobie Gillis), attempts to stop Goldfoot's plan to take over control of the world.

Years later Vincent recalled the film was meant to be "a musical and they cut out all of the music. They got scared. It could have been terribly funny. I thought it was a wonderfully witty script with wonderfully witty music and they cut it all out."

However executive producer Samuel Z. Arkoff remembers it differently: "As for Vincent's belief that we cut the music out of *Dr. Goldfoot and the Bikini Machine*, it may have been a momentary thought, but it wasn't part of the actual planning. We did not cut out any of the intended music."

Vincent and some of the cast of the film appeared in a musical special entitled *The Wild Weird World of Dr. Goldfoot* which was aired as part of the *Shindig* television series.

Before the film was released it went through a series of title changes. It started out as just *Dr. Goldfoot.* It was then titled *Dr. Goldfoot and the Sex Machine,* but quickly changed to *Dr. Goldfoot and the Girl Machine* before winding up as *Dr. Goldfoot and the Bikini Machine.* When the film was scheduled for release in England, the title was changed to *Professor Goldfoot and the Bikini Machine.* It was also released in some areas as *Dr. G and the Bikini Machine* as it was discovered that there were two respected doctors named Goldfoot living in England and they did not wish to offend them.

In 1966, Vincent made his first appearance on the Batman television series, a wonderfully comedic role for which he is still remembered through to this very day. "I was cast as a character named Egghead, with dialog by Stanley Ralph Ross splattered with EGGOSaggerated and EGGSplosive props. The script was art of its kind, carefully thought out and followed to the letter by the director and cast.

"I was amazed at the dedicated attention to the production in every detail. My make-up as Egghead was supervised by producer William Dozier himself and created by a master make-up artist, Ben Nye. My costumes were a triumph of camp, done by Jan Kemp. But the real surprise came in the inventiveness of the sets as imaged by the art director, Serge Krizman.

"In this Batman episode he let the range of his talent have free play and created one set in particular that could stand on its own in any pop art exhibition. Everything in this set, which was Egghead's hideout, turned up egg-shaped. The three-dimensional vistas in the background were egg cutouts on brightly colored flats. The furniture was halved hardboiled eggs on legs, but it was the mural on the wall, and the mobile that really brought out his talent. The mobile, from which Batman had to swing in his effort to overcome Egghead and his sidekicks, was a marvelous design of eggs on metal bars - almost a Calder creation and the mural was a fried egg sunny side up with a rasher of crisp bacon on an orange wall." One of the many memorable moments of series was the egg fight during the episode's climax, and as Vincent remembered "I was required to hit Burt Ward (who played Robin) with an egg. The crew was fed up with Burt. So they had me throw two dozen eggs at him, and he had to stand there and take it.

"The reason I did Batman was because I had a child (daughter, Victoria) at that time who was very young and who watched Batman. Still I was thrilled to be on the Batman series," Vincent quickly added. "I really felt that it was one of the most brilliant television series ever done. The imagination and the creativeness that went into those shows were extraordinary. They were way ahead of their time. The sets alone had all of the imagination of a fairy tale. These characters were wonderful and marvelous actors did them and they were great fun.

"I did a lot of these types of shows for my children and for the child within me. I am a real case of self arrested development. I don't ever let myself grow up all the way.

"Children wander down the most wonderful paths in life," Vincent continued. "We sometimes find it too muddy for us when we grow older. Or too dangerous, children have no fear and fear of life, I think destroys it." During this period he also appeared on numerous television shows (he would appear in over 5000 television shows during his entire career) including: *The Man From U.N.C.L.E., The Hollywood Squares* (over 900 appearances), *The Red Skelton Show, Voyage to the Bottom of the Sea* (as an evil puppeteer in *The Deadly Dolls* episode) and as a pseudo-vampire on *F Troop.* Stage-wise he portrayed Captain Hook in a West Coast revival of *Peter Pan.*

"*Dr. Goldfoot and the Bikini Machine* did quite well at the box office," recalled Executive Producer Samuel Z. Arkoff. "Good enough to encourage us to capitalize on the Goldfoot name with a sequel. I had talked to Fulvio Lucisano, who co-produced many of our Italian productions, and he felt that if we made the next Goldfoot a US-Italian co-production, he might be able to lure Mario Bava (a cameraman turned director, who turned out the classic Italian vampire films *Black Sunday* with Barbara Steele and *Black Sabbath* with Boris Karloff) to direct it. This arrangement would also allow us to split the costs of making the movie, as well as take advantage of a substantial subsidy from the Italian government.

"We talked Vincent into reprising his starring role as Dr. Goldfoot. Two Italian comics, Franco Franchi and Ciccio Ingrassia were cast in the film, but they overpowered everything Vincent was trying to do on the screen. Unfortunately, although they stole nearly every scene, they weren't funny and neither was the movie."

This time Vincent as the evil Dr. Goldfoot planned to start a war between the United States and Russia so he and the Chinese could take over the world. Arming his female robots with explosives, Goldfoot programmed his Girl Bombs to seduce the NATO Generals and once they get them alone, the robots are programmed to explode. Then with Goldfoot masquerading as a look-a-like general, ("They couldn't afford another English speaking actor, so I ended up playing two parts." Vincent recalled), he would be able to carry out his plan to take over the world. Enter bumbling secret agent Bill Dexter (singer Fabian) who, with two idiot assistants, Franchi and Ciccio try to foil Goldfoot's plan.

"*Dr. Goldfoot and the Girl Bombs* might have been saved but for some unusual heroics by my own nephew Ted Rusoff," Arkoff continued. "I had sent Ted to Rome to do some work for us, and when he first met Laura Antonelli, the female star of the film, he was swept off his feet. Antonelli was a beautiful young woman, and Fulvio and I figured that the picture would have a lot more box office appeal if she removed her clothing when the cameras rolled. She appeared quite willing, but Ted seemed shocked that we would even suggest that she disrobe.

"Overcome by his newly developed crush, he became very protective of her and told me, 'She's a serious actress, Sam. It would be insulting to ask her to take her clothes off!' Ted sat Antonelli down and pleaded his case,

'You don't have to take off your clothes. If you tell them no, they're not going to force you. I don't think you should do it.'

"Antonelli gave it some thought, and then followed Ted's advice. Her clothes stayed on. If Ted weren't my own flesh and blood, I might have fired him on the spot. The real irony is that Antonelli later became a big star in Italy, and one of the reasons was that she was willing to take off her clothing at the drop of a clapboard.

"Years later Vincent told me, 'It was the most dreadful movie I've ever been in. Just about everything that could go wrong did. At one point they even lost the soundtrack to the whole movie! They literally lost it!'

"Without the soundtrack, the entire production had to be dubbed. Unfortunately, however, the actors had done so much ad-libbing during the filming that they couldn't use the script as a guide, and none of them really remembered what they had said. They did the best lip-reading they could. It was a real nightmare."

On August 30, 1967, Vincent was elected Chairman of the US Department of the Interior's Indian Art and Craft Board. And later that Fall saw Vincent returned to the *Batman* series as the infamous Egghead, only this time he was reduced from a dangerous villain with a great brain to a cowardly, immature buffoon, spending part of his time riding around on a donkey chasing after his fiancée, Olga, Queen of the Bessarovian Cossacks played by Anne Baxter.

Actress Yvonne Craig, who portrayed the dual role of Barbara Gordon and her alter ego Batgirl, remembers an incident which could have proven tragic for Vincent. "Vincent Price was my favorite villain; he was bright, witty, sexy, and fun to work with. And when I ran over him by accident with my motorcycle, he took it very well.

"We were doing a scene where he was supposed to ride on the back of Batgirl's motorcycle. It was a bike that had been customized so that it had no shock absorbers on it. They had taken the shocks off in order to make those big batwings. So, it was really a rough ride to begin with.

"It was also bigger than anything I needed. Adam West had complained that the motorcycle he rode--the one with the sidecar--didn't have enough get-up-and-go, so they made up for it by giving me one that had more than I needed. Fortunately, they put an automatic starter on it, so I didn't have to kick-start it. That could have taken all day. And it was so heavy that if I would get it just a little bit off its center of gravity, I'd have to drop it and pick it up again because I couldn't wrestle it back to where it belonged.

"So I told Vincent, 'I've never ridden with anyone on the back of this motorcycle, and if it looks like we're going to dump it, you'd better jump clear.' He said, 'All I have to do is stand up and you can ride out from under me.' It sounded logical because he was so tall.

"We did the scene, but the boom mic was in the shot. So we had to do it over. This time I was directed to ride into the scene faster. Now, when you give a bike gas, you turn one way, and when you brake it, you pull it back the other way. But I have small hands, and in braking it I was still letting some gas trickle in. We rode into the scene and stopped. He jumped off the back end and ran around in front of the bike; just as he got in front of me, the bike leapt forward and bounded over his foot. Then he jumped clear, and I hit him again! And he said, 'Well, had I known we were going to shoot the scene this way, I would have shouted OLE! He was a good sport.' Craig later sent Vincent a bottle of Dom Perignon with a note attached which read: 'If you don't want to drink it, soak your foot in it.'"

Actress Anne Baxter, who had worked with Vincent before, recalled that "working with Vincent was a delight and Vincent had a lot of fun as Egghead. He hated the makeup, though, it took forever and it was very hot."

Although they had worked together previously and had fun during *Batman*, Baxter admitted not long before her untimely death in 1985, that "I didn't get to know him well, I did know George Macready, and they were very close friends, and had ran an art gallery together. Vincent loved to talk about art."

"Vincent as a consummate actor really enjoyed his roles in our pictures," declares Samuel Z. Arkoff. "However, there were some roles that he did that he didn't enjoy. There was a period in the 1960's when horror pictures didn't do very well. We had this contract with Vincent to make so many pictures a year, so we put him in odd pictures like the two *Dr. Goldfoot* films and the one I call the whorehouse picture, *The House of 1000 Dolls*."

While on vacation in Tangiers, American businessman Stephen Armstrong (George Nader) and his wife Marie (Ann Smyrner) befriend Fernando (Sancho Gracia), whose fiancée Diane (Maria Rohm) has disappeared. Fernando traces Diane to a brothel called the House of 1000 dolls, but in doing so loses his own life. Armstrong decides to find his missing friend and soon finds that magician Felix Manderville (Vincent Price) and his assistant Rebecca (Martha Hyer) are involved in the white slave trade. Using Marie as bait, Armstrong and the police are led to the mysterious brothel where Manderville falls to his death and Rebecca is revealed to be the head of slavery ring.

"The film was shot in Madrid," remembers Producer Louis "Deke" Heyward, "in a palace that had belonged to a Spanish prince who was a member of the House of Hapsburg. The palace had later turned into a whorehouse, which was kind of setting the pattern for what the picture was about.

"I remember casting the B-girls, at various gin mills in Madrid! Vincent approached me when we had about five girls there and he whispered, 'Deke, please, give 'em some garlic. They stink!' Which is beautifully anomalous to me! *Thousand Dolls* was done in partnership with Harry Alan Towers. We had some horny scenes there, and I wondered how we got away with it. There's a lot of nudity in the film that was excised for the American version.

"One day I came onto the set, which was a jail set, and I saw a guy with a stovepipe hat, a beard, a wart on the left side of his face, and a frock coat. I struggled to think of the scene to be shot, because standing before me was Abraham Lincoln! I went over to Harry and I said, 'Harry, what are we shooting?' and he said, 'Just be calm.' What had happened was, he had a copy of the script of *Abe Lincoln in Illinois* that he had submitted to the Spanish censors to get permission to shoot and so whenever the censor came by, there was Abe Lincoln walking back and forth."

For his next film, Vincent traveled to South Africa to star in *The Jackals,* a remake of the 1948 film *Yellow Sky*, in which five greedy fugitives take an old prospector, Vincent, and his granddaughter (played by Diane Ivarson) hostage in the hopes of stealing the old man's gold. The film had limited theatrical release before it was shunted to network television and home video.

Chapter Twenty-One

Vincent, the Witchfinder
or
Poe Meets Cromwell

After a successful four-week trial period in Boston, Vincent opened on Broadway in January 1968 in the musical *Darling of the Day*, which was based on the novel *Buried Alive* by Arnold Bennett. The play co-stared Patricia Routeledge (later the star of the British sitcom, *Keeping Up Appearances*) who won the Tony award for Best Actress in a Musical. Yet the play was a colossal flop and closed after thirty-two performances and a loss of $700,000.

Vincent then traveled to England to star in the film version of Ronald Bassett's novel *Witchfinder General*, known in the US as Edgar Allan Poe's *The Conqueror Worm.* AIP added a voiceover by Vincent reciting Poe's poem in order to cash in on the still-popular Poe craze. The film was directed by Michael Reeves, who committed suicide shortly after the film was released.

"Michael Reeves was a very bright director," recalled Executive Producer Samuel Z. Arkoff. "He wrote a script based on a best-selling book in the U.K., *Witchfinder General*," a story about a witch burner in Cromwell's era. Reeves sent it to us with the intent of getting some financing. The book had never been published in this country, and I just didn't think anybody in the U.S. gave a damn about Cromwell and such. By this time Jim Nicholson and I were fairly expert on Poe, so we looked at the poems and found one called *Conqueror Worm*, which fit pretty well in a way; although I guess a title like that could've fit a hell of a lot of things! So we went in on it, and it was released in the U.K. and such as *Witchfinder General*."

"English producer Tony Tenser had director Michael Reeves," remembered Producer Louis "Deke" Heyward, "and he had a script called *Witchfinder General*, which was in some sort of condition, but not completely correct; and he had some good locations scouted. What he didn't have was the full amount of money for total production, and he didn't have a star. We had a contract with Vincent Price, so what we did was make a trade. We gave 'em Vincent and a few dollars, and in exchange we got western hemisphere distribution rights."

During the English civil war, lawyer Matthew Hopkins (Vincent Price) is made Witchfinder General, and given the backing of the Puritans to hunt down and extract confessions from the witches which they believe populate England. Hopkins, who receives a fee for each confession, uses various torture devices and techniques and, together with henchman John Stearne (Robert Russell), go from town to town doing "God's work."

During one of their visits they torture the local priest, who is falsely accused of witchcraft. But when his young niece, Sara (Hilary Dwyer) offers herself to Hopkins, he agrees to turn him loose (but he is eventually killed anyway). When Hopkins goes off to another town on business, Stearne rapes Sara. When her fiancé Richard Marshall (Ian Oglivy), who is a soldier with Cromwell's Royalist army, returns to visit Sara, he learns of Hopkins and Stearne's actions and after first marrying Sara, vows revenge and rides off after them. Learning Marshall is after them, Hopkins kidnaps Sara in the hopes of capturing her husband.

Marshall is soon captured and is forced to watch Hopkins torture Sara but soon manages to escape from his bonds and blinds Stearne with the heel of his boot and hacks Hopkins to pieces with an axe, while a hysterical Sara watches. But before he can finish him off, Marshall's fellow soldier, Swallow (Nicky Henson) arrives and puts Hopkins out of his misery by shooting him, causing Marshall to snap because he wasn't able to finish him off.

Director Michael Reeves, although happy he was making the film, was far from happy with his star. "When I went on location to meet Michael Reeves for the first time," recalled Vincent. "He said, 'I didn't want you, and I still don't want you, but I'm stuck with you.' He could have been a wonderful director but he had no idea how to talk to actors.

"Prior to *Witchfinder General* Michael Reeves had made a film for me called *The Sorcerers* with Boris Karloff," recounted Co-Executive Producer Tony Tenser. "His first film was a horror film shot in Italy called *The She-Beast.* He really was almost at the state of being a genius. He was a very, very clever young man.

"On the day that we introduced them, Michael Reeves just wanted to get on with it and make the film his way. Vincent Price, who even then was a veteran, was sort of showing his superiority.

"During the witch burning scene, Vincent gives this speech to his friend (just after the burning and before they go off) and he was really hamming it up. Now Michael Reeves went up to him and said, 'Vinnie, please don't move your head about.' And Vincent said, 'Young man, don't move my head about. Thank You!'

"They shot the scene again and this time Michael said to him, 'Don't wave your arms about.' I mean, he was deliberately doing it. So, Vincent replied, 'Young man, don't move my arms about. Thank You!'

"Well, they shot it again and this time his voice goes over the top. Now there are a lot of people there playing the villagers and it's costing a lot of money. So Michael said, 'Vinnie, why are you hamming it?' Vincent Price then drew himself up to his full six-foot four and looked down upon Michael Reeves who was only six-foot one and said to him in his best stentorian voice, 'Young man, I have made over 70 films, how many have you made?' and Michael Reeves said, 'Two good ones!' Vincent Price laughed louder than anyone else and that broke all of the tension."

"Michael Reeves originally wanted Donald Pleasence for the part of Matthew Hopkins," remembered co-star and Reeves' friend, Ian Ogilvy. "To Mike, the character of Matthew Hopkins was a little, ugly, ineffectual man. When Donald was going to do it, Mike was going to have a scene in which he would get up on his horse in front of a bunch of villagers, and fall off on the other side, because he couldn't even ride. He was meant to be a pathetic Napoleonic character who was bitter about his own inadequacies. It all changed when Vincent came along as he was rather handsome and strong looking. Had Donald played Hopkins, I doubt that it would be considered a horror film, but it wouldn't have gotten as much of a release as it had with Vincent.

"When the deal came to be done, Vincent came with the package. Mike shrugged his shoulders and said, 'Oh well, okay, But, how are we going to stop Vincent from hamming it up, like he did in the Roger Corman Poe movies? This is much grittier and more realistic, and I don't want him to do that.' This caused the great battle between Mike and Vincent.

"Mike was always prepared to make the best of a situation. He wasn't an idiot. He knew that getting Vincent meant that we would have a bigger budget, and the movie would reach a wider audience. However, he was understandably a little nervous that Vincent might give a full high camp performance, which worked well in the Poe series, but would have been unsuitable for Witchfinder. So, he was determined to come on quite strongly with Vincent.

"This is why a lot of the problems arose on the set. Vincent didn't terribly want to be in England. He didn't terribly want to do this film. He had never heard of this young director, who was relatively inexperienced. And he was faced with this kid actually telling him: 'Could you take it down a bit?' Mike would have been happier not to have done that. He was the last person to want to antagonize anybody. But he knew that unless he did it, he would end up with a larger-than-life performance, which he didn't want.

"Vincent had already been on the movie for about a week before I arrived. I got myself all kitted up for my first morning's work, which was a riding shot. I had a huge horse, which was very fast and almost completely uncontrollable. I was trying him out, cantering him down the driveway to the vicarage. There was a black shape sitting in a ditch. As I rode past, I heard: 'Oh my God! Look at her! She's so fucking pretty! She rides that fucking horse so well! I hate her!' That was my introduction to Vincent. He was capable of being very funny, in a 'Queenie' sort of way.

"It was bitterly cold and uncomfortable in the wilds of East Anglia. We weren't staying at a nice London hotel. It was a bit Spartan, and Vincent wasn't used to that. He preferred shooting in a studio. The only things that really interested him were the antique shops. He loved them, and would go off to them all the time.

"I remain fond of Vincent. I never had any personal problems with him at all. He was a tremendous showman. I remember him being in the hotel bar in the evenings, and he was a perfectly cheerful and delightful companion. I was aware that he wasn't all that pleased to be there, but he was nothing if not a professional."

The climax scene of the picture had Ian hacking Vincent with an ax, and as Ogily recalled, "Vincent wasn't at all pleased. It was very late at night, and terribly cold. We were working under tremendous pressure. We had to be out of Orton Castle by a certain time in the morning, and had numerous set ups to do in a very short time. Vincent did not want to wear padding. He told Mike, 'The kid can pull his blows.' Mike said, 'No, he has to actually hit you.' It was a rather hard rubber ax, and would have bruised him if he was unpadded. Mike insisted that I hit him, so it was very tricky. Eventually, Vincent did wear some padding, but it was still a difficult and angry night."

On the subject of the real Matthew Hopkins, Vincent recalled "He was a real sort of small-league Hitler, in that he believed in what he was doing. I think that probably over the years he talked himself into believing it and for all the wrong reasons. For money! For fame! For everything wrong! If he'd really been a religious zealot, who he pretended to be, perhaps he would have been quite justified in what he did.

"I didn't see Matthew Hopkins simply as a sadist. In the first place you have no identity with the audience if you play a man who is one hundred per cent a black character. He has to have shades of grey."

"AIP insisted that four nude scenes of topless women in a tavern (scripted by co-producer Louis Heyward) be shot for the "'Continental

Version'," recounted Ian Ogilvy. "Those scenes were not in the original English print. They were completely gratuitous. Mike used to show me the telegrams from Sam Arkoff, saying, 'In these scenes, we would like an alternative version shot in which the innkeeper's girls bare their breasts.' Mike would hoot with laughter, and tell me, 'Look at how ridiculous this is! I'll do it, but there's no way that will be in MY version.' Mike wasn't terribly pleased about that."

Chapter Twenty-Two

The Horror Star Goes West
or
Vincent Meets Elvis

While in England, Vincent was scheduled to make a cameo appearance in the film *The Magic Christian*, but shooting on *The Conqueror Worm* ran over time causing Vincent to bow out of the film.

Vincent then signed to appear opposite Boris Karloff, actress Barbara Steele and horror film veteran Michael Gough in *The Curse of the Crimson Altar* (aka *Crimson Cult*) but when Karloff asked for extensive script rewrites, the shooting schedule was pushed back. Vincent, who had other commitments, dropped out of the project. He was replaced by Britain's Dracula, Christopher Lee. Vincent would later work with Karloff a few months prior to his death in 1969 on the Halloween episode of *The Red Skelton Show*, in which the pair sing the humorous song, *The Two of Us*, which parodied horror films.

"I believe horror is much less harmful than violence in films," Vincent declared. "I'm quite serious about the films I make. They are pure escapism and therefore harmless. No one believes them or takes them too seriously. In America these films are released to coincide with the school holidays. I'm convinced they do no harm to children.

"Many of them get rid of their hate on us instead of on their parents. Their nightmare is only while they're watching the picture on the screen, which takes place as they're munching popcorn and ice cream. They know it's not for real.

"These kinds of thrillers are fun to make, too," Vincent added. "I love them. After all, an actor ought to enjoy his work. Otherwise why do it? I love everything I do, drama, melodrama, comedy, tragedy or farce. And I have done them all, as all actors should.

"What I really like to play is comedy, even slapstick," Vincent admitted. "I love fun. At heart, I suppose I'm really a comic, but although I have played many a comedy role in my time, my build and general appearance are somewhat against the really slapstick stuff I'd love to do. I have to be content with 'sending up' some of my more macabre characterizations, as I did in the *Dr. Goldfoot* movies and *Comedy Of Terrors* in which these men find their undertakers' business has fallen off, so they have to create a little of their own. It was a marvelous idea.

"There are some actors who believe that they should specialize in one kind of acting only. They may be limiting themselves to tragedy and never discover that they could be brilliant in comedy."

Scheduling changes also caused Vincent to bow out of a guest-starring role on the Star Trek television series in the episode *And the Children Shall Lead*, as the evil Gorgon, the Friendly Angel. The part was recast with producer Gene Roddenberry's attorney Melvin Belli. Vincent was later signed to star with Christopher Lee in Hammer Films' *Taste the Blood of Dracula*, but when the budget was cut, Vincent was released from his contract and his role divided up among three less expensive actors.

Vincent next signed to play Dr. Van Helsing opposite Christopher Lee in director Jess Franco's Spanish version of *Dracula* (entitled *Count Dracula*), but when the project was delayed, Vincent left for another project and the part was recast with Herbert Lom.

While still in England, Vincent appeared on British television in a production of Henry James' play *Washington Square* re-titled *The Heiress* in the role of Dr. Sloper (a part originated on Broadway by Basil Rathbone).

Vincent returned to Hollywood to film his only real western *More Dead than Alive* in which Gunslinger Killer Cain (Clint Walker) leaves prison after 18 years and is unable to find work until he takes a job with traveling showman Dan Ruffalo's (Vincent Price) shooting show. This angers resident gunman Billy Eager (Paul Hampton), who constantly challenges Cain to a shootout. Cain eventually quits the show, but is soon ambushed by Luke Santee (Mike Henry) who seeks revenge for failing his attempt to break his brother out of prison. Rescued by Monica Alton (Anne Francis), he recovers quickly and rejoins Ruffalo's show as the star attraction. Eager still continues to confront Cain, causing him to quit once more and move in with Alton. Eager subsequently goes crazy and kills Ruffalo, who in turn is killed by Santee. Cain helps capture Santee and plans to live his life with Alton but is soon killed by Rafe Karma (Craig Littler), who seeks revenge for the death of his father at the hands of Cain years earlier.

Vincent finally got the chance to star opposite British Horror King Christopher Lee in another Poe-based story *The Oblong Box*, in which nobleman Julian Markham (Vincent Price) keeps his disfigured and violent brother Sir Edward Markham (Alistair Williamson) locked in an attic room. Sir Edward suffers from a curse brought upon him by an African witch doctor years earlier for the murder of a child. Edward arranges with family lawyer Samuel Trench (Peter Arne) to help him fake his own death so he can escape without his brother finding out that he too met with a witch doctor that he hopes will be able to cure him. Once sealed in his coffin, he is buried at the local cemetery, where he is to be quickly exhumed by Trench. However, before Trench can rescue him, he is dug up by local grave robbers who plan to sell his body to Dr. Neuhartt (Christopher Lee).

The now-mad Sir Edward revives in the doctor's house and forces him to assist him in getting his revenge on Trench and the witch doctor that left him to die in the grave. After murdering Trench, Dr. Neuhartt and a few others, he is eventually shot by Julian but not before learning that his brother actually committed the crime for which he was blamed. Just before dying, Sir Edward bites Julian on the hand transferring the disfiguring curse to him. This makes the curse little more than a communicable disease.

"The story was sent to us from America, written by an American, and we had to try to re-adapt and save it," recalled director Gordon Hessler. "Chris Wicking, who is an absolute horror buff, rewrote the script. We only had three weeks to shoot it, and the budget was very small, we're talking about $175,000, maybe a little bit more, but it was an incredibly small amount."

The first team-up of Vincent Price and Christopher Lee was far from satisfying as Lee was given a small role and had barely any screen time with Vincent. When he was asked why he agreed to accept such a small part in the film, Lee replied, "I did the picture because I wanted to do a picture with Vincent Price."

The role "I played was that of an anatomist," recalled Lee. "I played him as a man who is driven by this demon partly for decent reasons. But everything got out of hand, out of control, because he couldn't stop. He was a man who, in the interests of science, wanted to learn about the human body, and was reduced to dealing with grave robbers and resurrectionists. This caused him to become a bad character."

"Vincent Price was an extraordinary man," director Gordon Hessler fondly remembered. "We had a prince from Nigeria come to lunch with us at the Shepperton Studios; we were showing him around the place and we asked Vincent if he wouldn't mind coming along. Many actors have to talk about themselves or their careers and so on, but not one word of that from Vincent. All he talked about was African Art, by region, and in such detail that this prince was absolutely amazed!

"Vincent had a wonderful personality," continued Hessler. "Christopher Lee, however, was made of much sterner stuff; very enacting, very correct.

But he was very well educated and has a great deal of charm. I enjoyed working with him as well."

Vincent's penchant for art not only amazed the African prince but also Executive Producer Samuel Z. Arkoff, who recalled a time when "I visited Vincent in the London hotel, where he was staying, (during the filming of one of the later Poe films) in what struck me as the worst section of the city. And I was shocked at how simple both the hotel itself and Vincent's own room were. No elaborate suite with comfortable sofas. No room service. Instead, it was a small, bare single room, just large enough for Vincent's lanky six-foot-four frame, that didn't even have a toilet of its own. When he had to use the bathroom, he walked down the hall.

""'I don't get it,' I told Vincent. 'We're paying you $80,000 for fifteen days' work, and we've increased your expense money to $1,000 a week. With that kind of money, can't you afford something better than this room?'

""'Sam, if you loved art as much as I do, maybe you would get it," he explained. 'I'm buying art with the $1,000 a week. Who needs a toilet?'""

Vincent returned home to make a cameo appearance in the Elvis Presley film *The Trouble with Girls* as Mr. Morality, a lecturer on morals in Presley's 1927 traveling show. Vincent's only reason for doing the filming was in meeting Presley. "I was really excited about meeting Elvis," recalled Vincent. "But to try and meet him was rather difficult because he had about thirty people; bodyguards, secretaries, managers, etc. around him. You sort of had to put your hand through a great crowd to meet him. But he was a very nice man."

Vincent's final Poe film of the Sixties was *Spirits of the Dead*, although he had almost nothing to do with the film itself, as Executive Producer Samuel Z. Arkoff explains: "In 1969 we put Poe's name on a French Italian coproduction entitled *Histories Extraordinaires (Tales of Mystery and Imagination)*, even though the picture had been completed before AIP ever bough the distribution rights. It was actually three short films in one, each based on a Poe story, and each directed by an important director: Roger Vadim, Louis Malle and Federico Fellini. The film was originally a four-parter. I forget who the 4th director was, but the piece was too long, so we cut that one out completely. We re-titled it *Spirits of the Dead*, added some narration by Vincent Price and a song by Ray Charles, and released it in the US.

It was the most expensive of the Poe pictures (although we bore only a small portion of the costs) but it wasn't the type of Poe feature that our audiences were used to. It had more of a European flavor to it, which didn't have the same broad domestic appeal that our own Poe pictures had.

It was a satisfactory grosser, particularly in view of the small price we had paid. All our Poe movies did well, and in fact, no AIP picture we produced ever lost money in our first decade, and very few were money-losers after that.

Chapter Twenty-Three

Vincent Price, Superman
or
Lucy Scares Vincent Price

The 1970's brought about several changes in both Vincent's personal and professional life. In 1970 he re-teamed with Christopher Lee and Britain's Gentleman of Horror, Peter Cushing, in the disoriented film entitled *Scream and Scream Again*.

"We got a pulp magazine-type story called *The Disoriented Man* by Peter Saxon," recalled director Gordon Hessler. "Which if you read it, you knew it was just trash, but the ingenuity that Chris Wicking brought to it made it a film of a much grander scale. He showed his potential talent on that because it really was just pulp, he really uplifted it, made it something very, very different."

"Gordon Hessler didn't like the screenplay," continued Screenwriter Chris Wicking. "He didn't feel producer Milton Subotsky could deliver what they wanted...I got a call from Gordon requesting I read the book and then Milton's screenplay. The book gave me goosebumps. Then I read Milton's script, which was totally flat; it was like watching a soufflé dying, it just caved in after awhile.

"Gordon and I discussed it at length. He saw the police material as *Coogan's Bluff* country. The one radical thing we did which changed what Milton had done, which came directly from the book, was take out the blobs from space. We wanted to do a Don Siegel-style horror film. *Coogan's Bluff* meets *Invasion of the Body Snatchers*, and we needed something stronger than lumps from another planet. So, we took the aliens away and implied that Vincent Price's mad doctor character was responsible for the superhuman creatures.

"We wanted to investigate science and politics, so we used a lot of material from news headlines, material about transplants and genetic experimentation."

So, when a crazed blood-drinking psycho sex killer named Keith (Michael Gothard) terrorizes the women of London, Superintendent of Police Bellaver (Alfred Marks) is brought in to investigate. Keith is finally captured but manages to escape by tearing his hand off to escape from a pair of handcuffs and then jumping into a vat of acid located at a nearby house owned by mad scientist Dr. Browning (Vincent Price).

Meanwhile, an agent for an unnamed Eastern European country, Konratz (Marshall Jones) has been systematically removing his superiors before arriving in London to stop the ongoing investigation into Keith and Browning. Konratz kills Bellaver before arriving at Browning's lab to try and kill him as well. Browning is the mastermind behind a plan to create a race of super humans (of which Keith was one) using body parts from helpless victims. Konratz, who is also one of the super humans, is finally destroyed by super human Browning who then in turn is destroyed by super human government agent Fremont (Christopher Lee), who believes the world is not ready to learn about Browning's experiments.

Unfortunately, the teaming of the reigning kings of horror was a disappointment. Cushing's part as Marshall Jones' superior was a last-minute cameo, in which he has no interaction with the other two. While Price and Lee fared better in their roles, they had only one scene together.

When asked to recall his part in *Scream and Scream Again*, Vincent all but blocked the film out completely except he thought "That was an odd film. It starred Peter Cushing, Christopher Lee and myself, but, for the life of me, I don't remember us ever shooting a scene together. As a matter of fact, the only thing I remember about that film is that I die at the end by falling into a vat of acid or some such nonsense."

This was Christopher Lee's second film with Vincent, and while his memories of the film were less cloudy than Vincent's, all that he could recall was that "This was the first time that Vincent and Peter and I ever appeared in the same film. However, we were all three virtually defused. I had about eight minutes of screen time and Peter even less.

"I played the head of the aliens, but in point of fact, he is supposed to be the head of British Intelligence. At least I did have something to do on the screen. I shot one whole sequence in Trafalgar Square. If you can remember your lines with all the traffic, and the crowds of people behind the cameras watching----you can do anything.

"At the end of the film I dispose of Vincent in a vat of acid. I remember I stared at Vincent and through sheer will power, force him back, back, back, until he finally, quite willingly and without my saying a word, immerses himself in a vat of acid. I'll never forget that stately figure, desperately trying to keep a straight face, and me, too, stepping back slowly and with great dignity, and then quietly sinking into a deep vat of noxious-looking liquid. But he never lost his composure. Of course, who would want to do that scene a second time?" However, they did do the scene a second time as Lee continued, "I was very fond of Vincent and great respect for his acting skills, however, the yellow tinge of the acid bath made it look like Vincent had suffered some terrible natural mishap on a grand scale, so the first take we did was completely ruined by our both laughing as we fought to the death!"

The film was never designed to be a vehicle for all three horror stars; it was a last minute decision by producer Louis Heyward to try and get all three stars together in one picture, in the hopes the name value help the film at the box office.

Peter Cushing defended his small part in the film by stating that "I will accept any part big or small if I feel my contribution will mean something, and not be a disappointment to those who go to see my performances in particular. Naturally, I prefer a large role because I love to work and need to work for many personal reasons apart from the obvious."

Vincent's next film *Cry of the Banshee* was the last of the Poe films, although Poe had nothing to do with this story. Vincent portrayed magistrate and witch hunter Lord Edward Whitman, who slaughters a coven of witches but allows their leader, Oona (Elisabeth Bergner) to escape. Vowing revenge, she calls upon the devil to send her a demon with which she can take her revenge on Lord Whitman and his family. Enter Roderick (Patrick Mower), Lord Whitman's new groom by day and demon avenger by night.

As the members of Lord Whitman's family are killed off by the demon or Sidhe (it wasn't a banshee despite the film's title) as he is called, local priest Father Tom (Marshall Jones) seeks out Oona's new hiding place and with Lord Whitman's youngest son slaughters her and the other members of her coven.

Meanwhile, Roderick, who has been having an affair with Lord Whitman's daughter, Maureen (Hilary Dwyer), attacks her, causing her in turn to shooting Roderick in the face, thus killing him. The Sidhe, who can only be destroyed by fire, returns to life and subsequently succeeds in killing Lord Whitman's remaining children before driving Lord Whitman off to certain death in his private carriage.

"Again, we were sent the script from Hollywood, we read it and we were all unhappy with it," remembers director Gordon Hessler. "It was a dreadful script, what we got from AIP was something unbelievable, and so I asked if I would be allowed to change it.

"Chris Wicking and I went to Scotland and we were planning to do a completely different, very, very interesting movie. We wanted to shoot *Cry of the Banshee* there; all the witchcraft seemed to emanate from Scotland, The

Land of Witches, and we thought that would be a wonderful place to film it. As a matter of fact, while we were doing research in Scotland we met a number of witches! We were trying to get inspiration to do something very different, but as it turned out we were never really given the power to do that. We would have had to change the script so much that the AIP people in London got worried. They felt that the original script had been approved and pre-sold, and if we changed it very drastically we might be cutting our own throats.

"They said: 'Ten percent is the maximum amount you can change,' so that was about all we could do. What Chris wanted to add into it was that those of the 'old religion,' the people that everybody thought were so terrible, were actually the good witches. But as I said, we rewrote it so far away from the original script that Hollywood had sent us, that Deke Heyward got a little worried and said, "Look, this is not the story that everybody's bought. You're going to have to go back to the original concept."

Elizabeth Bergner, who portrayed Oona the witch, was well known for her many appearances in the films of director Ingmar Bergmann. This was her first film in 29 years and there has been speculation as to why she agreed to appear in a horror film after working in so many classic films. The real reason can be found in her comment to Vincent Price who asked her why she decided to take the role of the witch, she answered: "I wanted to be seen!"

While Elisabeth Bergner wanted to be seen, director Gordon Hessler wishes the demon was *not* seen, as he was not happy with the demon makeup. "Banshee cost maybe $450,000….$500,000 maximum, with perhaps four weeks shooting but we just didn't have the money to do the makeup the right way."

Banshee was the first of a number of films to be promoted as Vincent's 100th film, and to start off the celebration, the cast and crew held a special party in Vincent's honor at the end of shooting. And as director Gordon Hessler remembers, "We had an incredible party, everybody dressed in costume. After-picture parties are always so boring and so uninteresting, so I said, 'Anybody who wants to come to this party, executives included, had to wear a costume.'

"We got all the costumes from the Richard Burton movie, *Anne of the Thousand Days.* We had rented them from Berman's and they were marvelous costumes. Everybody had to wear one of those costumes, including Arkoff and Nicholson. Now, Vincent was very upset at the time for some reason to do with his contract, and he was having a fight with Arkoff, I don't really know what the details were. And Vincent didn't want to come to the party. I said, 'Vincent, you've got to come, this party is in your honor.' He refused and refused, but I finally persuaded him to come. But by the time he arrived, he had drunk too much."

Vincent and Sam Arkoff were fighting over the money details of his new contract. Vincent wanted more money and the ever frugal Arkoff balked. At the time, Arkoff was grooming actor Robert Quarry as a new horror star, after his starring role as *Count Yorga, Vampire*. Arkoff was supposed to have threatened to replace Vincent in future pictures with Quarry. Eventually, Vincent and Arkoff worked out the details, but Vincent always felt somewhat threatened when Quarry costarred with him in his last two films for AIP.

"What we had done, we'd got a big cake and there was a naked girl supposed to pop out of it. And Vincent was supposed to cut the cake. I had told Arkoff he had to make a speech, to present the cake and all that sort of thing, but when Vincent found out that Arkoff was going to make the speech, he said, 'If he does, I won't be there to cut the cake!' So, we had to rush back to Arkoff and tell him not to make the speech!

"I remember also that we couldn't find a knife to cut the cake, and Vincent, who was roaring drunk, said, 'Use the knife that's in my back!' I thought, 'God, this is going to be disastrous,' but everything turned out all right, the party was great fun, a lot of liquor was flowing, we had a band and dancing and I think everybody enjoyed themselves."

Everyone except the nude girl (and maybe Vincent), as co-star and veteran horror film actor Robert Hutton remembered, "I had known Vincent Price for years and years, but I had never worked with him, so that's why I did the film. It was shot at Grim's Dyke, which was the house that belonged to W.S. Gilbert of *Gilbert and Sullivan* fame. We were there in the dead of winter, and it was cold because they didn't have any heating! *Cry of the Banshee* was supposed to be Vincent's 100th movie, and after shooting they gave a big party for him in the house. And they had a girl come out of a cake, a nude girl. This was another first for me; I had never seen that before. The poor thing was freezing to death, naked as a jaybird, and Vincent was very embarrassed because that isn't his cup of tea. A nude coming out of a cake, that isn't Vincent Price, not at all."

After completing work on Banshee, Vincent returned to the US to spoof his own horror image on an episode of the Lucille Ball series, *Here's Lucy*, entitled *Lucy Cuts Vincent's Price.* When Lucy buys a painting at an auction, she suspects that there might be a valuable masterpiece hidden underneath, so she goes to Vincent Price's house to have it appraised. Unaware that

Vincent is shooting his new horror film at his home, Lucy thinks he is a crazed monster while he mistakes her for an actress who was to star with him in the new production.

"After I finished all the Poe films I did *An Evening of Edgar Allan Poe*, a one hour television special for AIP in which I did four Poe stories: *The Tell-Tale Heart*, *The Pit and the Pendulum*, *The Sphinx* and *The Cask of Amontilado.* Absolutely pure Edgar Allan Poe, without a word by anybody else, no changing of the plot, just as monologues presented with action, sets and costumes. His wife Mary designed all the costumes. AIP showed it to some exhibitors and television people. They said, 'It's too serious, not like the real Edgar Allan Poe,' but it was the real Edgar Allan Poe, it won all kinds of awards. It's probably the best Poe thing I ever did," declared Vincent.

Vincent next appeared in an unsold pilot entitled *Mooch Goes to Hollywood*; it was produced by actor comedian Jim Backus, and was an unsuccessful attempt to sell a series starring the dog that would later be known as *Benji.* The pilot also starred James Darren and Jill St. John.

Vincent followed it with his first made-for-television film, called *What's a Nice Girl Like You?* in which Vincent and assistant Roddy McDowall try to pass off Bronx girl Brenda Vaccaro as the daughter of a wealthy socialite, in order to extort money from the real girl's father.

Actress Brenda Vaccaro had wonderful memories about working with Vincent. "When I worked with Vincent during the film, I was with one of the finest actors one could wish to meet. Much more to work with! I remember we were off camera at one point and he said to me as he put his arm around mine. 'I know it's soon time to get ready to say our lines but I just love what I'm doing. I'm in love with acting' I loved and adored being around him and working with him was a like being in a dream! I will never forget how enthusiastic he was about everything!"

Chapter Twenty-Four

Vincent Goes Over the Rainbow

or

I Learned This Trick from Charlton Heston

In 1971, Vincent created his first recurring horror character, Dr. Anton Phibes in *The Abominable Dr. Phibes* (his role in *The Fly* films was a sympathetic one and Dr. Goldfoot was an over-the-top comedic role), the horribly disfigured musical genius who seeks his revenge on the team of doctors he feels is responsible for the death of his wife, Victoria (Caroline Munro). Using his knowledge of religion (he has a doctor's degree in theology), he does away with each member of the surgical team with the help of the mysterious Vulnavia (Virginia North), by killing them in accordance of the ten plagues of Egypt brought down upon the Pharaoh by Moses.

As the medical men are killed off, the police, who are always one step behind Phibes, join forces with chief surgeon Dr. Vesalius (Joseph Cotton) to locate the remaining members of the team. But when his son Lem (Sean Bury) is kidnapped by Phibes, Vesalius evades the police and rushes to his aide. As Vesalius operates on his son to retrieve the key (placed inside his son's chest by Phibes) which will unlock the operating table before an ever-descending flow of acid reaches the boy's face, Phibes rejoins his dead wife in his underground tomb, awaiting the time when the planets will be in the correct position to revive him.

"It was a wonderful part for me," recalled Vincent. "It had a super script and Robert Fuest was one of the best directors I've ever worked with. It's also the first time I've acted with Joseph Cotton in thirty-two years, not since the days of the Mercury Theater."

"Joseph Cotton was just like Boris Karloff, the original gentleman," remembered producer Louis Heyward. "He also was not in good health at that time, but he went home and he studied, and came in the next day knowing his lines letter-perfect, attempting to contribute, using every one of the tricks that he had acquired over years in the business to enhance the picture. He was a big plus!"

Actress Caroline Munro spent the entire film lying in a padded coffin, as Phibes' dead wife Victoria, recalled "Vincent was such a funny man. He used to come into the makeup room at 6:00 a.m. with a great bowl of homemade pate for us to eat, which was lovely."

"I find almost anything funny, and myself funniest of all," admitted Vincent. "I find the minute I take myself seriously I've got to laugh because it's so ridiculous. It's what gets me through an awful lot of films, this sense of the ridiculous. However, Phibes was something I had to take very seriously, when I was doing it so it would come out funny.

"All the same it was agony for me because my face was covered with plastic, and I giggled and laughed the whole time, day and night, and the makeup man and I were practically married because the makeup kept dissolving and he had to patch me up every five minutes.

"Phibes was also very difficult to portray, you see, he has no throat. He can only speak if an extension cord from an electric-light socket attached to a receptacle in his neck keeps him functioning. He's all right as long as someone doesn't blow a fuse!"

This, of course, caused great problems for co-star Joseph Cotton who, as Vincent remembered, "They covered my face with collodion, which is like new skin, so that I couldn't move. I was immobile, I always learned the lines but I never had to speak them, (they were dubbed in later, when Phibes spoke through his electronic voice box), which made Joe very angry. He used to come to me and say 'You're unfair. You're not speaking the lines, and I'm having to remember all mine and say them,' and I said, 'But I remember them, Joe.'

"You can take it from me that horror films are hard work. In the movies I made with Boris Karloff, whether the scripts were great or mediocre or sometimes even downright bad, we all worked terribly hard to make them good. It isn't true what people say about comedy or horror films not being serious art. Those people think only in terms of problem dramas, but every single work of fiction has seriousness behind it. And that goes for comedy most particularly. There is this funny thing: all the classic horror pictures really had a seriousness of intent."

The Abominable Dr. Phibes was an immediate hit and AIP quickly produced a sequel in 1972, *Dr. Phibes Rises Again.* The film picks up right where the first film left off, with Phibes joining his dead wife in eternal slumber. Then a few years pass and the planets move into their proper position, causing the mechanism inside Phibes' underground tomb to return him to life. It is now the proper time for him to return with his wife, Victoria

(Caroline Munro), to Egypt to obtain a supply of a magic elixir which will return her to life.

Returning to the surface, Phibes finds his house reduced to rubble and the parchment containing the directions to the source of the elixir missing. Suspecting archeologist Biederbeck (Robert Quarry) of the theft, he plots to join him on his trip to Egypt. Once there, Phibes and Vulnavia (Valli Kemp) systematically do away with Biederbeck's men until only the archeologist and his wife, Diana (Fiona Lewis) remain.

Phibes kidnaps Diana and imprisons her upon an ever-rising platform beneath a ceiling of spiked snake heads. He then gives Biederbeck the choice of saving his wife by surrendering the key to a secret passageway or joining him through the passageway at the expense of his wife. Biederbeck, who is over 100 years old and needs a new supply of the elixir to stay young, gives Phibes the key. As the police rescue his wife, Biederbeck begins to die of old age, as Phibes with the body of his wife sails his barge down the passageway to find the elixir of life, while singing *Over the Rainbow.*

"Vincent was very funny, recalled actress Fiona Lewis." He said, "I love doing this movie, because the costumes are so good." That's all he ever said about the role of Dr. Phibes, and it seemed a damn good reason to do a picture. He was great to work with because he was permanently in a good mood. He had a marvelous sense of humor and kept everybody buoyant. The working atmosphere was very good when he was around."

The costumes weren't the only reasons Vincent did the film, but it was also "Brian Eatwell's wonderful sets; he turned Phibes into a visual masterpiece," recalled Vincent. "This puts it into a class above the average horror film where they use a lot of fog and dreary Gothic sets. Bob Fuest, who was a set designer before he turned director, realized at once that to make this film different and to give it integrity as a Grand Guignol horror picture, it had to have a difference.

"The 1930's were a great period and it hasn't been used in this type of film before. It's much more horrifying to set the story in a period with which many people easily identify than in a creepy mansion in some ancient time and country unknown to them."

Vincent was in such a great mood during the making of this film that his co-stars found it amazingly difficult to keep a straight face whenever he was around, as actress Valli Kemp remembered, "I played a mute character in that film, and I found it's harder not to speak than to speak because you have to give out your feelings without using words. I found it difficult having to keep a straight face through some of the scenes because just before a shot, Vincent was likely to pat me on the bottom and say, 'Go on!' and joke with me and I'm supposed to go on and be serious.

"I did one scene with Vincent in which I was playing the violin and he takes a grape from the fruit bowl and shoves it into my mouth. He then takes another grape and shoves that into my mouth so I now have two grapes in my mouth and I daren't swallow them because if I did, I'd burst out laughing. He then picked up a pineapple and tried to put that into my mouth as well, but then he shakes his head when he realizes it was too big, the pineapple that is, and he puts it down. This was all in the film and it's hysterical as it was complete improvisation and I didn't know anything about it."

Valli Kemp wasn't the only one to fall victim to Vincent's good humor as actor Robert Quarry continues, "The hardest acting I ever did in my life were the scenes I played with Vincent. I had to keep a straight face and play it with anger while Vincent's mugging. He knew I was gonna go crazy. He said, 'Just wait till you do a scene with me. Joe Cotton couldn't stand it.'

"After the first take, which I blew, and Vincent's loving every minute of it, because he knows what he's doing to me, I thought, I'll just relate it to somebody I really hate, in real life, and just look at his ear. Vincent said, 'You did better than Joe Cotton did!'"

"Vincent Price was a lovely man. He was a terrific, marvelous guy. We put each other on so terribly all of the time, some people thought we were at odds about something, but it was just our way of showing affection. We had a good time. And for the first week of production, I was the juvenile. I was with Vincent, Peter Cushing and Hugh Griffith, and I said to myself, "My God, it's the first film I've been on in so many years, where I'm the juvenile.

"The thing about this type of film is that you can joke before and after but during the scene you have to play it straight. It's Hamlet all over again. The secret in doing this type of film is that at the moment of shooting you have to play it very earnestly and break up afterwards."

Chapter Twenty-Five

How to Murder Your Wife-To-Be
or
Peter Cushing, Spider Lover

Returning to the US, Vincent continued to make frequent television appearances on *The Hollywood Squares*, *The Carol Burnett Show*, as well as *The Brady Bunch*, *Columbo*, *The* (Canadian produced) *Hilarious House of Frightenstein*, *The Mod Squad*, *Night Gallery*, *Get Smart* and a special appearance in old friend Helen Hayes' *Snoop Sisters* television series in the episode entitled *Black Day for Bluebeard*, in which he played a horror film star who is accused of murdering his wife. He also found time to publish *The Vincent Price Treasury of American Art.*

After doing a cooking series on England's BBC-TV entitled *Cooking: Price Wise*, Vincent went on to star in what would be one of his favorite films *Theater of Blood.*

When Shakespearean ham actor Edward Lionheart (Vincent Price) fails to win the Critic's Circle award, he kills himself by diving off a high balcony into the river. Lionheart, who somehow manages to survive the fall, together with his daughter, Edwina (played by *The Avengers* TV series star Diana Rigg) and a group of homeless drunks plan to take revenge on the critics who snubbed him.

Lionheart manages to lure each critic into his clutches and then proceeds to do away with them by recreating the death scenes from a number of Shakespeare's plays as critic Peregrine Devlin (Ian Hendry) and police inspector Boot (Milo O'Shea) try to stop him.

Soon, Devlin finds himself the sole surviving critic and in the hands of Lionheart, who offers to spare him if he will reverse his decision and give him the award. Devlin refuses, and almost joins his late friends, but is rescued by the police. Lionheart later loses his will to live when Edwina is killed. After setting fire to his old theater, he carries her dead body to the roof where he falls to his death as the building collapses.

"This was one of the most ingeniously inventive films I have ever made," Vincent fondly recalled. "It was quite unlike anything I'd ever done before. The screenplay was so funny and original. And when I first heard all the big names they had assembled for the cast, I simply couldn't believe it.

"It was a marvelous role because I got to play eight Shakespearean parts in it, which is a feast for any actor. And I got to knock off eight critics. It was a story dear to the heart of any old actor. It was a dream to make and very real to me. I really understand the man who is doing his very best and yet is unrecognized.

"Actors hate critics," Vincent continued, "because there are too few critics, in the proper sense of the word, around today. They are writers who pride themselves on their own following and cleverness. There are some who are wonderful, Brooks Atkinson, for instance. Also, Kevin Thomas, who in his review of *Theater of Blood* for the *Los Angeles Times*, said that if the horror genre was taken seriously in this country, as it is in all the other countries of the world, that this film would win every Academy Award. And he's a fellow who doesn't really like this kind of film."

On August 17, 1973, Vincent's wife Mary filed for divorce after 24 years of marriage. She received custody of their daughter Victoria in the settlement. Early in 1974, Vincent married his third (and final) wife, the Australian actress Coral Browne, whom he had first met during the cemetery scene in *Theater of Blood.* From the moment they met, the two were an item. They were constantly sneaking off to the dressing room to spend time together, which as a result caused frequent reprimands by the director for returning late to the shoot.

While the details of his divorce from Mary Grant were not made public, his antics with Coral could have been at the root of it.

For his next film, Vincent re-teamed with Peter Cushing and Robert Quarry in *Madhouse* (originally promoted by AIP with the more appropriate title of *The Revenge of Dr. Death*). Vincent portrayed Paul Toombes, the star of the *Doctor Death* series of horror films, who suffers a mental breakdown when his fiancée is murdered in the Doctor Death style at a party.

Years later, Toombes, having recovered from his breakdown, returns to England to star in a television series based on his Doctor Death character, and moves into the home of his old friend, actor-turned-writer Herbert Flay (Peter Cushing).

As the series begins filming, the Doctor Death murders begin again and pretty soon Toombes begins to believe that he is committing the murders without knowing it. When his new assistant is found murdered, Toombes suffers another breakdown and, locking himself inside a studio, sets fire to the place with the cameras running. Later, when Flay watches his friend's last minutes on film, Toombes appears in the room and forces a confession out of him. With Toombes out of the way, Flay would be allowed to take over the role of Doctor Death, a role he felt cheated out of years earlier. Flay battles it out with Toombes, but soon falls to his death. Believed to be dead, Toombes, with the help of Flay's disfigured and mad wife Faye (Adrienne Corri), uses makeup to assume Flay's appearance so he can take his place on the television series. The film ends with Vincent singing over the closing credits.

"I think horror stories end up more successful if they're done the Corman way," declared Vincent. "By which I mean to say, letting the audience in on the secret that the actor is enjoying it. Sometimes, however a scene is so totally preposterous it is almost impossible to do. In the film, dear Peter had to fall into a tank of spiders! It's very difficult to fall into a tank of spiders and be Brando!"

"I like Spiders!" countered Peter Cushing. "One of Vincent's great qualities as a gentleman is his manner and attitude to all who come within his orbit. No matter what their status, everyone received the same charming courtesy and attention."

"Peter," Vincent thought, "was a very wiry little fellow, but he was one of the strongest men I ever knew in my life. I had to do several fight scenes with him in the film. My God! He can throw you! He doesn't fake it at all. Nobody warned me about this, and I was sort of battered and bruised. He was a very realistic and very serious-minded actor, but he was also a very gentle, sweet man and I am very, very fond of him."

Actress Linda Hayden remembers one memorable scene in which she managed to surprise Vincent. "I played an aspiring actress who used her evil ways to try to get a part in Vincent's *Doctor Death* film. There's this scene where I'm supposed to walk up to his bed where he's asleep, and he wakes up and is startled to see me. They decided they wanted me in this low-cut dress. Now, I'm not a very busty person, and I never have been. I'm always cast in those roles and somehow got away with it. Anyway, before the scene was shot, the people in wardrobe and makeup were strapping my boobs up in this low-cut black dress. Now the scene was only a walk across the room to wake Vincent up, and we'd rehearsed it, but never when I was wearing that dress. So, the director yells 'Action!' and I walk in---and they'd worked wonders on me---and I lean over Vincent, and he opens his eyes and sees my tits looming in his face. He cracked up. He couldn't believe what he was seeing. He laughed his head off. He knew damned well they weren't mine, or what was mine was not very much."

Vincent's next appearance came in the sequel to the 1971 film *Percy*, a British sex comedy about the world's first successful penis transplant. In

Percy Progress a nuclear explosion releases a chemical into the water supplies of the world turning every man impotent except for Percy (Leigh Lawson) (Hywel Bennett played Percy in the original film), the recipient of the world's first successful penis transplant, who was out sailing when the water was contaminated.

Discovered in South America by a British journalist, he is returned to England where he becomes a national treasure. As he is the last potent male in the world, the United Nations sets up a commission to select the best suited women from every country of the world to mate with Percy in order to ensure a continuing population.

Percy is later kidnapped by invalid Stavos Mammonian (Vincent Price), the world's richest man, who wants him to mate with his wife, Clarissa (Elke Sommer) in order to give him an heir. Although made in 1974, the film did not see release in the United States until 1979 when producer Joseph Brenner (who had released *Naked Terror*) released it under the title *It's Not the Size That Counts*.

Vincent was next supposed to star in a new AIP film called *The Naked Eye*, but script problems caused the project's cancellation. Later that year he was voted the Grand Prix award for Best Actor by *The International Festival of Science Fiction and Fantasy Films.*

A film version of Shakespeare's *Troilus and Cresida* was planned for 1975, but was abandoned. So, Vincent toured during the summer of 1974 in a traveling stock company of the musical *Oliver* in the featured role of Fagin.

In 1976, Vincent narrated *The Devil's Triangle*, a documentary film about the mysterious disappearances of ships and planes in the Bermuda Triangle. The film was produced, written and directed by Richard Winer, with music by King Crimson. The film had a limited theatrical release by UFO Distribution on the top half of a double bill with the low budget science fiction film, *UFO: Target Earth.*

Chapter Twenty-Six

Vincent's Explosive Finish
or
Rock 'N' Roll, Monster Style

During the later part of the 1970's, Vincent made only non-horror films. "It wasn't that I was ashamed of my horror films," Vincent pointed out. "I've made a very successful career out of doing them and a lot of what I have done in the genre have turned out to be classic films. It's just that there was much more to my career than horror films."

The first was a 1976 remake of the Orson Welles film *Journey into Fear*, in which geologist Graham (Sam Waterson) finds himself the target of an assassin who works for the oil companies of the Middle East. As he tries to escape from Turkey with the help of Kopeikin (Zero Mostel) and Colonel Haki (Joseph Wiseman), he finds himself on board a steamship headed for Greece with an odd group of passengers including the assassin and his foreign agent superior Mueller (Vincent Price), as well as Turkish agent Kuvetti (Donald Pleasence) sent by Haki to look after him.

Graham is eventually captured by Mueller and his gang and taken to a deserted mansion. Graham manages to escape and kills Meuller with a flare gun, (one of Vincent's more spectacular death scenes).

And while on location in Athens, Greece, Vincent was relieved of his wallet containing $2,000. Chasing the pickpocket down the street, he soon found himself in an alley confronted with three thugs. Rather than put up a fight, he wisely forfeited the money.

On February 22, 1977, Edith Barrett Price passed away at the age of 70 and while Vincent and Edith were no longer close, they did remain friends till the end. Later that year Vincent appeared as the on-screen host and narrator in the British concert film, *The Butterfly Ball.*

And then *Scavenger Hunt in 1979*, in which toy tycoon Milton Parker (Vincent Price) dies leaving his vast fortune to the winner of a scavenger hunt presided over by executor Bernstein (Robert Morley). Parker's sister Mildred Carruthers (Cloris Leachman), aided by her son, George (Richard Masur) and crooked lawyer Stuart (Richard Benjamin) try everything they can to keep Parker's other relatives and members of his household staff from winning the estate. In the end, Mildred loses when the others join forces and decide to split the estate rather than let her get it.

"The key to my life is that I am in love with the whole profession of acting,' said Vincent. "I don't particularly give a damn where it is or what it is in. I probably should be more selective but I have a very rich and wonderful life."

While Vincent had a rich and wonderful professional life, it's hard to believe that he felt the same way about his personal life. He was married three times and he had two children (who were twenty-two years apart in age), whom he alienated himself from. From the time he married Coral, his family and friends were pushed into the background in favor of Coral's, and it wasn't until after her death in 1991 that Vincent and his daughter were able to reconnect again. He always said he wished he was a better father.

Vincent's final film of the decade was entitled *Days of Fury*, a theatrical documentary for which Vincent used his velvet-toned voice to recount the many natural disasters and catastrophes which have befallen the planet Earth. The film had a very limited theatrical release. Soon, Vincent would find himself returning to the genre that gave him stardom. "Almost against my will I became a star of horror films," Vincent admitted. "There was nothing I could do about it. Indeed, I was quite flattered to be asked to take over the mantle of such eminence as Boris Karloff, Lon Chaney and Bela Lugosi.

"Quite suddenly, after fifteen years in Hollywood, I was really in demand, but to play really nasty chaps in movies calculated to frighten filmgoers out of their seats. So I took to my new career with relish. I thought to myself, if I'm going to do it, I'll do it better than anybody else. And I have kept that thought in front of me ever since.

"Now without fame, you really don't survive in this business. You've got to have some kind of identifying reputation. Mine was being a villain." However, fame can be fickle as Vincent recalled, "I was sitting in an airport one day on my way somewhere, and a lady came up to me. And I was sitting there minding my own business which I do pretty well. And she came up and spread her legs, and she said, 'You are, aren't you?'

"And I said, 'Oh, I don't know about that.'

"She said, 'Oh yes, you are! Aren't you?'

"She said, "I know you movie actors, you don't like to be recognized. You are Boris Karloff. Aren't you?'

"Well, I said....this is really true! And I said, 'No, Madam, I promise you I'm not Boris Karloff.'

"She said, 'Oh, come on! Why don't you admit it?'

"And I said, 'I'm not Boris Karloff. He's dead.'

"She said, 'He is? Well then, who the Hell are you?'

"She left before I was able to tell her I was Christopher Lee!

"But it really is quite extraordinary. People get you all mixed up. Fame doesn't mean a thing. It really doesn't."

In 1980 Vincent returned to England to star in what was to have been an all-star horror film, entitled *The Monster Club*. After all the promises fell through, Vincent wound up hosting a hodgepodge of second-rate horror tales while trading quips with an obviously bored John Carradine. The only remarkable thing about this film is that it was the first and only time Vincent portrayed a real vampire.

Vampire Erasmus (Vincent Price) invites horror author Ronald Chetwynd-Hayes (John Carradine) to a nightclub for monsters in return for giving him a taste of his blood. Once at the club, Erasmus offers to give Hayes a vast supply of material for his stories. He then relates the story of the Shadmock, a strange being who can destroy living flesh by whistling and a movie director who stumbles upon a small town populated by ghouls and the half human girl he finds there.

He is also entertained by several rock bands, a stripper who removes not just her clothes but her skin as well. Plus he is treated to a new film by a horror movie producer, which shows what it was like growing up as the son of a vampire. In the end, Hayes is inducted into the membership of the club, as the representative of the greatest monster on the planet, MAN!

Despite the film's shortcomings, Vincent loved the film, "I hadn't been offered a script as good as this one in years. It was neat, precise and very funny and it had music.

"I was offered countless scripts, which of course I turned down because in trying to be modern, they became pornographic and had a lot of dirty language. I wouldn't do smut because lots of people are offended by it and the ideal audience for these films is children. There is no graphic blood or gore in this at all. In fact, it's quite moral, or to quote a line from the film, 'No Nudity, No sex...a little violence perhaps."

"My original idea for this picture was to put the top six horror names in it: Vincent Price, Donald Pleasence, Christopher Lee, Peter Cushing, John Carradine and Klaus Kinski," recalled Producer Milton Subotsky. "I wanted the ultimate horror film!

"But Kinski wanted too much money, Lee wasn't interested and Cushing turned down several of the film's choice roles, claiming he didn't like the subject matter. Perhaps he thought it was going to be gruesome and disgusting. I told him it was a joke and supposed to be funny."

"Other actors seemed to have turned their backs on these sorts of films," remarked Vincent. "It's very silly to turn your back on something that has made you extremely successful. It would be like if John Wayne had said he'd never play another cowboy. For heaven's sake, they aren't all the same part! They are different characters, and as often as not; the films aren't even horror stories, they're Gothic tales!

"I always frighten people with the hope that they will giggle afterwards. My pictures don't frighten me and I don't think they frighten the kids either. What I loved about *The Monster Club* was that it was not a violent film. It was not anything except amusing and entertaining. I never took myself too seriously. The minute I took myself seriously I had to laugh. It got me through an awful lot of films. In fact, it got me through life too."

While co-star John Carradine had nothing to say on the subject of *The Monster Club*, he did have nothing but praise for his longtime friend and fellow actor: "Vincent Price is one of the great unknown humorists of our time---a strong wit, an observant eye and a warm heart, coupled with the heartiest laugh. He is an amiable art lover and a gentle critic. He would offer advice but his criticism would only be given in the most positive sense. A gentleman whose artwork was in awe of its owner. A gentleman, but then there are many, but this gentleman has the capacity to calm the actor that is new in front of the camera. A gentleman's gentleman!"

"Vincent Price was a very jolly fellow," remarked director Roy Ward Baker. "I liked him quite a lot. John Carradine was a charming man, absolutely sweet. He was totally riddled with arthritis. It was dreadfully sad, because he was such a nice man.

"I thought *The Monster Club* was an awful failure. Quite frankly, I was frightened of it going in, because the script wasn't any good. Even Milton Subotsky himself said the script was no good. I was able to do a bit photographically with the Stuart Whitman segment, but the other episodes were pretty straight forward. The Donald Pleasence segment was a one joke idea stretched too thin. The material was entirely lacking.

"There were two main problems with the rock and roll aspect. First, Milton couldn't possibly afford to get the bands that should have been in it. Secondly, whoever the bands would have been, by the time the film was released, their songs would be out of date. It was a no-win situation. I wanted to cut as much of that as possible. I thought the rock bands were the biggest bore of all, but then, I'm not a rock fan.

"By the time I got into it, and realized what it was all about, it was too late. There was no question of me walking out. But I knew damned well that I was simply cutting my own throat. It was ridiculous. It was an impossible task. Milton had set up some very interesting and far-sighted notions, but he was unable to fulfill them."

The Monster Club never saw a theatrical release in the United States, but instead was included in a package of films sold directly to local television stations by the film's distributer, ITC Entertainment. However, while still in England, Vincent began a seven-year stint as the host/narrator of the BBC Radio series, *The Price of Fear.*

Vincent ended the year by lending his voice to a feature-length Claymation version of Walt Kelly's *Pogo* comic strip. The film produced as *Pogo for President,* eventually saw limited theatrical release before turn up on video under the title *I Go Pogo.* Also in the cast were Jonathan Winters, Ruth Buzzi, Arnold Stang, Stan Freberg and Jimmy Breslin.

"I am certainly the most unforgettable character I have ever met," declared Vincent. "And I think I am very lucky to have met me."

Chapter Twenty-Seven

The House of Old Fiends
or
Vincent Price Thrills Michael Jackson

Two years later in 1982, Vincent and John Carradine returned once again to England to join old friends Christopher Lee and Peter Cushing in *The House of Long Shadows,* a remake of *Seven Keys to Baldpate*, which was a creaky murder mystery written by Earl Derr Biggers, the creator of fictional detective Charlie Chan. The story, although updated, was neither a horror film nor a comedy. The first and last team-up of all four then-surviving horror masters suffered from a bad script, poor editing, and in Vincent's own words, "They hired a WOMAN editor who thought she was making a horror film and cut out all the comedy!" and a miscast Desi Arnaz, Jr.

When American mystery novelist Kenneth Magee (Desi Arnaz, Jr.) arrives for a book signing tour in England, he makes a bet with his agent Sam Allison (Richard Todd) that he can write a novel in 24 hours. Allison sends him to an old deserted manor house in Wales, where he attempts to use the atmosphere of the old house to help him write the book. As he settles down to write, he is constantly interrupted by the arrival of several strange people, all members of the Grisbane family (Vincent Price, John Carradine, Sheila Keith, Peter Cushing and Christopher Lee) at the house, who involve him in a series of horrible murders. However, when it looks like he is going to be the next victim, his agent shows up and admits he set up the entire thing with a troupe of actors to prevent him from finishing the book and collecting the bet. But in a double twist, the entire story (complete with the fake ending) turns out to be the story Magee set out to write and returns successfully to London to collect on his bet.

"Christopher, Peter, and Vincent were all taken by the screenplay," remembered screenwriter Michael Armstrong. "It was written with them in mind and they found the idea of sending themselves up very appealing. The film was very funny and very literate. The characters wax poetical about philosophy and things like that, so it's definitely not like *Friday the 13th*.

"Surprisingly, the film went without a hitch, which considering how rushed everything was, is a miracle. Everyone found it a great pleasure to work on the film, especially with Vincent around, as he had such a dry wit. For example, during the filming of Chris Lee's death scene, Vincent swept on to the set in his cape, intoning in a rather loud voice, 'I just love to see Chris bleed!'

"As there was a lot of night shooting, all were concerned about keeping warm, but it was Lee who made a point of demanding thermal underwear as a safeguard for keeping pneumonia at bay. Subsequently, a large order for thermal longjohns and related undergarments was sent to Damart, Britain's leading thermalware suppliers.

"We've all worked together before," remarked Vincent. "But never as a foursome. It was sort of a joyful class reunion. This wasn't a horror movie. It was an old fashioned suspense thriller, Today's horror films are just too far out and gruesome for people like us."

"There's nothing subtle about an axe falling onto somebody's face," concurred Christopher Lee. "There is nothing left to the imagination of the audience. However, we had a lot of fun and had a lot of laughs. Cold house, cold weather, every one of us got sick.

"There was one humorous incident that occurred during filming that all but sums up Vincent's wonderful dry wit. It happened while the crew was preparing the set for the next shot. A bat suddenly swooped in through an open window creating a furor amongst British technicians. The bat frantically flew up into the rafters of the old manor house where the film was being made and then lodged itself in the draperies of the high windows for the duration of the shot. When Vincent entered the room to film the next scene, he was quickly cautioned by director Pete Walker that there was a bat loose on the set. Vincent wryly quipped, 'Anyone we know?'"

Although scheduled for a theatrical release in the United States, distribution problems between Cannon films and M.G.M. developed causing the film to be released directed to video. However, it did receive a theatrical release overseas.

While in England, Vincent appeared in a British television version of Gilbert and Sullivan's *Ruddigore*, which Vincent described as "Marvelous! Gilbert and Sullivan were considered trash. Now, we have discovered their enormous musicality and how it is classic trash. It was the greatest challenge of my life working with all-British cast in England, it was really wonderful. I never worked so hard in my life. I was a basket case at the end of it, but it was worth it." The special later aired on PBS and was also released to the home video market a short time afterward.

Also in 1982, foreign film producer Georges Chamchoun announced the production of a new horror film entitled *Altinai* which was scheduled to star Vincent Price, Robert Powell, David Hemmings and Price's *Phibes* co-star Caroline Munro in the title role of Altinai, the Wolfwoman. Makeup was supposed to be created by Tom Savini, and music conducted by Miklos Rozsa. Unfortunately the producer was unable to raise the necessary funds and the project was never made.

A year later, Vincent teamed up with then-popular British comedians Kenny Everitt and Pamela Stephenson to a make of spoof of splatter films aptly titled *Bloodbath at the House of Death*.

Years after a mass murder occurs, in a secluded country house, psychic researchers Lucas Mandeville (Kenny Everett) and Barbara Coyle (Pamela Stephenson) along with a team of experts, return to the house to examine reports of multiple hauntings coming from the house. Unbeknownst to them, the townspeople are members of an alien demon cult run by the Sinister Man (Vincent Price), and soon find themselves being first murdered and then replaced by alien look-a-likes.

"When I signed for *Bloodbath*," recalled Kenny Everitt, "I insisted that my director, Ray Cameron, sign up Hollywood's Vincent Price to play the villain. I had been a Price fan for many years, ever since *House of Wax* and probably before that. To have him in the picture gave the comedy horror flicker a real touch of class. He was marvelous to work with and, of course, a great actor who has brightened up a score of mediocre scripts. I adored him."

"It was a funny idea, but very English," Vincent recalled. "It didn't turn out very good, which was a pity. I really only did it as a great friend of mine wrote it. I just had a cameo in it. It was fun to make, but I didn't really see it."

The film, which cost one million dollars to make, never received a theatrical release in the US but instead was released directly to video.

Vincent followed *Bloodbath* by narrating Michael Jackson's popular album and video *Thriller*. "Quincy Jones, who is a musical genius, called me up," declared Vincent, "and asked 'Would you like to do this song with Michael Jackson?' I'd known Michael since he was a little kid when he appeared with his brothers on the *Hollywood Squares*. I think he's an extraordinary talent. Quincy asked if I would like to do this 'rap' on the record. I said, 'What is this rap?' He said 'it's sort of a poem that comes in the middle of the song.' So I went down to the recording studio and did it."

"Afterwards, they sent me a tape of this song *Thriller*. One night, I played it for the head of one of the movie studios, who came to my house for dinner. After he heard it, he said 'Well, Vincent, you finally hit the bottom! I mean, being popular in films, on television, going around lecturing at colleges, that's all fine. But doing a rock video? You have hit bottom now!' Later, as it sold its 20 millionth album, people began to change their tune. I didn't do it for the money, because I didn't have a percentage of it. It was just fun to do. It was a wonderful piece of music, and it was great fun reading the poetry that had been written for me. You know, to be identified with the most popular record ever made is not just chopped liver! It had really done me a lot of good, because it gave me a new audience."

In the fall of 1985, Vincent returned to television as Vincent Van Ghoul, the animated host of *The Thirteen Ghosts of Scooby-Doo.* As Van Ghoul, Vincent joined Scooby, Shaggy, Daphne, and Scrappy-Doo in trying to recapture the thirteen ghosts that had been accidentally released from a sealed chest. This Saturday morning cartoon series was released to celebrate the canine detective's sixteenth year on television.

Vincent also spent several years hosting the PBS series *Mystery*, a role he subsequently passed on to his *Theater of Blood* daughter, Diana Rigg.

In 1986, Vincent joined the cast of a low-budget horror anthology film called *From a Whisper to a Scream*, as the town librarian who relates four horror tales to a reporter played by Susan Tyrell. The film ran out of money and production was halted for months before it was finally completed. It then had a limited theatrical release in 1987 under the new title *The Offspring* before being quickly released to home video.

After murderess Katherine White (Martine Bestwicke) is executed in prison, reporter Beth Chandler (Susan Tyrell) pays a visit to White's uncle Julian White (Vincent Price), the librarian at the local Oldfield library. He tries to convince her that his niece had fallen victim to the curse of the town by relating the following four tales of horror that have been committed by the inhabitants over the years.

A man murders his sister and then spends the night having an incestuous relationship with her corpse, causing the birth of a mutant monster nine months later. This becomes the basis of the title The Offspring.

An injured man is rescued by a centuries-old ex-slave-turned-hermit who restores him to good health. The man wanting the secret of the hermit's eternal life plots to steal the secret, but the hermit gets the upper hand and condemns him to an eternal life of torment.

A small town girl falls for a glass eater from a traveling sideshow, but the sideshow owner is a voodoo priestess who refuses to let him go off with her so she revokes his glass-eating powers which causes all of the glass he has eaten over the years to reappear through his skin. The girl soon takes his place as a human pincushion.

Finally, union soldiers are captured by the children of rebel soldiers who enact their revenge for the torment the union soldiers did to their parents. In the end, the reporter also falls victim to the evil of the town and kills the librarian before continuing on her way.

"Susan Tyrell and I were the link between four separate stories," related Vincent, "incidents that have taken place in this Southern town, in the past. I played the librarian who kept records of the town's terrible history, the records being written in blood on pages made from human skin!"

"I truly believe in this kind of low-budget filmmaking. There is something about young people attempting something of quality on a low budget. I find that knowing a movie cost $24 million, going to the theater and seeing none of it on the screen is very disturbing. I'm convinced that you can get good production values and do imaginative things on a limited budget.

"And it doesn't bother me that they had to stop production on this film halfway through because they ran out of money. I've worked on a number of productions that were plagued with money problems. As long as my check is good, that's all I care about."

At this point in his life he could have retired, but his wife Coral's fears of running out of money made him push onward. It wasn't until after her death that he discovered the millions of dollars she had back home in British banks that he realized he could have indeed retired and not have had to work as much as he did.

The film was the brainchild of director Jeff Burr who, along with fellow filmmaker Darin Scott (who later went on to produce *Tales From the Hood* and *Menace II Society*), persuaded the local businessmen of Dalton, Georgia (the town where Burr grew up) to buy shares in his movie instead of their usual practice of investing in real estate. Burr managed to raise a hefty quarter of a million dollars, and then set about to find a cast he could afford. "We went to Vincent before we started shooting and he liked the script, but he said 'I don't know, I'm kinda busy. Show me some stuff when it's done,'" Burr recalled.

"So then we went back to him and showed him one episode of the film and he liked it well enough to do it. We only had him for two days. I wish we could have done more with him, quite honestly, but it was at a point at his life where he was not in particularly great health.

"He was a great guy to work with. He had no reason to listen to me. He knew he was the biggest star there and he could have easily run roughshod over me. But he was an incredible gentleman and it was a great thrill just to have Vincent Price listen to my direction.

"I'm sure it was very similar to the Boris Karloff thing in *The Sorcerers*, where you just feel so happy that he's there. Vincent was getting on in years, but giving it his all. He never stopped talking from the time we started shooting until we wrapped two days later."

During the short time he worked on the film, an interesting incident occurred that reunited Vincent with old friend Roger Corman, as Jeff Burr fondly recalled. "I had worked for Roger Corman in 1982 as an intern in his advertising department, so I called up Roger and asked his advice. We were shooting on Roger's stage in Venice, California. I asked him to come down and so there was this great reunion. My only regret is that I didn't get a picture taken. Roger looked at Vincent Price sitting in a chair with a glass of wine in this Gothic library set. He said 'Jeff, I have a feeling I've directed this movie before.'"

Chapter Twenty-Eight

Vincent Sings Again
or
Vincent, the Juvenile

Vincent's next film was a masterpiece of casting. He was chosen to provide the voice of the evil Professor Ratigan in the animated Disney film, *The Adventures of the Great Mouse Detective.*"

When mouse toymaker Flaversham (voiced by Alan Young, star of TV's *Mr Ed*) is kidnapped by bat Fidget (Candy Candido), daughter Olivia (Susanne Pollatschek) goes off to find mouse detective Basil (Barrie Ingham), in the hopes of getting him to help her find her father.

Along the way she meets Dawson (Val Bettin), who helps the child find Basil and later joins them on the trail of her father, who has been kidnapped by the evil Ratigan (Vincent Price), who plans to use the toymaker's skill to create a clockwork version of their queen, with which he plans to takeover the government after removing the real queen from the throne.

"For the longest time, we didn't even know what the character was going to look like," recalled animators Mark Henn and Glen Keane. "Early concepts depicted him as being thin, weasely and ratlike, which, design-wise, were too similar to Basil. We found the voice for Professor Ratigan while watching the 1950 movie *Champagne for Caesar*. We had originally decided to view the film since it starred Ronald Colman, and we were considering his voice as a possible model for Ratigan's. Vincent Price played one of those bigger-than-life cads, and, as soon as he came on, we all said, 'That's our guy.'""

"Ratigan is the ultimate villain!" stated Vincent. "I played it by exaggerating because it was an exaggerated character. It needed humor and humanity to make the film work, and I think I gave it just that."

The film, which gave Vincent his last opportunity to sing on film, also featured Basil Rathbone as the voice of Sherlock Holmes despite the fact that he died in 1967. His voice was borrowed from a recording made prior to his death.

Around the same time he played host as well as guest star in a made-for-video program featuring four "spooky" stories entitled *Escapes*. Also released that year was a syndicated made-for-TV special called *Dracula, the Untold Story*, in which Vincent played host and narrator to old movie trailers and travel footage of Dracula's castle in Romania. The one hour special failed to sell and was released directly to video, complete with blank spots where the commercials would have gone.

In 1987, Vincent teamed up with Bette Davis (the first time since 1939), Lillian Gish, and Ann Sothern in the well-received *The Whales of August* in which he played a white Russian with a creaky accent.

The story of two sisters, Sarah Webber (Lillian Gish) and Libby Strong (Bette Davis) who, after growing up in the same house, return years later during the twilight of their lives to once again live out their remaining years together while being visited on occasion by aging White Russian Mr. Maranov (Vincent Price), rich widow Tisha Doughty (Ann Sothern) and handyman Joshua Brackett (Harry Carey, Jr.).

"It was a very dear story about nothing," recalled Vincent. "I played a white Russian, a mysterious man who was given a handful of jewels by his mother as a young man. That's his legacy. He's down to his last jewel. What he does with his life is live with people. He attaches himself to a family or to a woman. He's a wonderful listener and a great storyteller. He moves from one place to another and the people support him. He's not a bad man. He doesn't rob them. That's simply how he exists.

"I was 76 when we made it and I was the juvenile. It was a great thrill working with those ladies. First of all, looking at their faces is an extraordinary experience. I met Lillian over 50 years ago and she was beautiful then and she still was. But we'd never worked together before. I had always been a fan of Lillian. I had worshipped her as a movie actress. When I was in college at Yale, I had saved enough money to come to New York to see her make her stage debut. When she walked out on the stage, the audience just fell apart. One of the greatest performances that will ever be seen on the screen is Lillian's performance in *The Whales of August.* I did *Elizabeth and Essex* with Bette. I'd known her for quite a while and I thought, 'Thank God, we get along.' It's much better to get along with the leading lady than not to. But she was wonderful to work with.

"We filmed the picture on Cliff Island off the coast of Maine and there was no place to meet. I've been on locations all over the world. There's usually a bar, a dance hall, a movie theater. You just hoped to God the crew would ask you to dinner. They were on another much more comfortable island. But you had to get there by boat and the ladies couldn't do that.

"When I told my wife Coral Browne that I was going to do the film with an elderly cast for Alive Productions, she quipped: "May I suggest they change the name to Just Barely Alive Productions.""

"Vincent pulled off the role beautifully," director Lindsay Anderson proudly remarked. "He was grateful to have a real role and not go out as a comic ghoul."

The film had a limited theatrical release and was quickly rushed out to video, and probably the reason why it didn't fare well in the theater can best be summed up by its star Bette Davis: "It was a delicate script, but I wondered if anyone was interested in these old dames."

Vincent then followed the film by hosting a video tape horror quiz, *Creepy Classics,* sold through Hallmark Card shops at Halloween.

Vincent returned in 1988 with a featured role in the action horror comedy flop, *Dead Heat.* After a shootout with two reanimated bank robbers, police officers Roger Mortis (Treat Williams) and Doug Bigelow (Joe Piscopo) trail the corpses to a company once owned by the recently deceased Arthur P. Loudermilk (Vincent Price), where Mortis is accidentally killed.

Using a machine created by Loudermilk's company, Mortis is returned to life, but he has only a few hours before his body falls apart to find the truth behind the zombie killers.

He eventually learns that Loudermilk is still alive and is planning to sell his reanimation process to his rich business friends in return for half their fortunes. Mortis and the now-reanimated Bigelow put an end to Loudermilk's plans as well as the machine, his assistant Dr. McNab (Darren McGavin, TV's *Kolchak, the Night Stalker*), and several zombies before going off together into the unknown.

"I thought it was a very cute script," Vincent explained. "I played the fellow who sponsors the machine and tries to get his rich friends to go on into eternal life. It was the kind of small part that pays off. It was well written, a little humor, preposterous in the right way, and adds to the plot. It wasn't just a familiar face walking by, which bores the shit out of me."

And while his film roles became few and far between, and his need to keep active and unfounded belief he needed the money, he continued to make television appearances and numerous commercials.

"I love doing commercials, it's a challenge, and to sell somebody on something in thirty seconds is so exciting. I knew a lot of people at the beginning of their acting careers who thought doing commercials were selling themselves down the drain. I don't think that is true anymore. I think they feel that they have something to do, something to sell. I tried to be sort of selective with my commercials."

Vincent later joined friend actor-director Dennis Hopper and actress Jodie Foster for the 1989 crime thriller *Backtrack*. Unfortunately, the film company that produced the film went bankrupt causing the film to get a direct-to-video release a year later.

When her car breaks down near an oil refinery, artist Anne Benson (Jodie Foster) goes off to find help, but stumbles upon mobster Leo Carelli (Joe Pesci) and his goons carrying out an execution. With the mobsters hot on her heels, Benson makes it back up to the highway and makes it to the nearest police station where she meets with Federal agent Pauling (Fred Ward), who is assigned to the case. But when she spots mob lawyer John Luponi (Dean Stockwell) at the police station, who was present at the execution, she flees for her life.

Meanwhile Carelli, fearing the displeasure of mob boss Mr. Avoca (Vincent Price), send his goons to rub her out but only manage to kill her boyfriend Bob (Charlie Sheen) instead.

After the failed hit, Avoca sends professional hitman Milo (Dennis Hopper) after her. Milo, who is also Avoca's son, becomes obsessed with Benson who, rather than kill her, professes his love and kidnaps her instead, turning his back on his profession and family. Benson eventually falls for him and together they set out to turn the tables on Carelli and the mob before running away together to raise sheep in New Zealand.

"One of the overriding reasons for my not doing many horror films is that most of the scripts I have received are overly violent and contain a lot of unnecessary gore," declared Vincent. "I hate gore-for-gore's-sake kind of films. But it is not like I'm totally against gory and violent films. Lord knows I've been shot, stabbed; I've died a million different ways over the years. But a film must have a good storyline and an overall quality to go along with these elements and you don't see much of that in many of today's horror films."

Despite his dislike for modern gore films, Vincent agreed to appear as the on-screen host and narrator for British film producer Dick Randall's gore-fest theatrical documentary entitled *Don't Scream: It's Only a Movie!* It incorporated footage from his previously-produced horror films (*Don't Open Till Christmas Slaughter High*, etc.) and dozens of public domain horror features. The film never had a theatrical or video release in the United States. After Randall died in 1996, the film surfaced as a home video release from a Japanese video company (in English with Japanese subtitles).

Chapter Twenty-Nine

Vincent's Final Creation

or

Vincent, the Immortal

In 1990 Vincent was reunited with director Tim Burton (Vincent had narrated Burton's five-minute animated tribute to the horror star apply entitled *Vincent* years earlier) as the creator-inventor of title character *Edward Scissorhands*. The featured cameo was a fitting swan song to Vincent's long theatrical film career.

The story of a strange mechanical boy named Edward (Johnny Depp), created by The Inventor (Vincent Price of whom David Kehr of *The Chicago Tribune* describes as "incredibly ancient, fragile and as Burton photographs him, beautiful") and discovered in an ancient castle by Avon Lady Peg (Dianne Wiest) who, believing him to be lonely, takes him home with her. There, the boy with the strange hands (made of several different types of scissor blades) tells how his inventor father died before he was able to give him real hands.

He soon becomes the toast of the town, but when he falls for Peg's daughter Kim (Winona Rider), her boyfriend Jim (Anthony Michael Hall) becomes jealous and arranges for him to be arrested for a crime he didn't commit. Soon, the townspeople turn against him, forcing him to retreat back to the castle where he was found.

"I have always thought that Frankenstein was really one of the great, puritanical gothic novels," Vincent remarked. "It's this great moral tale: don't fool around with God's work. This film, too, has that. This creature Edward Scissorhands has been created by the old man out of love. And love can be frustrating when it's not complete.

"One of the things I was dying to know when the picture was released was if people will realize (because it all happens very quickly) that when Edward was created, he came out of a cookie cutter. My character, the inventor, picks up a heart-shaped cookie and looks at it and then looks at the machine, and he thinks if I could put that heart into him....

"I thought it was very lucky that we had Johnny Depp. In all my scenes with him, he was so into it, and yet he had this smile on his face because he knew who this boy with the extraordinary hands was.

"There was wonderful cartoon madness in Burton's work, a kind of madness that doesn't exist anymore in film." Vincent never lived long enough to see Burton's creative genius flourish to even higher levels.

Later that year he provided the voice of Edgar Allan Poe in a parody of the poem *The Raven* in an episode of *Steven Spielberg's Tiny Toon Adventures*, and in October 1990 he was given a Lifetime Achievement award by *The Horror Hall of Fame.* Vincent, who was too ill to attend the televised ceremony, was presented the award on film by long-time friend actor Roddy McDowall.

In 1991, as Vincent approached his 80th birthday, his wife Coral Browne, who had been suffering for the past year from breast cancer worsened and on May 29, 1991, a scant two days after his birthday, she died two months shy of her 78th birthday.

Despite his delicate health (he was recovering from a broken hip, as well as suffering from Parkinson's Disease) and the death of his wife, Vincent appeared to a standing ovation on the *2nd Horror Hall of Fame* special in October 1991 to present the award for Best Horror Film of the Year.

In the Spring of 1992, Vincent rejoined Dennis Hopper in the Turner Network Cable film *The Heart of Justice,* which subsequently aired on February 20, 1993. Reporter David Leader (Eric Stoltz) is assigned to investigate the shooting death of Austin Blair (Dennis Hopper) and the subsequent suicide of his attacker Elliot Burgess (Dermot Mulroney). However there is more to the story than he first thought. At first he believes that the mentally unstable Burgess was suffering from paranoid delusions that Blair had been spying on him and his rich socialite family in order to use their lives as the topic of his latest book.

However, with the help of his sister Emma (Jennifer Connelly), he soon learns that Blair had indeed been spying on them and had included the family's secrets in the book (Emma was having an incestuous affair with her brother, as well as having an affair with Blair). Leader eventually falls in love with Emma and agrees to kill the story and run away with her to Seattle. However, after he destroys all of his evidence and quits his job, he is abandoned by Emma who got everything she wanted: to get revenge on Blair who used their relationship as the focus of his book, to be rid of her unstable brother and the elimination of the reporter who could have exposed all of the sordid details of her secret life.

Vincent appeared briefly at the beginning of the film as Blair's friend, Reggie Shaw, who has lunch with him prior to his murder and sometime later reappears to chat with Leader about Blair. Despite the limited screen time, Vincent gave his best and the most natural performance in the film.

Knowing his time on Earth was coming to an end, Vincent reflected on what was to come. "I have no sort of fear of the ending of life because I think it must be a beginning too. I don't know where, or what or why. I am a religious person but I am not going to sit up on a cloud playing a harp. I don't believe that. But I do believe it is a beginning. I don't think that life can be useless and just finished. I approach life as though it were a challenge. I know too many people in my profession who are perfectly content with their position in life, I'm not. I think if I have one regret, it was that I didn't stay in the theater a little longer than I did. But then I was brought up in movies and I loved movies as an audience. I wanted to be in movies, but then the little bit that I was in movies at the beginning of my career, I really knew that I had to always be in the theater, too."

In the Fall of 1992, due to his failing health, Vincent finally retired from show business and on Monday October 25, 1993, Vincent Leonard Price, Jr. died at the age of 82. The reported cause of death was lung cancer complicated by Parkinson's Disease. He was later cremated and his ashes scattered over the Pacific Ocean.

His second wife, Mary Grant, passed away on March 2, 2002 at the age of 85.

There is an interesting post-script to Vincent's long career, in that a Vincent Price film long thought never to see light of day finally saw release nearly two years after Vincent's death.

The film, which began in 1976 under the title *The Thief and the Cobbler*, was released to the theaters at the end of August 1995, under the title *Arabian Knight*.

This animated feature was conceived by *Who Framed Roger Rabbit* creator Richard Williams in the early 1970's. The story deals with a beautiful princess, a shy young cobbler, and an incompetent thief who brave great danger to recover three magic golden balls that once protected their city, only to have been stolen by the King's evil advisor Zigzag (played by Vincent Price). The production suffered numerous setbacks including the loss of half of its recorded soundtrack and a constant lack of production funds. The film was scheduled for release in July of 1992 by Warner Brothers, but the film was not completed on time, so Warners dropped their option on the film. The film was taken over by the Completion Bond Company, who ordered the creation of fifteen more minutes of footage to be added to the already-completed film as the film was lacking sufficient story content. The film was then set for a 1993 release, only subsequently to be sold to Miramax films for a summer 1995 release. The film, which had been compared to Disney's *Aladdin*, lasted only a short time in the theaters and disappeared. Of all the actors associated with the original version of the project, only Vincent's voice remained intact. It was as if Vincent returned from the dead, to make one final appearance.

Vincent once said, "I'll go on acting until I die. They will have to bury me before I retire, and even then, my tombstone will read, 'I'll be back.'" And he was right, he did come back.

Vincent once summed up the difference between the Horror films of today with the classics of yesteryear by stating that "one of the big mistakes in the films they make today is that they try to bring the old horror films up to date by doing the most ridiculous thing, by making them dirty! It's so silly because they don't need that. They don't need violence superimposed on them. They are frightening in their own mood.

"Some of them are really terrifying, but I don't think they will last because they don't have that kind of humor, that kind of gentleness about them which makes a fairy tale. The difference between a fairy tale and a horror tale is:

MAGIC!"

The Phibes Report

During the course of my research for this book, I came across a rarity in the history of the *Dr. Phibes* films, an unused October 1972 draft of *Dr. Phibes Rises Again* written by James Whiton and William Goldstein, the writing team who wrote the first film.

Director Robert Fuest based his script for *Dr. Phibes Rises Again* on the characters created by Whiton and Goldstein, but aside from a few minor ideas he borrowed from them, he wrote a completely different version than what was uncovered in the script. So, here now for the first time is the story of *Dr. Phibes Rises Again* by James Whiton and William Goldstein.

Dr. Phibes Rises Again

Years after lying embalmed next to his wife, Victoria, Anton Phibes is once again returned to the land of the living when the moon and the planets come into alignment, thus activating the elaborate mechanism of his crypt. After dusting off the clockwork musicians which have stood guard over the crypt, Phibes returns to the surface and his mansion in Mauldine Square. He then drives to the St. Daffodil Home for the Criminally Insane to rescue the now acid-scarred Vulnavia from her years of imprisonment.

Returning with her to his seemingly abandoned estate in the English countryside, he performs miraculous reconstructive surgery and restores Vulnavia to her former beauty. Phibes and Vulnavia then begin the process of restoring the estate to its former glory in preparation for the return of Lady Phibes. This includes the revival of the all-new 17-piece Dr. Phibes Mechanical Marching Minstrels, a more advanced and far more mobile version of his clockwork minstrels.

At the same time, Emil Salveus and his fiancée Daphne are visited by Dr. Steuben, a noted psychic. Salveus gives Steuben a small golden key, which he claims is the key to his salvation. Steuben then tells him of the house in Mauldine Square and of the Phibes crypt beneath it. Using this information, Salveus drives to the house and descends (and armed with a deadly silver dart gun) via the organ into the crypt, only to find his prey, Phibes missing.

Suddenly, he is attacked by the clockwork musical guardians. After a short battle, he dispatches them with the dart gun and then places one of them in the crypt next to Victoria. Taking a gold ring from off his finger, a ring embossed with a pentagram and the Greek letter Psi, he places it in the mechanical man's hands.

Several hours later, Salveus arrives with the body of Victoria Phibes in a large gas-filled glass cylinder at the Institute of Psychic Phenomena. Joining Salveus at the Institute are Sir Judah Ibo Adibo, the cultural attaché to the Abyssinian Embassy, Charles Carruthers, an apothecary, Walton Wren, the Arch Vicar of Dulwich, Lady Peune, a rich invalid and society matron, and Colonel DeLancey Trenchard, a retired army man and military historian, who is also the Institute's managing director. Using Victoria's body as a bridge to the other side, they hold a séance in which they manage to call up the devil, but only for a short while.

Enthused by their result, each of the members clamor to use Victoria to further their own needs in psychic research. While Salveus goes off to hatch his revenge scheme on Phibes, he leaves Victoria in the hands of Lady Peune, who plans to use Lady Phibes to reach the long deceased Lord Herbert Peune in the spirit world.

With the estate in readiness, Phibes returns to the crypt to retrieve his beloved wife, only to find her body missing and his mechanical men destroyed. Finding the ring Salveus left behind in the crypt, Phibes knows what has happened and together with Vulnavia goes off to seek his revenge against those who have stolen his wife.

Traveling to the Institute, Phibes stumbles upon Colonel Trenchard, dressed as a Carthaninian soldier, gluing toothpicks together in the shape of a fort. Phibes sneaks up behind him and applies a sleeper-hold to the unsuspecting man. Then picking up one of Trenchard's many gluepots, he begins to pour the sticky stuff over the head of the motionless man. After empting several pots of glue, Vulnavia wheels in a large fan and turns it on the now totally covered body of Colonel Trenchard. Once the glue has hardened, Phibes picks up a large mace from among Trenchard's vast weapon collection and strikes Trenchard with it, causing his body to shatter into a thousand pieces, just as if he were a plaster statute. Phibes then picks up the Institute's membership list and gleefully leaves with Vulnavia.

Returning to his estate, Phibes writes the names of the six remaining members of the Institute on pingpong balls and intermixes them with the others contained in a bingo calling machine. He then proceeds to systematically pick pingpong balls until the name of one of the six members is chosen, namely Charles Carruthers.

Meanwhile, Salveus arranges to have an embalming and tanning apparatus (complete with a 500 gallon tank of acid) installed in his townhouse cellar, under the pretext of using it to properly mount several big game trophies.

Having selected his next victim, Phibes travels to Carruthers' lavish home with a large carboy filled with hundreds of black leeches. Finding his way into Carruthers' cellar, he arrives just as Carruthers prepares to take a bath. Locating the proper water tank, Vulnavia pours what appears to be bathing salts into the tank. As Carruthers soaks in the tub, purplish vapors fill the room causing him to fall fast asleep. Phibes then empties the leeches into the water supply and as the water continues to fill the tub, the leeches are drawn through the pipes and onto the unconscious Carruthers. A short time later, Phibes enters the bathroom, and views with delight the leech-covered body as he turns off the faucet. Tossing the pingpong ball with Carruthers' name on it into the tub, he returns to his estate to choose a new victim.

Sergeant Schenley (Inspector Trout's former partner) and Inspector Witherspoon are called into investigate when Carruthers' housekeeper reports the murder to the police. Alerted to this bizarre death and of the death of Colonel Trenchard, former Detective Inspector Trout pays a visit to his old boss Superintendant Crow on the belief that Phibes has returned from the grave.

Meanwhile Phibes, having selected Sir Mastic Mateland, a symphony conductor, as his next victim, journeys to the Mateland home and, finding Mateland seated at his dinner table, once again performs his infamous sleeper-hold. Vulnavia then wheels in a large vat of oversized lobsters and, while pouring a tureen of melted butter over the now semi-conscious Mateland, Vulnavia bastes him with lemon slices. Phibes then removes a large pair of tongs from his robes and proceeds to hand the large crustaceans to a now-gloved Vulnavia, who places them in Mateland's lap. While Phibes and Vulnavia sit down to dine, the lobsters use their great claws to pinch the clothes and the flesh from Mateland's body. Upon their completion of both their and the lobster's dinner, Phibes pops the pingpong ball into Mateland's mouth before returning to his estate.

Believing Phibes may have returned, Trout is re-teamed with Sgt. Schenley. Trout and Schenley pay a visit to the asylum in the hopes of getting Vulnavia to help them in their search for Phibes, only to find she was removed from their care a week earlier by a distinguished gentleman, namely Phibes.

After several days in Lady Peune's care, Victoria is visited by Arch Vicar Wren. Disappointed that she was unable to reach her late husband, she reluctantly turns the glass-encased woman over to the vicar, who claims he wants to use her to reach the spirit of Sir Thomas More. While Wren transports Victoria to his parish, Salveus and Daphne rehearse his planned confrontation with Phibes.

Believing the pingpong balls are Phibes' new calling cards, Trout decides he'd better pay a visit to the remaining members of the Institute. Choosing the most vulnerable, Lady Peune, Trout and his men set off on their way, completely unaware that Phibes at that moment is paying a visit to Lady Peune.

Phibes, dressed as the spirit of her late husband, distracts the old woman long enough for Vulnavia to enter with two large cylinders containing helium. Phibes then straps a harness to the back of Lady Peune's wicker wheelchair. Opening the valves, the helium is released, filling a large balloon hidden in the garden foliage. Lady Peune, believing she is going to join with her husband's spirit, is completely unaware that Phibes has tied her to the chair with a white weblike material. Opening the overhead windows, Phibes and Vulnavia watch as the large aerialist balloon, the wicker chair and its occupant slowly sail upwards towards the sky, just as Trout and his men arrive at the house. As Lady Peune sails to her death, Phibes deposits the pingpong ball in the house before leaving with Vulnavia.

Miles away, Arch Vicar Wren, dressed in Arch Bishop's robes, prepares to call forth the spirit of Sir Thomas More in the hopes of using his knowledge to become the Arch Bishop of England. At the same time, the ancient half-witted caretaker, Proby, is preparing to vacuum the chapel with a very old and very large industrial-type vacuum cleaner. Both however are interrupted by the arrival of Trout. Unable to convince the Vicar he is in danger, Trout leaves policemen posted outside the chapel and goes off to warn the other members of the Institute.

Later that night, after Proby has finished his work and returned to his room, Wren bolts his door, locking the old man inside, and then proceeds to perform a black mass in the hopes of calling up the devil to do his bidding. During the ceremony a skeleton dancer appears, followed by a black-cloaked figure. Wren, shocked by these apparitions, collapses before the altar. Then, from out of the darkness, the cloaked figure (who in reality is Phibes) pushes the vaccum cleaner from its resting place to the altar. Vulnavia, having removed her skeleton costume, assists him with the huge machine. Phibes forces open the Vicar's mouth and then shoves the vacuum hose deep inside his mouth. Turning the machine on full power, the vacuum sucks out the Vicar's internal organs as well as everything else.

Phibes, having recovered his wife, returns with her to his estate and attempts to revitalize her, only to find that her heart has been surgically removed. Enraged, Phibes goes on a mad search for the list of remaining members. Since Salveus has no listed address, he settles for the other remaining member, Sir Judah Ibo Adibo.

Adibo, who is under police protection, is unaware of the figure who stands on the rooftop directly across the street from his Embassy apartment. Phibes, dressed as Robin Hood, sounds a hunting horn which sends the police below off in a different direction. With the police distracted, Phibes fires a heavy iron arrow through Adibo's window. Attached to the arrow is a long cord. While Abido sleeps undisturbed, Phibes, attached to a harness and carrying a wicker basket, hurtles down the cord and in through the window. Phibes then empties the contents of the basket into the room and then with the help of Vulnavia and a hand winch returns to the opposite rooftop and safety.

Back at his estate, Phibes ponders the last remaining name on the list, Emil Salveus. Using the oversized scoreboard, with which Vulnavia has been dancing out her messages to him (via an oversized typewriter keyboard located on the ballroom floor), Phibes rearranges the letters in the name and finds they now spell out *Lem Vesalius*, the son of Dr. Vesalius, his old enemy and chief surgeon who he believes murdered his wife Victoria.

Back at the vicarge, the old caretaker Proby manages to free himself from his room only to find the church decorated with Satanic artifacts and the Vicar propped up before the altar. His ears and nostrils sealed with small corks and a surgical zipper sewn over his mouth, Proby opens the zipper and unknowingly lets the air out. The sudden blast of air frightens the old man away. Hours later the police discover the remains of Wren who, with his insides now inside the vacuum cleaner and all the air released from his body, he resembles an empty bag of skin. Fearing for Adibo's life, Trout returns to the Embassy, only to find him lying in bed like a limp rag doll covered with dozens of deadly cobras.

Meanwhile at Emil Salveus' (alias Lem Vesalius) townhouse, Daphne accidentally stumbles upon the box containing the well-preserved heart of Victoria Phibes. Later that day, she confronts her fiancé with the news of the heart and demands to know just what he is up to. He then tells her of his first encounter with Phibes, how he was made the pawn in a game between his father and Phibes, how Phibes implanted the golden key above his heart and how his father rescued him at the last minute from an acid bath. But the toll was too much for the old man, as he died a year later. Believing himself cursed, the Vesalius, bearing an ugly red scar (caused by the surgery), searched the world of the occult in the hopes of removing the Phibes curse from his life forever.

Daphne, realizing that Vesalius is quite mad, threatens to leave him. Vesalius, whose mind has snapped, manipulates the mechanical chessboard on his desk. As he does, a corresponding floor tile is activated and in moments Daphne is sent on her way to the acid bath in the cellar.

A short time later, Phibes arrives at the townhouse where he confronts Vesalius. Having tied the box containing Victoria's heart to a small ceramic elephant, Vesalius positions it in the center of the floor. He then informs Phibes of the box's contents and then watches as Phibes tries to retrieve it without falling through one of the many trap doors to certain death below.

As Vesalius is about to activate another trap door, he is startled by the appearance of Daphne. She holds her arms out to hold him, but he unwittingly backs away from her and onto the tile floor and through the trap door opened by Daphne, who then removes her false face to reveal Vulnavia underneath.

Returning to his estate, Phibes prepares to return Victoria's heart to her chest, but upon opening the box, he finds not the heart but a note from Daphne to Vesalius informing him she placed the heart in the custody of the police as she couldn't bear the thought of him with another woman, even a dead one.

Furious, Phibes throws the empty box across the room and then searches for a folder in a wall cabinet. Moments later, Inspector Trout receives a telephone call from Phibes. Trout challenges Phibes to meet him at high noon at Wembley Stadium, if he wishes to reclaim his wife's heart.

As noon approaches, Trout and his men swarm over the stadium. They don't intend to let Phibes escape this time. When noon arrives, Phibes' car pulls up outside and Phibes marches through the corridor and out onto the playing field, where Trout is standing with the heart. As Phibes comes within a few feet of his enemy Trout taunts him, but Phibes rants about being immortal and never making mistakes. Angered, Trout grabs Phibes by the throat and violently shakes him about, only to have him come apart in his hands. This is not Phibes, but one of his clockwork marvels outfitted with a recording device. As the police swarm onto the field to join Trout, the real Phibes, dressed as a policeman, joins them and in the confusion easily makes off with the box containing the heart of his beloved.

Phibes and Vulnavia race back to the house as fast as they can, as the box containing the heart has developed a small leak and the preserving fluid is slowing draining out. With the police hot on their trail, Phibes returns to his operating room to restore the heart while Vulnavia activates the Marching Minstrals. As the police arrive at the house, the minstrels march out of the house and prepare for an attack.

Inspector Crow leads the attack against the mechanical men. As the police are batted about and struck by the minstrel's musical instruments, Trout and Schenley enter the mansion but are nearly hit by an arrow fired from Vulnavia's bow. She then calls out the remaining minstrels to continue the attack.

Phibes having restored the heart to his wife, quickly attaches a variety of electro-shock devices to his wife's body and in a few minutes, after years of lifelessness, Victoria Phibes returns to life and greets her beloved husband. As the police attempt to break down the door, Phibes disconnects his wife from the machine and as the spark of life drains from her body, he wheels her out into a dark corridor.

Having disposed of the minstrels, the police move towards Vulnavia, who takes her own life with a jeweled dagger while falling across Phibes' organ which sounds a fatal chord.

Phibes, having sealed himself and his wife inside a secret cellar room, opens a door to a large walk-in freezer. Setting the controls to absolute zero, he wheels his wife into the freezer and then shuts the door behind them. Setting his wife in one of a pair of elaborate lounge chairs, Phibes settles into the other and then, taking Victoria's hand in his, he awaits what is to come. While upstairs, the police ponder the complete disappearance of Phibes. On the scoreboard is a final message from Phibes: KEEP ON TRUCKIN'!

So ended what would have been the second chapter in the Phibes saga.

Despite the rejection of the script, writers Whiton and Goldstein did not give up in the hopes of writing a third *Phibes* film as Executive Producer Samuel Z. Arkoff explains: "The original writers wrote a script for a third Phibes film but we didn't pay for the writing. Since the second one didn't do that well, we turned down the third one. I'm not saying we lost money, we made a little, but what was a novelty with the first one was no longer really a novelty with the second one. It wasn't different enough in a sense."

The story doesn't end there. In 1982 Laurel Entertainment announced the production of a new *Dr. Phibes* film. In the hopes of raising capital and interest in the film rights, they circulated a ten page outline of the plot of the new film.

The tale takes place fifty years after the first film (it completely disregards the second film). Phibes arrives in New York harbor at the helm of the HMS Victoria Regina and with him a crew of his clockwork robots. Once safely docked, Vulnavia and a complement of clockwork sailors unload the glass cylinder containing the body of Victoria Phibes.

Phibes believes that by coming to America he will get a new start on life. He plans to revive his dead wife and hopefully she will bear him a son.

However, his plans would soon fall victim to the inhabitants of the Wormwood Institute, a haven for eccentric geniuses presided over by the ancient Hector Wormwood, who would give anything to live forever. It is one of these geniuses who determines through his massive calculations that Phibes is arriving in New York.

Wormwood and the others conspire to find Phibes and learn the secrets of life and death. Finding the yacht, they board the vessel in search of Phibes, but find only the cylinder containing Victoria, as Phibes and Vulnavia have gone off to find suitable penthouse accommodations.

Among the intruders is a young 12-year-old genius named Lester who, upon seeing the gas-shrouded cylinder, turns off the preserving gas. As the vapors dissipate, the perfectly-preserved body of Victoria becomes visible. Wormwood, believing the gas will restore his youth, cracks open the case, but in doing so the polluted New York air enters the cylinder and in seconds Victoria is reduced to a prune-like mummy.

Returning to the yacht hours later, Phibes swears revenge on the members of the Institute. His method is love; since they destroyed the only thing he loved, he will destroy them with the only thing they love. For example, a woman member who loves horses will be surgically altered to look like one. An Oriental man who loves chocolates will be turned into an Oriental chocolate statue. The killings will continue until only Wormwood will be left and he will be destroyed with lobsters.

Besides killing off the geniuses, Phibes also must obtain the vast quantities of exotic human hormones and glandular extracts to rehydrate his wife before he can revive her.

This film of course was never made, however two years later in 1984 Laurel Entertainment announced the production of a new *Dr. Phibes* film, this time entitled *Phibes Resurrected* (the previous one did not have an official title). The script was to be written by James Whiton and William Goldstein, the original writing team of the *Phibes* series.

Interestingly, the script actually has two titles, the second is entitled *Phibes Resurrectus: the Ultimate Love Story.* What makes it interesting is that when they offered AIP the second *Phibes* script it had three different titles on it: *Dr. Phibes Rises Again, The Bride of Dr. Phibes,* and *Phibes Ressurectus.* What even makes it more interesting is that this script that Laurel was promoting in 1984, as a new *Phibes* story is the same script Whiton and Goldstein submitted to AIP in 1971 with about fifteen to twenty percent new or altered material.

The major differences are in the settings and in one of the deaths. Instead of rising from the crypt with his wife, Phibes returns to England in a giant balloon, having arrived from an undisclosed location to travel to a cemetery to remove her from the crypt. Gone are the house in Mauldine Square and its underground crypt.

Phibes rescues Vulnavia from the asylum on a black motorcycle and not his infamous touring car. Salveus is now a short man with "a stunted soul," which he blames on Phibes, despite the fact that Lem Vesalius was played by a rather tall young man in the first film.

Gone also is the black mass that the members of the Institute used to call up Satan; instead the mummy of the Egyptian goddess Isis is called forth. Gone also is Sergeant Schenley; he is instead replaced by Sergeant Tom Harmon although Trout and Crow still remain a part of the story.

The script also details the use of film footage of the death scenes from the first film and a more graphic detail of Vicar Wren's death, which includes a pingpong ball stuffed into his mouth instead of the zipper, the lifeless body flying around the room like a deflating balloon as the air escapes from his mouth, finally coming to land atop a large cross.

The death of Abido was changed by death from the cobras to the more ingenious death by immersion in a vat of chlorine, from which his corpse emerges blanched white in color and looking like decayed human flesh.

The final attack by the clockwork minstrels against the police was altered so that the mechanical minstrels are dressed for some unexplained reason as cowboys, while Vulnavia, dressed as an American Indian, fires arrows at the approaching police.

After the police dispatch the clockwork cowboys, they find Vulnavia's Indian clothing lying discarded upon the organ, but she is no where to be found.

Like in the original script, Phibes takes his revived wife into the freezer to remain until a future time. On the scoreboard, the message now reads: I SHALL RETURN! followed by the song, *New York, New York*. This can only lead one to believe that the abandoned story outline for the *Phibes* adventure in New York was next on the drawing board, had this tale been made.

Also included with this new version of the script was a partial projected cast list. It proposed that Dr. Phibes would be played by David Carradine, Vesalius by Paul Williams, the psychic Dr. Steuben by Orson Welles, Vicar Wren by Roddy McDowall, Dr. Womber (the head of the asylum) by Donald Pleasence, Proby the old caretaker by John Carradine, Abido by Sam Jaffe and in an ironic twist, Coral Browne as Lady Peune.

Laurel never made a *Phibes* film and the idea was abandoned or so it would seem as Sam Arkoff reveals: "The fact is that quite honestly David

Carradine would never have been good in that role. The only reason that it was good the way it was, was because Fuest did give it a very good art look for the price and Vincent was bigger than life, as usual. Which is exactly what that role is, bigger than life. As a matter of fact, one of the writers, James Goldstein, keeps coming to me, wanting to make another Phibes film. Old scripts never die, they just get a title change and float around."

"Due to the nature of our original deal, Goldstein and Whiton kept the rights to the Phibes' characters and only recently Goldstein has returned again trying to make another one."

There is a postscript to the *Phibes* saga. Besides the two drafts of the script and the proposal outline, I also uncovered a treatment for a script titled *The Seven Fates of Dr. Phibes* written by Paul Clemens (the star of the film *The Beast Within* and the son of actress Eleanor Parker) and then Monsterland Magazine editor, Ron Magid.

The plot dealt with Phibes and the revived Victoria returning to England after passing through the River of Life (from the end of the second film) to reclaim the set of seven Greek god statuettes that were taken from their house in Mauldine Square and return with them to the island of Crete to take their place among the gods. Along the way they kill off the collectors who possess the statuettes and battle a man who possesses the secret of eternal death.

This story treatment would be considered nothing more than the writing of two fans, except for one thing. The treatment I uncovered came complete with a copy of a hand-written letter addressed to Clemens by Vincent Price on his own stationary.

The letter tells of Price's love for the new story and that he would be interested in reviving the part of Phibes if he could get the film produced. The letter unfortunately is not dated (nor is the treatment) but it might be safe to believe they were both written in the early 1980's, around the time of the other proposed *Phibes* films. But like the others this story was never made, which leaves Dr. Anton Phibes and his wife Victoria where we left them, sailing down a long tunnel to find the river of eternal life.

THE MANY DEATHS OF VINCENT PRICE

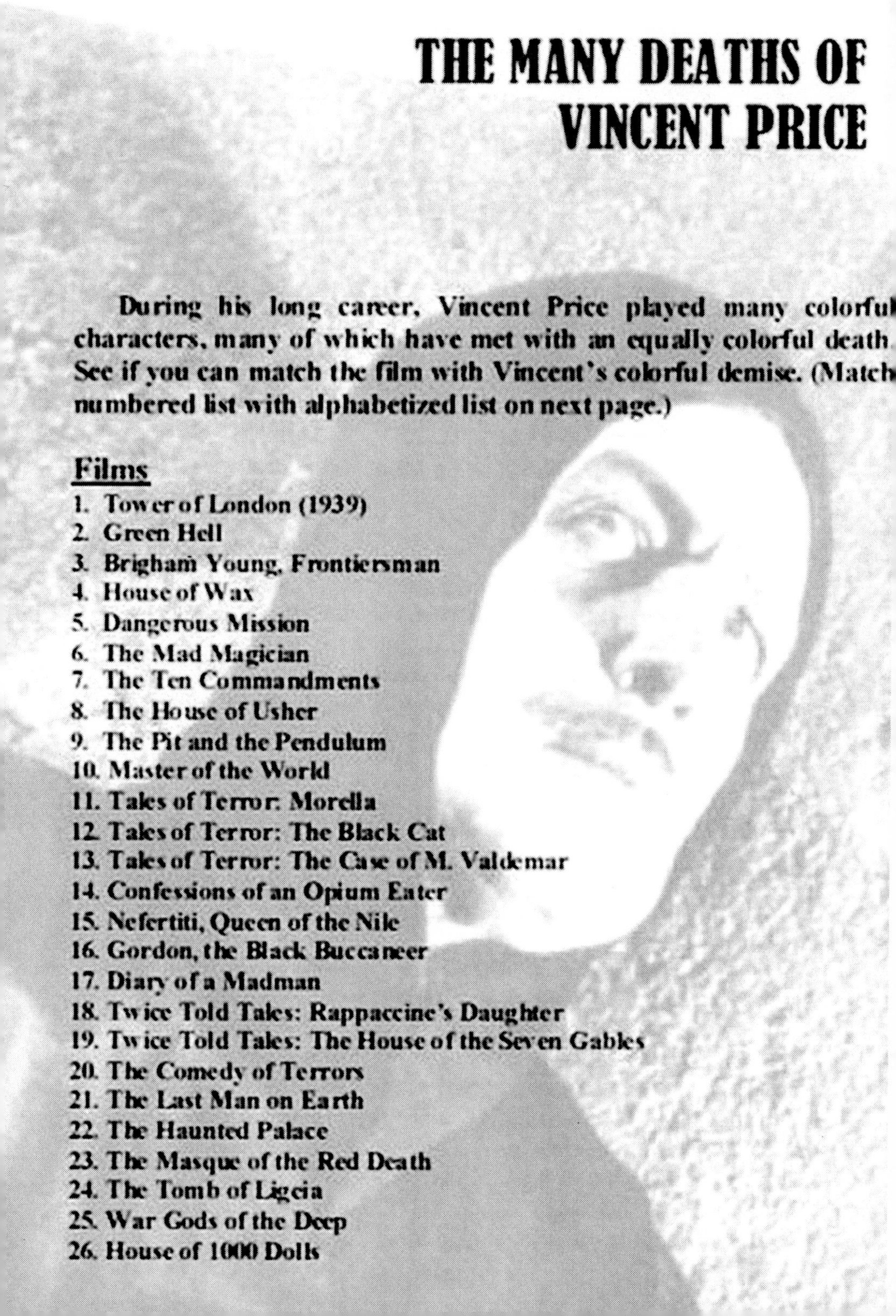

During his long career, Vincent Price played many colorful characters, many of which have met with an equally colorful death. See if you can match the film with Vincent's colorful demise. (Match numbered list with alphabetized list on next page.)

Films

1. Tower of London (1939)
2. Green Hell
3. Brigham Young, Frontiersman
4. House of Wax
5. Dangerous Mission
6. The Mad Magician
7. The Ten Commandments
8. The House of Usher
9. The Pit and the Pendulum
10. Master of the World
11. Tales of Terror: Morella
12. Tales of Terror: The Black Cat
13. Tales of Terror: The Case of M. Valdemar
14. Confessions of an Opium Eater
15. Nefertiti, Queen of the Nile
16. Gordon, the Black Buccaneer
17. Diary of a Madman
18. Twice Told Tales: Rappaccine's Daughter
19. Twice Told Tales: The House of the Seven Gables
20. The Comedy of Terrors
21. The Last Man on Earth
22. The Haunted Palace
23. The Masque of the Red Death
24. The Tomb of Ligeia
25. War Gods of the Deep
26. House of 1000 Dolls

27, Conqueror Worm
28. More Dead Than Alive
29. Scream and Scream Again
30. The Abominable Dr. Phibes
31. Theater of Blood
32. Journey into Fear
33. House of the Long Shadows
34. Bloodbath at the House of Death
35. The Offspring
36. Backfire

Deaths

A. Shot with 16 poison arrows
B. Shot and then buried in an avalanche
C. Decayed until corpse dissolved
D. Burned and then later thrown into a vat of boiling wax
E. Drowned in a vat of wine
F. Strangled until neck snapped
G. Shot with arrows
H. Strangled and then had a burning house fall on him
I. Shot several times and then falls through a plate glass window
J. Dies in explosion over the ocean
K. Sealed behind a brick wall and asphyxiated
L. Strangled by skeletal hand and then had a house collapse on top of him
M. Drowns in a sewer
N. Strangled in a burning house
O. Falls into a deep pit
P. Knifed in throat
Q. Run through with a sword
R. Burns to death
S. Commits suicide by grabbing on to a poisonous plant
T. Poisoned
U. Speared through the heart
V. Falls several stories from balcony
W. Burned at the stake
X. Died from the plague
Y. Incinerated in a crematorium
Z. Blinded, strangled, and had a burning house collapse on top of him.
AA. Axed then shot to death
BB. Extreme old age
CC. Shot multiple times
DD. Falls from rooftop into burning building

EE. Falls into a vat of acid
FF. Axed
GG. Self-embalmed
HH. Caught in explosion
II. Accidentally set on fire
JJ. Shot in chest with flare gun and explodes into flames

Answers:

1:E, 2:A, 3:I, 4:D, 5:B, 6:Y, 7:F, 8:H, 9:O, 10:J, 11:N, 12:K, 13:C,
14:M, 15:G, 16:Q, 17:R, 18:S, 19:L, 20:T, 21:U, 22:W, 23:X,
24:Z, 25:BB, 26:V, 27:AA, 28:CC, 29:EE, 30:GG, 31:DD, 32:JJ,
33:FF, 34:II, 35:F, 36:HH

Interior photo credits:
Title 1: From "Scream and Scream Again" ((1970 American International Pictures)
Contents page: Vintage photo
Title 2: Vintage photo
Intermission Title: Vintage photo
Quiz Title 1: Vincent Price in "The Pit and the Pendulum" (1961 Metro-Goldwyn-Mayer)
Quiz Title 2: Vincent Price in "Last Man on Earth" (1964 American International Pictures)
Quiz Title 3: Director Tim Burton with Vincent Price on the set of "Edward Scissorhands" (1990 20th Century Fox)

About the Author

Joel Eisner is the author of three successful TV pop culture books including the bestselling *The Official Batman Batbook* (selling over 100,000 copies worldwide). He has co-written *Lost in Space Forever* and *Television Comedy Series: An episode Guide to 153 TV Sitcoms in Syndication.*

His most recent book is The *Official Batman Batbook, Revised Bat-Edition,* a newly updated and enlarged version of the original *Batbook* which surpasses the original in both scope and content.

Upcoming projects include a film and TV trivia book and a pop culture series of books called *Attack of the Rubber-Suit Monsters* dealing with the hundreds of films and television series featuring actors in rubber monster, gorilla and robot suits.

TV Historian Joel Eisner received a B.A. in Media Arts and an MBA in Marketing from Long Island University.

He has published numerous interviews and articles in such magazines as *Starlog*, *Starblazer*, *SFTV*, and *Collecting Hollywood.* He has been quoted and his works have been sited in numerous publications.

He lives in New York City with his wife Sharon, his son Jeremy and their dog Sparky.

Mr. Eisner is available for inquiries at
PRICEOFFEAR@HOTMAIL.COM

www.downwarden.com/blackbedsheet

Check out these other titles from the #1 source for the best in independent horror fiction,

BLACK BED SHEET BOOKS

Whispers in the Cries
by Matthew Ewald 978-0-9833773-6-8

Hunted by the shadowed entity of his grandfather's past and its brethren of demonic beasts, Randy Conroy must survive the nightmare his grandfather could not. A thrilling ghost tale of the Queen Mary and haunted souls.

Wherewolf by Franchisca Weatherman 978-0-9833773-7-5

When a pack of werewolves hits a small southern town, the local Sheriff realizes this is one case he can not solve alone. He calls in the F.B.I. to help him take down the killers that are taking the lives of the local teens. When the wolves abandon the town for the streets of New Orleans during Mardi-Gras celebrations, the hunters become the hunted in an all-out war where no one may survive....

Fractured Time by Alan Draven 978-0-976994787

Donovan Vicar is a "feeler," a man who feels the vibrations of people around him. He embarks on a late bus ride to seek out Timothy Crane, a man rumored to be dabbling in black magic, and finds himself in 1957 and a town plagued by missing young women.

Charla by Alexander Beresford 978-0-9833773-4-4

Charla kept her unsettling hatred towards her daughter Amelie a secret for so long, but over time it became harder for her to quench her morbid impulses without raising concerns. One lonely dawn, Charla ...divorced, pained, unhappy... ignited events which invoked a horrible demon to disrupt her twenty-five year old's picture perfect life. She put her terrifying scheme into action ... and the demon began its wave of hell.

www.downwarden.com/blackbedsheet

Electric Angel by Sue Dent 978-0-9769947-9-4

Because of her cancer, Anna Chadwick wouldn't live long enough to carry her twin infants to term. Yet she wanted nothing more than for them to have a chance at living. Learning one would be stillborn didn't lessen her desire.

It would take a miracle....so she prayed for one.

When an electrical entity arrives to take the place of her stillborn, some would reflect that prayers aren't always answered the way we'd expect them to be.

The Everborn: Special Edition by Nicholas Grabowsky 978-0-9842136-0-3

The Everborn concerns the offspring of fallen angels that have lived among us since the dawn of man. Throughout the ages, they live life after life in normal society until each one falls in love and fathers their own child. Before that child is born, they undergo a rapid degeneration into a fetal state before they disappear entirely and become reborn into a new life. When an Everborn is reborn as a set of twins, one a soulless serial killer on a quest to be born again into a sinless life and the other a kind-hearted ghostwriter for a world-famous rock-and-roll horror novelist, a banished Watchmaid claims her role in an ancient prophecy to use the soulless twin as a means to re-enter our world and bring about its destruction.

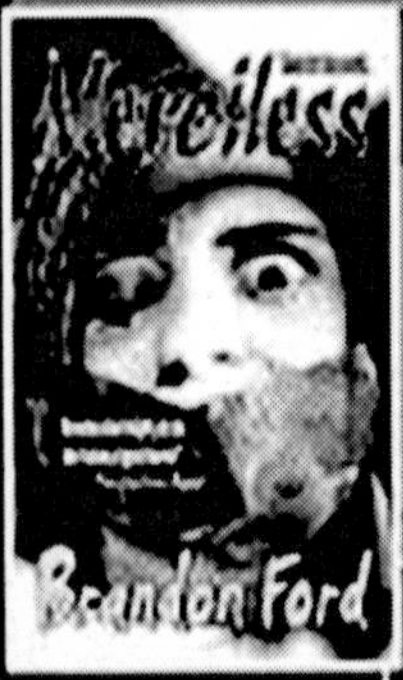

Merciless by Brandon Ford 978-0-9886590-0-1

Kyra and Claire are strangers, but by the time their crisp autumn eveni comes to a close, they'll have formed an unbreakable bond. Kidnapped gunpoint, they are bound and savaged by a madman whose purpose is impose pain and suffering. He is ruthless. He is relentless. He MERCILESS.

The Return of Spring-heeled Jack by Jennifer Caress 978-0-9858829-7-6

Spring-heeled Jack is a British urban legend, first appearing in 1837. Eye witnesses tell of a man who could leap several stories in the air with little effort. Some say he could breathe blue fire, others say he lured women out of their homes and attacked them by clawing at their faces. By all accounts he was a thief and a menace. Sightings of Spring-heeled Jack continued for several centuries and crossed numerous continents, but he has been mysteriously absent from the 21st century. Until now.

www.downwarden.com/blackbedsheet

Blood Verse by Patrick James Ryan

978-0-9886590-3-2

A collection of horrifying tales and poetry covering a wide spectrum of horror themes both familiar and original, and altogether chilling. From a new voice in horror, BLOOD VERSE will haunt your nightmares.

Blood Related by William Cook

978-0-9858829-4-5

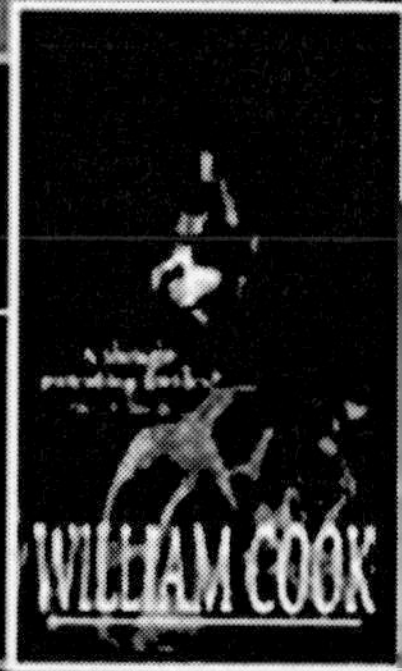

"Blood Related is a nasty but nuanced take on the serial killer genre. Cook's bruising tale of twin psychopaths who are as cold as mortuary slabs is not for the weak-kneed."
- Laird Barron, author of Occultation

Morningstars by Nick Kisella 978-0-9858829-0-7

While at his dying wife's bedside, Louis Darque, a recently promoted detective, is confronted by his absentee biological father, a demon named B'hal. The demon offers Louis the chance to save the life of his wife if he 'works' for him on earth. He informs him that because of his mixed blood he has certain demonic traits, such as immortality and the ability to travel to and from Hell. While Louis attempts to solve a series of murders on Earth and battles in Hell, he finds he has a twin brother: Obscure. In an effort to save the world from their father, the two team up to fight B'hal on his own turf...

Spinner by Dustin LaValley

978-0-9858829-2-1

"In Spinner Dustin LaValley has created a new twist on the serial killer mythology, with one of the most memorable characters in recent crime fiction. The author has mapped the depths of human depravity, and is an all-too-willing tour guide. Just pray you can keep up - you don't want to get lost along the way." - John Edward Lawson, Stoker Award finalist, author of The Troublesome Amputee and Last Burn in Hell

Chophouse by Horns 978-0-9842136-8-9

A sinister night falls over the relaxed rural community of Dominic County, and a restless evil plots its escape from years of confinement. Before the light of day would return to the quiet woodland town, many came to believe that the gates of Hell had broken open and the Devil's minions were rampantly spreading terror and death there....

www.downwarden.com/blackbedsheet

Jeremiah Black

by Jason Gehlert   978-0-9858829-9-0

Jeremiah Black is unwittingly trapped in Hell after heroically saving h family from a serial killer one fateful night during the 1890's. There he fin himself propositioned by the Devil himself. Resurrected and immortal, he forced to kill his wife and entire bloodline over the course of the next centu in order to appease the Devil. When Inspector Granger, through a fre mishap of Black's blood mixing with his own while wounded, finds himse immortal, he seeks to end Black's reign of terror.

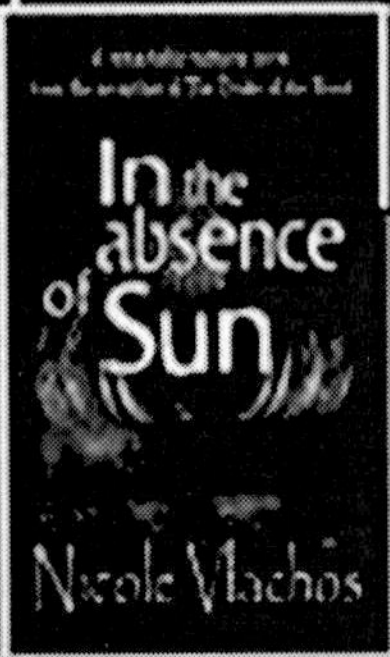

In the Absence of Sun

by Nicole Vlachos   978-0-9858829-1-4

Vampires are being abducted and murdered in the cit London. A fragmented coven is forced together to try uncover the truth, but wounds time has been unable to drive them deeper into danger. Faced with comp destruction, they must find a way to overcome grievances loss, if they are to survive. Soon, the question becomes n they can save their world, but if they can save themselves.

Red Simon: Vampire Punk

by B.L. Morgan   978-0-9858829-5-2

What would happen if an abused, ignored, angry teenage boy was given the power to make all of his tormentors pay for what they did to him? Red Simon: Vampire Punk answers that question with buckets of blood. A bullied teenage boy is murdered and comes back as a vampire to take gruesome revenge on everybody who mistreated him. He's tracked by police, a private detective and a vampire hunting priest. Simon develops a group of followers who want the same kind of vampire powers he has.

Dead Batteries

by Rey Otis   978-0-9858829-6-9

Selena Rodriguez died. Not for the first time. Now she's leapt back into something resembling real life after enrolling in a cutting edge clinical research study – one which included installing a radical new artificial heart where her broken one used to reside. "Third times the charm" becomes the mantra of her well-meaning nurses. The Zeus 3000 has given her a second second chance at a normal life after receiving the heart of a young girl – and rejecting it. Finally home – one which Selena inherits after her family is taken from her prematurely – she must navigate closets full of skeletons and a new haunt – since awakening from surgery Selena can hear and see things she has no business hearing or seeing. In this fast-paced Paranormal Sci-Fi melange, the pharmaceutical giant responsible for her newly found health hides dark secrets, an ancient race and a threat to everything she holds dear.

FRED WIEHE
Aleric: Monster Hunter
Aleric: Monster Hunter
by Fred Wiehe
Clean Freak
by Sean M. Davis
BLACK BED SHEET
Clean Freak
Mythic Blood
Shannon Lee
WWW.
Downwarden.com/
blackbedsheet
The best in independent underground horror fiction on the planet.
Order wherever books are sold.
You must order *now*.
Mythic Blood
by Shannon Lee
The Clock Tower
The Clock Tower
by Antoinette Heathfield
Shadows in the Dark
Shadows in the Dark
by Tom Sawyer
TOM SAWYER
Nicholas Grabowsky
Red Wet Dirt
"Nicholas, I salute you!"
--Clive Barker
Red Wet Dirt
by Nicholas Grabowsky
Rusty Nails, Broken Glass
S.C. HAYDEN
Rusty Nails, Broken Glass
by S.C. Hayden